Individualism

Government by We the People

By Frater Ponderator

© 2007, 2017

A MASS MEDIA PUBLICATION

Individualism

Government by We the People

By Frater Ponderator

Published by:

MASS MEDIA
PUBLICATIONS DIVISION
PO BOX 1411
Cranberry PA 16066

ISBN 978-0-9988148-0-3

Table of Contents

PART ONE

Individualism

Government by We the People

Be mindful, 90% of the world's wealth is owned by 5% of the world's population.

There is a trinity of ailment which afflicts today's society. The apex of which is Ignorance, which spawns first Irresponsibility, which in turn creates Sloth. Because of this, the masses are dependent upon *others* for all of their needs instead of themselves. This propagates power and growth to those who supply the need, effectively creating powerless slaves of the masses who, through lack of hands on experience, have increased their ignorance of fulfilling their needs, imprisoning themselves to dependence upon the 'need suppliers'. The free Individualist, however, has power over all individual needs by fulfilling all of them oneself. With such independence, the individualist is not subject to the forces of other individuals. This rule over oneself successfully vanquishes all vices which lead to corrupt systems on a number of levels as will be shown in this document. By constantly working directly with those things necessary for survival, one gains in wisdom, elevating one mentally, spiritually, and physically, which continually distances oneself from the slavery of dependence, causing the control of the 'need suppliers' to progressively diminish, leading to true freedom, that of independence.

Today's Ignorance has been purposefully compounded by the need suppliers by withholding the methodology of fulfilling each need, (successfully veiling the simple sources and processes); and causing all valuable information to have a high price (while still concealing pertinent knowledge); and furthermore, by inflating government and law to unnecessary complexities which only assist suppression by binding the lay while leaving loopholes and veils for the corrupt. All compounded with continual mass marketing hypnosis encouraging the masses to relax, think less, and rely on the need suppliers. In their unceasing deception with false reasoning and concealed facts they grow in power and suppress their brethren. They literally feed off of this 'ailment' of man, an aliment which they initiated, encourage and sustain. However, if all men created what they need for themselves, as the Individualist, these parasites would then die of starvation and fall away from mankind so that man may continue with all of its might on the path of evolution. Otherwise, the society will continue on its hollow materialistic path and successfully continue to devolve into inept, wasteful beasts with unrivaled skill to consume all leaving naught but unparalleled pollution.

0. Preliminary Notes

Detail

With any subject, detail can be added infinitely. As the reader will see, this document addresses many topics, on each of which an entire book could be written. Therefore it is made known that further research into all of the topics presented is encouraged as each subject shall be addressed only so long as to make the Individualistic stance and reasoning clear. The subjects that contain great detail are here included in that way to show often concealed notions which assist the Individualistic stance as well as enlighten the reader.

Definitions

To begin any discussion on any concept one must first clearly define all definitions of the concepts to be used to discuss the initial concept. The focus of this discussion is a philosophy called Individualism, which has its own perspective on government, economy, divinity and how they relate to the individual. Therefore the subjects of government, economy, and divinity will be described in detail and used to clearly define the Individualistic position in each subject, before moving on to describe how Individualism can be applied to the present world.

One phrase that will be occasionally seen throughout this document is "need suppliers". This is the Individualists' label for any hustler, merchant, dealer, manufacture, salesman, contractor, tradesman, scientist, engineer, lawyer, etc. who will do anything for money at the expense of one's fellows and the environment. Thus they are all categorized as such to varying degrees. The only ones who do not fall into this category are they who create in harmony with man and the environment, from the raw materials to the finished product, from its packing and shipping and even to its labeling, truth and harmony will be present through the entire procedure. The product having a definite meaning and purpose. This phrase "need supplier" is not to be confused with the Bourgeoisie. For the Bourgeoisie is a generalized term and not concerned with the methods of production, such as if they are destructive or not, and the profits, whether they were had by the exploitation of man or by respecting him. Bourgeoisie also represents an upper class, as the phrase "need supplier" is classless, for a thief or murderer can be of any social class.

I. The Individualistic Understanding of Government

Government by *We* the People – The Populus.

"OMNES HOMINES AUT LIBERI SUNT AUT SERVI"
(All men are freemen or slaves)

"The mania for giving the Government power to meddle with the private affairs of cities or citizens is likely to cause endless trouble . . . and there is great danger that our people will lose our independence of thought and action . . . and sink into the helplessness of [one] who expects his government to feed him when hungry, clothe him when naked, to prescribe when his child may be born and when he may die, and, 'in fine', to regulate every act of humanity from the cradle to the tomb, including the manner in which he may seek future admission to paradise." -- Mark Twain, Samuel Langhorne Clemens

Unfortunately, the present day entity, separate from the people and acting only for the benefit of the selfish cells who compose it, wrongly entitled 'government', is overly complex and exercises too much power and control over the individual for selfish gain instead of truly governing; which is a word whose origin is kubernan (Greek) and gubernare (Latin) both of which mean "to steer". Normally this steering would be implied to the benefit of the masses instead of steering to the benefit of the "elite" few as in today's society. Over time many more domineering variations to the word appeared such as, "to guide or direct" "to regulate" "to exercise authority over" " to control the actions or behavior of" "to keep under control, restrain" etc. This is where the fine line of Individualism is seen. All theses definitions are correct if they apply to One individual wielding power over oneself to direct and regulate one's own actions and steer one's life in such a way as to evolve in harmony with The Creation. The instant another is put into the equation the word is no longer government, it is simply slavery. No one should wield power over anyone but one's self. No matter how you look at it, how you justify it, what you call it, or to what degree, when one being controls another being the one being controlled is a subject, a servant, a slave.

Presently, the American society is a direct contradiction to the authority invested in "We the people" by the United States Constitution.   The authority has gone instead to the government which is now a separate entity from "the people" and controls them as a dictator. The majority is not truly involved in decision making, for they have no say on the individual policies, and often they do not even hear the details of them. The only say they have is to who gets into office, and their only choices are between the lesser of the liars, which are mostly self-serving profiteers with no concern for the Union or the people they are supposed to represent. The government has successfully become a kleptocracy, with no representative effectively representing anyone unless given "incentive" of some nature. All positions are bought and paid for. The only consensus that is heard is the one who spoke with the most financial influence. How many of these supposed representatives have not put into action things which they said they would have? Hired staff to enforce their own personal goals, instead of the goals of the people. How many laws and policies were never brought into public light until after they were passed? The very forces which control the masses are these laws and policies seldom brought to public attention. The very word policy comes from the Latin word "apodixa" which means to display or make known!

The ability to choose the individual in office yet not have that person strictly legally bound to the obligations of those they represent is completely pointless. The effect is a public who believes that they are contributing and in control when they are completely in the dark and powerless, just as is the puppet figure who supposedly represents them is to corporate forces. Furthermore, no matter who wins the vote, there is always complaining of some portion of the masses about the ruler. If the "ruler" is taken out of the picture, the burden falls upon the individual, where it has always belonged, who then can complain not, except that the burden of one's own fate be upon him.

Such is the argument about voting and how valuable the present vote is. First, limited candidates limits the choice of rule, thus limits choice itself. The campaign for any position is such an expense that it immediately puts that capability out of the reach of the common man, limiting equality. The few candidates being voted for only mention a small number of policies while campaigning, and if elected may not even hold their word on those. The myriad of other unmentioned policies are their real work which the people should be informed of but which rarely come into public light, mocking representation. Also it is not the candidate that has power, the candidate once elected is moved by "campaign contributions" and "donations" by huge need suppliers engrained into the system. It is they who are the true shapers of the policies to their own selfish ends, making the vote even more meaningless. All these candidates are soon allied with them or heavily invested with them, if not, they either soon will be, else they will be demonized in the public eye. No truly free thinker is allowed to get too far in present day political affairs without pledging allegiance to their empire, lest they be "neutralized". For those who deny this power, know that of the Earth's 100 most wealthy entities, 51 of them are corporations, while the other forty-nine are merely countries. Lastly, the remaining worth of the vote is snuffed out by the Electoral College who is supposed to represent the majority's will but *does not have to*. One does not vote for the president, one votes for 538 people who will make that decision for you. In this world it is far too easy to influence that small amount of people. The Electoral College was erected in a time when the common man was not sufficiently educated. It is a thing of the past in the Individualistic society where knowledge and education are their crown jewels and the people make decisions for themselves, as is their authority to do so.

The individuals comprising the said government, especially in the larger more powerful departments, are far removed from the income level and stresses of the masses; therefore they have no affinity towards the wants, needs, problems and concerns of this vast majority. The Members of the House of Representatives and the Senate received a salary of $165,200 per year; Congressional leaders receive $183,500, Speaker of the House $212,100 per year. The average American salary is approximately $37,000, thus the lowest paid congressman makes about 4.5 times more than the average man. Furthermore, they have become involved in, and understand corrupt systems directly proportionate to how far they have progressed within government and are now allied with corporate powers and benefiting therefrom. Therefore their goals, incentive, and determination become that of the corporations while the people who they are supposed to represent are simply forgotten. This is why if one holds on to the concept of representatives they must be forced to disclose in advance all of their intentions to the people they are to represent and be bound by strict law to fulfill that contractual obligation. Nevertheless; the Individualist sees even this as unnecessarily complex and prone to corruption and chooses its own simplistic system of harmonically reflective civil management, a form of direct democracy.

Individualistic simplicity holds that there is but one right. One has the right to do whatever one wishes as long as it causes no harm. Harm in itself is the indicator that one has broken the universal right. This universal right can not be subdivided into infinite subclauses of ensnarement as in profane doctrines. A system is either universal and unlimited by being simply One, or it is limited and profaned into many, there are no other systems. A profane system can easily be distinguished because of its plurality. These systems of many rights have limited the infinite, which is One, causing the One right to be explained as a complex series of capabilities, such as "one can do this, but can not do that" madness, which only evolves into a tool for manipulation and control. Complexities as these are erected by corrupt governments, groups and other controlling entities masquerading as protecting "rights" while veiling this limiting and controlling aspect.

This danger is present within a constitution or "social contract". Which are based on limited "rights" allotted to the people by an entity separate from the people, which was brought into existence by the people. The entity called into being, "government", has a contract of duties to perform based on these "rights". Ideally the beast created is to remain slave of the people, and the people may at any time alter their contract with it. As necessary as the social contract is to any society, it must be carefully monitored as it instantly causes a separation which sets up a group to "govern" and another group to be "governed". This separation is profaned unity, which is fertile ground in which only corruption may grow. The Only social contract that is not divided as such is a contract where all are equal in all powers, thus all govern and are governed simultaneously with one universal right to each and all. This is the only constitution acceptable so as not to blossom into perversion. This truth is clearly seen in the profane social contracts of today, started in good faith, now impossible to change in favor of the people who created it, yet simple to change in favor of the government, the entity drawn into being by the people now is controlling the people.

"If we understand the mechanism and motives of the group mind, it is possible to control and regiment the masses according to our will without their knowing it." -- Edward Bernays on *"engineering of consent"*

In today's age the very definitions of forms government are widely disputed. And when practiced in reality they are more often than not, a synthesis of a few different types of governments yet only label themselves as one or the other. This has further convoluted their definitions. It is for this reason that the Individualists have decided to clearly define their methods of operation and intent so as to be free from ambiguity. Therefore the following simple unadulterated definitions of the major forms of world government are used in comparison to clearly indicate how Individualism is a unique system of civilization management.

A. DEMOCRACY

From the Greek word "demokratia": demos (the people) and kratein (to rule) which is from the Greek word "kratos" (strength or power). Thus it literally means "rule by the people" or "the people's power".

Defined by the cognitive science laboratory at Princeton University:

1. The political orientation of those who favor government by the people or by their elected representatives
2. A political system in which the supreme power lies in a body of citizens who can elect people to represent them
3. The doctrine that the numerical majority of an organized group can make decisions binding on the whole group

B. REPUBLIC

From Latin res (a thing, matter, affair) and publica (the public) thus literally "a public matter"

Defined by American heritage dictionary:

1. Any political order that is not a monarchy
2. A constitutional form of government especially a democratic one
3. Any group of people working freely and equally for the same cause

C. FEDERATION

From Latin foedus (league, treaty)

Defined by the cognitive science laboratory at Princeton University:

1. An organization formed by merging several groups or parties
2. Confederation: a union of political organizations
3. The act of constituting a political unity out of a number of separate states or colonies or provinces so that each member retains the management of its internal affairs

D. MONARCHY

From Greek mono (sole) Arkhos (ruler)

Defined by YETC Arizona:

1. A type of government in which political power is exercised by a single ruler under the claim of divine or hereditary right.

E. THEOCRACY

From Greek theos (god) and kratein (to rule) thus "rule by God"

Defined by the cognitive science laboratory at Princeton University:

1. A political unit governed by a deity (or by officials thought to be divinely guided)
2. The belief in government by divine guidance

F. AUTHORITARIANISM

Defined by American heritage dictionary:

1. Characterized by or favoring absolute obedience to authority as against individual freedom

Such as a state or organization whose leaders have the power to govern without the consent of those being governed and enforce this control and strict obedience of the citizens through the use of oppression extending even into their thoughts and actions of daily life.

Authoritarianism is mentioned here to show that the definition of Individualism has nothing whatsoever in common with it. As this is not a form of government, but is more rightly a system of slavery in many guises.

G. INDIVIDUALISM

Individualism defined as a practical method of existence without using labels of other types of government to avoid tarnishing the definition with their modern preconceptions:

1. A constitutional government of the people by the people whose supreme absolute power lies in each individual as one's own state and monarch, each being thoroughly embodied with the consciousness of the Divine and thereby elect one's own self as one's own representative to determine the activities of their society of unified individuals with their collective free Will which can do all but limit in any way any individual or group of individuals so long as they are causing no harm to any thing including the body of their constitution.

Individualism as defined using methods of types of government:

1. A direct democratic republican commune governed by every member of the population as divinely endowed individual monarchs whose collective free will acts as a symmetrical federal government.

Individualism is the synthesis of most major forms of governments to date. It takes the sovereign divine king from the monarchy and makes each individual a representative of this divine flux within him. It takes congress from the republic and makes each individual a member. It takes the unity of individuals cells operating together as a whole from the federation, it takes voting from the democracy, and with that determines the major and general desire of the people formulating the primary direction of work together as a republic. It does this all with the knowledge that The Infinite is all permeating, within man and without, thus all individual and collective activities will be divinely oriented as in the theocracy.

To accomplish these ends free unrestricted knowledge is the cornerstone of the Individualistic society. Knowledge alone is sufficient to guarantee all liberties, knowledge is not only wisdom it is also awareness. When knowledge is withheld the resulting ignorance causes dependence upon others, which is a control, thus true Independence is lost. When knowledge is withheld one cannot make sound decisions for one's self, let alone stop unsound decisions being made by others. This allows the establishment of regulations for certain individuals and groups that differ from that of others, thus true equality is lost. When these are lost, an unnatural complexity is formed in which people can then be easily misguided, deceived and controlled, and finally, true freedom is lost. Therefore the Individualistic system stresses one's responsibility for all of one's own actions and one's own welfare by utilizing a system of free unrestricted knowledge.

Hence, Individualism offers true independence, equality and freedom, with the most noble attempt to freely give each individual the highest and most complex knowledge available. Illuminating them to the limitless powers of the mind, body and spirit so as to assist them in their individual and collective decision making. Thus the collective result upon society will mirror the individual efforts, and the society as a whole will come closer to perfection.

The Individualists advise that this approach is critical in these dark times. As humans have now drifted so far from essentials that they no longer know what is essential, they are lost in a realm of useless material and ignorance, and have abandoned evolution and freedom by abandoning knowledge. Individualism takes this existing materialistic society and hews from it the pure and healthy body of direct democracy buried deep in the core, abused and forgotten. So corrupted is the old world that not much will remain when the work is completed. Countless tons of black debris will be chipped from its body, and the small form remaining will be polished back to sound vitality and breathed into life with unrestricted knowledge.

HARMONIC REFLECTION OF INDIVIDUALISTIC MANAGEMENT

The most perfect form of government has existed before our very eyes since humans came into being. It is simply nature, has it ever needed governed? The countless types of species are all acting in perfect harmony, from the microscopic to the massive whales, because each one is governing itself. This keeps the system at maximum power and efficiency because each individual cares for itself to the highest extreme, thus creating a collective whole unit which cares for itself to the highest degree. If any individual unit is for whatever reason rendered unable to maintain this high standard of care, such as being severely wounded, it is naturally removed from the system. Thus ensuring that no fault exists within the system and it continues at maximum efficiency. This same principle is further expounded in simply weak creatures, they cannot get food, or win a mate thus their fault is not allowed to propagate simply due to the stresses of the high standards of the system, the individual is therefore destroyed and the system survives. The Individualists call this the microcosmic system of management.

The attempted opposite of this system, profaned Macrocosmic management, one human governing many, propagates fault and weakness, jeopardizing the entire system because of the flaw of merely one individual. Not only because the one individual does not care for another as much as oneself, but by the thwarting of that efficiency principle at work in nature. Humans also can not get too weak for too long else they will be removed by nature's system, *unless* assisted by society. This assistance unnaturally thwarts the efficiency principle of the system. It is the only reason that weakness, ignorance and ineptitude exist in modern society, else these individuals would have either changed for the better or ceased to be. This mechanism becomes more serious when such flawed individuals sit in positions of rulership. As an extreme example, if one such individual takes without equally returning to those dependent upon him, thus hoarding energy, whatever its form, be it food, money, fuel, knowledge etc, the rest grow weak, and will die leaving the hoarder no slaves to continue his parasitic sustenance, causing his own demise. Thus from one, or a few, corrupt individuals the entire system is sacrificed. In contrast, within the Microcosmic system of the Individualist, only the corrupt individual perishes (or changes), simply ensuring a stronger condition of the collective whole because a fault was removed.

Macrocosmic government (governing many beings) is for God not man. The only Macrocosmic government which is not profane is The One (God) governing All (also God), all other human attempts are limited profane abominations. Man can only govern the microcosm, that is, himself, and he has no right to govern anyone else because to properly govern himself is more than a challenging effort which is rarely brought to completion in a lifetime save by very few enlightened geniuses. This is the high standard of the Individualist, to focus on the perfection of oneself so that the collective whole of the society is a direct reflection of their individual valiant efforts. Thus a noble society, a great and powerful civilization with an enlightened and divine government in harmony with all of creation is born. When all men govern themselves, the sum total *is* the government of the Lord God, the government intended for man since antiquity. It is the macrocosmic government of the many microcosms, the house of many mansions, the kingdom of God.

All profane Macrocosmic governments, with man governing man other than himself, are not only a psychosis, (asserting oneself as being capable to know others as well as one knows oneself, if at all) but a redundancy (why govern some one who is already governing themselves?) and a slavery (one individual gives up his *duty* to govern himself, immediately becoming a subject to the one individual who asserts direction – even if with good intent).

Individualism takes the existing government and equally divides it amongst the people making each individual a small yet complete reflection of the whole so that each individual intelligence is aware of the workings of the entire system (albeit on a smaller scale) and is therefore included in each operation. Every individual becomes an active, balanced working part of the system as opposed to present civilization where most action and contribution is severely bias, with less than five percent of the population active in government proceedings leaving ninety-five percent of them inactive. Very few possess a clear understanding of the detailed workings of the entire system. The Individualistic society naturally increases this awareness and participation from its individuals by their practicing of this government on a microcosmic scale. Government thus subdivided is consequently easier to comprehend, effectively creating a civilization of aware and informed souls who understand the importance of their relationship to all others, as well as their responsibility thereto. Thus being no different than the human body whose sum total of efficiently working cells is one self-governing unit.

IMPORTANT NOTE: For the remainder of this document the word "Government" when referring to an Individualistic form of true direct democracy shall be replaced by the word ***Populus*** so as to distinguish between a profane government separate from the people and a just government of the people. The word 'government' from hereon shall refer to any government other than an Individualistic government and shall further be written in italics to remind the reader each time of the distinction, as such: *government*

II. The Individualistic Understanding of Economics

A question which arises when evaluating economic systems is, "which one is more successful?" To answer that question the idea of success must be defined apart from the efficiency of the system which is merely an attribute which defines no end goal of the society. Is success; quantity and/or quality of material goods, constant growth of the system, stability of the system, military power, wisdom and/or happiness of the people, complexity, or simplicity, etc.? Just what is the end goal?

- Economy is from the Greek words oikos (house) and nomos (to manage), thus "house management."

Some accepted definitions of economy are:

1. The careful or thrifty use or management of resources, as of income materials or labor. – American Heritage

2. The system of production, distribution and consumption – cognitive science laboratory at Princeton university

3. The state of a country or region in terms of the production and consumption of goods and services.
– Wikipedia

– Economics is the study of this state and system defined as:

1. "The practical science of production and distribution of wealth", wealth being defined as "the stock of useful things" - John Stuart Mill

2. "The science which studies human behavior as a relationship between ends and scarce means which have alternative uses." - Lionel Robbins

The Individualist believes that the most noble "end" a human can seek is the perfection of mind body and spirit, all other "ends" are deviations from this path and wastes of time and energy to varying degrees. This is the Individualistic concept of economic success which consequently alters many economic mechanisms of the present world, rendering most of them useless if not pointless, as they do not contribute to this "successful end".

Economy began simply as self-subsistence. Such as simply producing food, water and shelter and distributing it to only oneself. Soon this grew to distribution amongst the people of the group, then evolved to Macro subsistence, even larger scale tasks performed by the few for the many with knowledge that they withheld from their brethren (by accident or purposefully) such as large scale farming. With the handing over of personal responsibilities to others an unnecessary complexity of economics is produced and a cycle of malignant growth is initiated. Soon services need rendered for the myriad of tasks neglected because of the one unnaturally doing things for the many has substantially less time to do those things he should be doing for himself. The exact same happens to all who become involved, such as those rendering the services now need services for tasks they too have neglected. Thus this cycle of nonsense grows only thickening ignorance amongst the people and further specializing their abilities and awareness, removing true independence by increasing dependency upon others.

As soon as "value" begins being placed on these tasks and services a whole new dimension of perversion is born. The initial over complexity may still have been being performed in a compassionate manner. Yet with value comes corruption as time is initially of equal value to all, hence the granter of services or macro-supplier raises prices so that they have more free time. This forces the people dependent on that good or service to have less time because they now have to work more. Therefore in the simplest state all beings have exactly the same spare time, when this complexity is erected time becomes a fluid commodity which flows from the many to the few. Thus whether they know it or not, those supplying a good or service upon which others have allowed themselves to depend upon, control those people. Soon this force is realized by some, and inequity enters man as he begins to prey upon his fellow brothers' trust and ignorance and the true need supplier is born. Prices are raised, lies are told for their reasoning. Deception in endless facets arises such as Goods and services that are not needed but the people are convinced in every way to utilize them, thus distorting their concept of essentials and simplicity, allowing further complexity which is by its nature a proportionate veil for deception. This cycle continues growth in complexity, specialization, alienation, ignorance, dependence, and deception creating distrust amongst the brotherhood of man and dividing them against each other in endless ways while taking time from the many and giving it to the few magnifying all negative emotions. As time is essential for happiness thus those with less time, begin to experience negative feelings. Before long these bottom end users, miserable and timeless, begin to desperately seek time by the same methods albeit more hasteful through severe lack of time, thus resulting in inferior solutions. Such as a prostitute or drug dealer. Both operating on capitalistic principles, with the value of their gain exceeding that of the expenditures. Thus, the most effective method becomes adopted. The easiest being simply theft, little work (time and energy)for exactly what is needed, the same practice that occurs constantly in modern business. Soon even Law is used to gain time or money, and thus, the circle of corruption is complete.

This is the formula of the need suppliers, the intermediate between private wealth and public interest, either real or synthetically generated. This is where the terrible relationship between the banks and businesses come into play. The majority of bottom end users are unable to do business with the merchants do to lack of time and money the system inflicts upon the masses. Thus the merchants, hungry for more time and eager to exploit this massive resource of people, develop the banks so that they can "assist" the people in doing business. The bank is really the only one doing business with the merchant, and enslaving the people for their "help". To illustrate the point, the merchant seduces a soul into a material object, this soul now needs money to quench this desire, the merchant's partner, or second face, the bank, lends a hand. The "Loan" goes from the bank, right past the individual, to the merchant. Thus, the bank directly pays the merchant to bait the people to enslave themselves to the bank who then also makes money off these already poor souls by usury increasing their desperation. The bank thus becomes the controller of the work force crippling them even further by usury taking the last of their time and money. Most likely the bank is a collection of wealth by a merchant or group of merchants to initiate this system of control. Over time the bank becomes strictly oriented to these self initiated monetary feedback loops, growing exponentially in power and control. Making bond slaves of the entire populace.

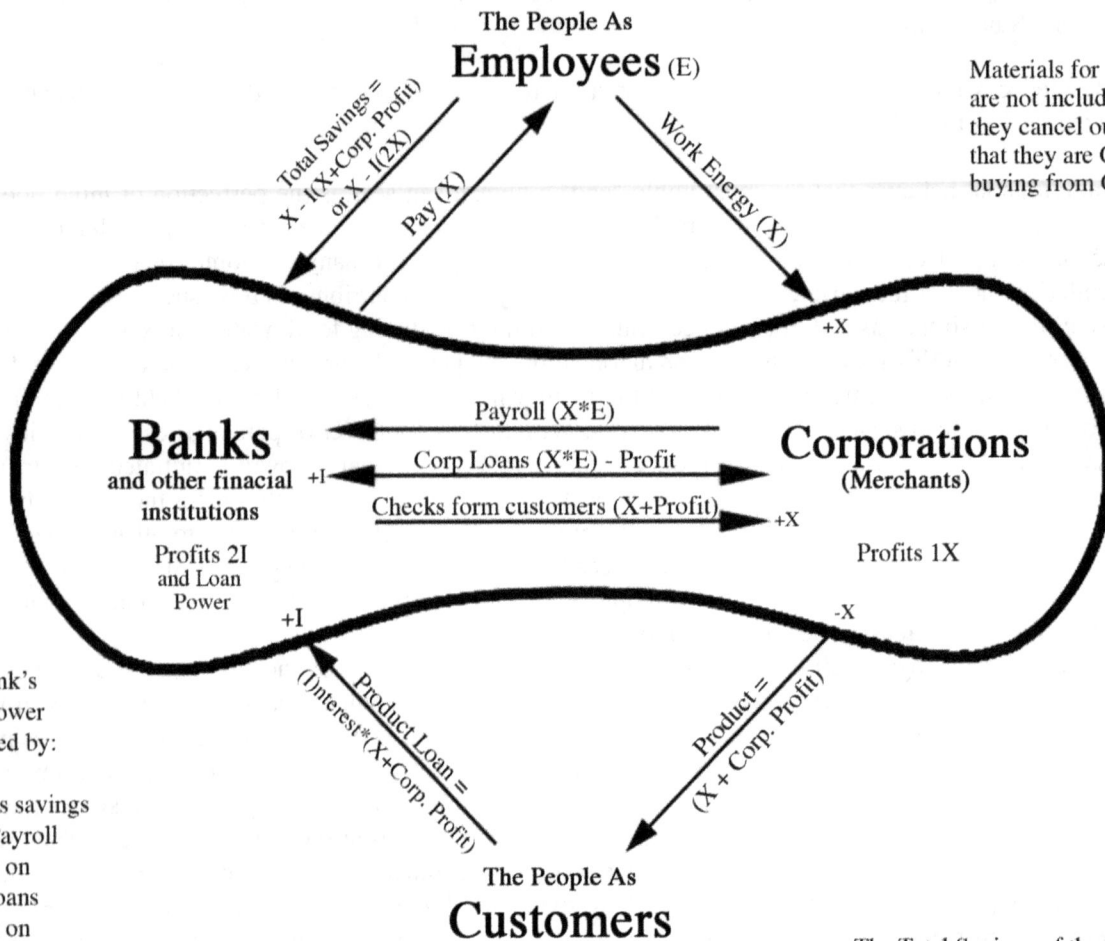

The People As
Employees (E)

Materials for product
are not included, as
they cancel out being
that they are Corps
buying from Corps.

Total Savings =
$X - I(X+Corp. Profit)$
or $X - I(2X)$

Pay (X)

Work Energy (X)

$+X$

Banks
and other finacial
institutions

Payroll $(X*E)$

Corp Loans $(X*E)$ - Profit

Checks form customers $(X+Profit)$

$+I$

$+X$

Corporations
(Merchants)

Profits $2I$
and Loan
Power

Profits $1X$

$+I$

$-X$

Product Loan =
$(I)nterest*(X+Corp. Profit)$

Product =
$(X + Corp. Profit)$

The People As
Customers

The Bank's
Loan Power
Increased by:

1. People's savings
2. Corp. Payroll
3. Interest on
   Corp. loans
4. Interest on
   Customer loans

All <u>Times</u> 9

I="Interest" which is money made on money. If 90% of
that money does not exist, it is money made on nothing.

The Total Savings of the People
shows that for every unit of work
expended, the people pay interest
on it twice. Of the small amount
that remains, 30-40% will be tax.

16

The handing over of one's own responsibilities to others in even the smallest degree initiates this process of individual alienation leading to a lack of understanding of the mechanics of the entire unnecessary system as well as methods of self subsistence. Subsequently breeding false convictions of how all things work together and the true purpose of life, leaving these individuals prey for wiser forces to take advantage of this ignorance ending in inescapable dependency. To avoid this information asymmetry and its repercussions delineated above, the Individualists believe in all power to the individual bar none. The single most important key to this is free unrestricted knowledge. Thus, The Individualists erect The Library of Accredited Free Knowledge and Instruction which teaches all the people Freely. Additionally vast improvements are made to the public education system of the minors. All necessities of self sustenance are taught as well as free access granted to all knowledge possessed by all mankind collected and clearly cataloged by LAFKI. With the masses enlightened, the cycle of dependency begins to reverse.

The Individualistic society's priority is not monetary or material gain; it is intellectual gain, resulting in efficiency of every industry, orchestrating them toward one goal, the evolution of mankind. Therefore, because its priorities are completely different from the pointless priorities of past systems, many laws of the dying world's economics do not apply. They are seen as incomplete and inferior distortions of truth, gross misconceptions which only serve to limit man.

Such are the concepts of employment, economic growth, supply and demand, privatization and specialization all flawed concepts which limit man because they are a resultant of a system which has forfeited individual responsibility. The initial creation of a macro supplier creates first privatization, then employment, then specialization, then a supply and a demand, then a monitoring of the cycle and forces implemented to achieve "economic growth" which is merely increased profit for the need suppliers at the expense of the masses.

Demand need not exist before supply, as humans can be convinced into a need. Supply and demand can only be considered true and natural laws when speaking of basic subsistence such as a fixed amount of people and a fixed amount of food which nature yielded that particular season. They become merely quasi-laws in today's economic complexity because the demand (decisions of the people) can be artificially implemented by marketing propaganda, incentives and price altering. Price itself is mistakenly looked at by some as a measure of relative scarcity, but withheld knowledge creates an illusion of scarcity when in fact there is plenty. Thus the entire system is based on illusions, therefore any "economic analysis" is also illusory to varying degrees. To maintain this faulty system it must be constantly monitored and meticulously altered by the proponents of the banks and the need suppliers so as not to allow its overdue collapse. Production and prices are therefore set to limit the market and maintain animation of this long-dead machine for the gain of only the need suppliers, the very reason for the insanity of paying farmers to burn crops. The control of these prices directly controls the people by controlling their decisions which are based on those prices.

Unrestricted free knowledge makes one less susceptible to faulty elements of this system such as the need for employment. Employment results in wages and unemployment. Wages empower only the bank, which holds the payroll money of the merchant increasing its own loaning power. Unemployment is something to be feared only in societies whose people are so specialized that they are incompetent in all tasks but one. Thus they are incapable of surviving without the help of the system when their specialized task suddenly becomes obsolete, which is the unfortunate destiny of the majority of pointless tasks in today's insane world. In the Individualistic society these problems do not exist because of the knowledge of self-subsistence. One needs not to work for another because one is generating all of one's needs by oneself. One works only by choice and interest, employment being sought and businesses being wrought because of the love of a particular thing, such as electronics, airplanes, engines etc. not for material gain out of desperation. Knowledge alone negates the need for employment thus negating the need for unemployment welfare, which taxes society.

Employers only encourage limitation in man by encouraging specialization of labor and cause it to become even more specialized by rewarding the individual with the higher output. The money paid out by the employer remains the same as his production efficiency increases because of increasing one workers wage while a less efficient worker is terminated to compensate. This increases the strength of only the employer because of the greater efficiency had for the same cost, and weakens the masses because another is unemployed who is too specialized to sustain himself, thus taxes society to sustain him.

Specialized labor further tends towards waste when a specialist has completed all tasks, he is then out of work. Therefore either the employer will create unnecessary work to maintain this individual or the individual will initially never allow the work to be complete by slowing his pace, or will create faulty works in need of constant repair. Thus the infamous slogan of materialistic waste is borne "Job Security" the direct result of specialized labor. If none of this can be maintained the individual is laid off and without self-sufficiency, now taxes society. Thus the supposed benefits gained through specialization are lost in its many tendencies towards waste.

The specialist may be superior to all in just one task but is impotent in all others. The well-rounded laborer is inferior in any one task but capable and aware of many. The Individualist sees a virtue therein. The sum total of all of these known tasks allows the practitioner insights and understandings, which will not appear in the strictly specialized individual, granting the potential for higher solutions. The specialist in a meaningless task has a meaningless knowledge, useless in one's own personal evolution. Thus, focus on simplifying tasks for less training time breeds deeper ignorance in the individual regardless of time saved in training which yields only profit to the company. Specialists, no matter their degree of mastery, will never improve the quality or purpose of an object which was poorly engineered or conceived, it matters not how perfect the specialists craft and assemble to the plans, the product will simply be a rapid and efficiently produced piece of junk. Many of today's products are examples of this, an endless sea of entirely meaningless, useless, unnecessary garbage contributing nothing to humanity, pushed upon them as a need, leading society further astray from their true priorities, while wasting the lives and minds of those who specialized to create them.

The Individualist realizes that most normal human beings will inevitably find one particular task especially enjoyable, a love. It is these paths which the Individualist is encouraged to pursue specialization in and none other. Specialization pursued in love creates an Artist. Hence both well-rounded understanding and artistic specialization are needed to keep an individual free from alienation to the endless methods of production. Creating high enthusiasm as a direct result of free unrestricted knowledge. Production in the Individualistic society will therefore be controlled by the desire of an informed people, so high production will not be a relevant factor to measure the success of their system. As focus upon production in terms of time neglects time used for more important things such as enlightenment of the individual. High production of useless things is waste and failure to the creator and the society. Most material goods of necessity are self-made by the knowledgeable Individualist, removing the need for many merchants, except for those few true lovers of a trade. These are true Artists and not just in the business for the money and control it may provide. All workers of the Individualistic society are capable of shifting to self-subsistence and creative pursuits at any time. Therefore abundance does not cause unemployment in the Individualistic society as it does in the present world, it causes an influx of time to the entire populace resulting in additional inspiration and innovation from forces which will later be explained in detail.

In the discussions below on economic systems a "publicly owned" means of production is described as owned by the people, not "by the state" or "by the government". These latter two phrases were meant to mean the same thing as "by the people" in their original systems because those systems have governments of the people in their ideal forms. However, this slight, seemingly harmless alternate definition injects fatal flaws allowing an entity separate from the people to control these important things thus deviating from the true intent of the original systems thereby not practicing the system intended regardless of public claims. This small twist in the definition and intent of the system is exactly what has demonized the good intent of socialism, and its archetype, communism. Twisted by power mad tyrants so that now the very use of the titles of these systems sends fear and hatred into the beholder. It must be clear that the Individualists do not defend the totalitarian *governments* of the past who falsely claimed to utilize these systems in the name of tyranny. The Individualists simply present the true noble intent of their ideal forms to shoo away darkness falsely connected therewith. The Individualists aim to show the misconceptions of each of today's economic systems and bring them all into equilibrium especially exhibiting how each can be perverted to a system of control simply by slightly distorting their definitions or mass understanding of their definitions. Individualism realizes that each system has a kernel of truth as well as a kernel of ignorance and attempts to extract the good of each system and compile it into the universal technique of Individualism by clearly defining their synthesis so as to be incorruptible. Once again "by the people" and "by the government" were intended to define the same group but now the latter speaks of an entity separate from the people, beware of these twists. The Individualist defines them all as "By the people" meaning exactly and only "each and every individual in the entire society bar none", and far from "publicly owned" as in the sense of purchased stock.

A. CAPITALISM

To quote the online encyclopedia Wikipedia pertaining to the definition of capitalism: "There is continuing debate over the definition, nature, and scope of this system."

Therefore, due to the variety of definitions, only one definition has been presented so as to avoid a "capitalism definition debate" which is not the in the scope of this work. The following definition sums up the Individualists' understanding of the basic concept.

Defined by American heritage dictionary:

1. An economic system characterized by freedom of the market with increasing concentration of private and corporate ownership of production and distribution means, proportionate to increasing accumulation and reinvestment of profits.

The freedom of true capitalism cannot be denied, but it is rarely practiced, if at all, in its ideal form due to countless laws, regulations and restrictions designed to control who and what comes to power. Yes it can be said that capitalism fuels incentive for each individual to get up and work hard for what they dream of, but makes no promises of fulfilling that dream. And the harder or smarter one works the greater will be the success, thus the amount of work energy and the efficiency of that work is directly proportionate to success, - ideally. This neglects to consider, however, families who have long had control of vast wealth and or corporations, and place their family members directly into power with little or no effort. It neglects the masses of middle class laborers who, some even with college education, burn every ounce of energy each day until collapsing in bed just to make ends meet. Yes it drives one to work one's hardest, possibly in haste, developing innovative new technology for great *personal* reward but neglects that it will also conceal new technologies such as disease cures because of the great market demand for them. For the same selfish profiteering reasons it will curb resources away from things that will hurt profit even if it is to the benefit of all mankind.

It is said that each individual is free to do whatever type of work they wish. However, people end up doing what makes more money, not what they love, and what makes money may not be what is best for human evolution, especially in these times where mankind has completely lost touch with the reason for incarnation and dwells in complete nonsense. Thus the initial person is alienated not only because of labor specialization but because of a task one is uninterested in and which evolves one's being to no extent during the long hours applied, nor does it assist humanity. Enthralled to fulfilling the dream of another at one's own expense. Thus it is a tragic waste of life force from the Individualistic point of view. Every ounce of time must be used for the evolution of self, all else is secondary.

This "freedom" of market concept is even further corrupted. All things in nature have limits, the Earth has a definite path, beings have definite life spans etc. So too must this free market have a limit so as to avoid corporations which become larger than nations exploiting the masses and the Earth, causing freedom to be in the hands of only the few. The limit is not applied to the freedom of activity, it is applied to size.

Once a business gets so large there is no logical reason for it to grow even larger save for power, control and other vices which fuel the egos of totalitarian madmen. As one can see in the definition, " increasing concentration of private and corporate ownership", here the definition is plainly admitting this fatal flaw. With an unlimited free market, businesses soon own all, and they then buy each other out until all things are owned by a mere handful of people. Thus the God given things such as land and resources, have false claim laid over them by man, forcing others to labor to receive what is truly owned by God and given freely to all men, not just a few. It is no different than the feudalism it evolved from, the business owner becomes the authoritarian despot, and through his hierarchy of officer/barons and foreman/knights he rules his serfs, the nameless employees nearly powerless to raise up in the company, a mockery of the proclaimed freedom. Thus one can see that the "freedom" of this system is directly proportionate to level of rank in a particular size of a company which is proportionate to wealth and power. The result is thus subtle slavery of the masses being that the higher the rank the fewer the available positions.

The Individualist believes the goal of human existence is the cultivation of the human mind body and spirit. Not the construction of the largest and most inharmonious machine or city ever built. Look at society, and honestly ask where is it heading, what is the ultimate goal? What more has it achieved since its ancient brethren besides unnecessary creature comforts and devises that in no way assist mankind's evolution or the welfare of the planet which sustains them. Man has moved virtually nowhere in evolution for thousands of years. His understanding of nature has been used to no constructive ends. If anything we have gone backwards and become ignorant to nature and bedazzled by our own magnificent pointless material creations. To this day we cannot build the pyramid of Giza yet we call our selves 'advanced'? Materialism is the cause, the focus upon only the physical has caused man to lose touch with his true nature, the infinite soul!

Proponents would say that capitalism does assist humanity, now this is where the definition and beliefs of life's purpose must be defined. The proponents judge the evolution of a nation and people by the sophistication of their material technology and level of production of these items which may or may not assist humanity's evolution. These proponents go as far as waging war on third world countries informing them that they are benevolently assisting them to evolve to the pointless materialistic state of waste and consumption possessed by the "advanced" first world countries. Hypothetically, say a nation had no creature comforts, and lived a ancient tribal life, yet were happy, prayed to their god every moment of life, and were strong in mind body and spirit such as the native American. Suddenly they were forcefully converted to materialism and forced to work and learn the "new" and "better" system. They became unhappy, stopped praying as much, and didn't have time to study the wisdom of their culture. They were no longer allowed to freely take what they needed from the earth because others now "owned" it. In which state were they successful? Are devoted monks less evolved than the rest of us when they denounce material possessions yet submerge themselves in a wealth of knowledge and a life of simplicity? This is not to say that the Individualist is a proponent for tribalism or a life of a monk, it is simply to show the alternate views of "success". It is not denied that technology is useful, but it must be guarded against so as not to become the main focus of existence.

The primary focus of capitalism is materialism, to have and to own. Its very definition includes "capital" which is material wealth. The Individualist does not dispute mans inherent desire and right to own, but it must be done so in a wise manner. How many people have not the things they need? How many people have things they never use or used only once? How many have purchased the latest trendy item which does nothing to enhance their mind, body or spirit? Material objects are vain and pointless unless they, as tools, can contribute to the ultimate goal of one's personal evolution.

Capitalism has made itself an object of such focus that it gains more attention than the goal of life itself. Life is not about pointless work, it is about meaningful work, which is individual evolution. Many live life the way they were told to live; get a job, get a spouse, have children, have your children get a job and spouse and have their children do the same etc. It is a never-ending cycle of servitude that achieves nothing, ignorant to the spirit of man, its importance and precedence. People then focus on work and making money more than living life and enjoying the majesty they dwell in. They focus on making this money as fast as possible regardless of the consequences, generating haste, because the system has taken away all spare time from them. Haste in turn generates inferior and unwise solutions which are irresponsibility, which generates nothing but corruption and pollution. It has been common sense for aeons that haste makes waste yet its practice governs our modern lives. Today everyone is trying to "get ahead", get ahead of what? Ahead of their fellow brother regardless if they feed him to the wolves? Or ahead of the machine that saps them of their most precious and aware hours of the day, and then taxes their tranquility of mind afterwards with silent threats of future despair if even more of their effort, in the form of capital, is not produced to quench the ever increasing cost demands of the need suppliers. It also may lead to one becoming one of those who profits by impassively deceiving and enslaving one's fellow brethren. To strive for only the pile of gold is directly ignoring the most important task in one's life – to strive to make oneself gold! The flaw of modern capitalism is that work energy is directed senselessly and hastily. All its solutions and fruits being only shortsighted, short term goals for the quickest possible self profit regardless of a bigger picture or a wiser long term solution, thus thoroughly selfish.

To look at capitalism from a static point of view it seems a noble system. But when set into motion over time it inevitably steadily increases in bias as delineated by the above definition. The haves become less and the have-nots become greater. The haves having everything and the have-nots having nothing, thus naught but a world of corporate tyranny results. The youth of the have-nots are forced to work unless they have come into great money, the chances of which are negligible, they have no choice but to deal with the machine at whatever job pays the best, regardless of their loves. An environment where one is forced to work is slavery. True every man must work for food, but natural tasks such as hunting, fishing or tilling, are not very time consuming or difficult when supporting just oneself. To put things into perspective, in this present day world the average man works six hours more per week than the average roman slave for the goal of others. His key to escape, the knowledge of self-subsistence, is kept from him. (a 1000 ft^2 garden worked 1/2 hour a day can support two people all year)

One major reason is generation. People are being born into biased conditions and each generation the bias increases. Another reason is the lack of size limitations on businesses. A large company has the power and wisdom of generations and buys out other companies, however large, yet less powerful. Thus these giant companies become immortal, no real competition exists. Even when two or more immortal companies find themselves unable to buy each other out they inevitably cooperate behind closed doors, thus creating a monopoly but technically not so. The playing field is therefore increasingly unfair as the system proceeds. The wealthy and large corporations, usually one in the same, get favored by *government* representatives through either contributions, or the politician being invested into the company, thus developing a higher degree of freedom and control over the laws and governing forces. The have-nots, needed by the haves to continue their parasitical existence, are subjected to lesser freedoms, not necessarily by law, but simply by their meager resources and conditions. Price itself puts much out of reach for the have-nots. Long hours take all their spare time putting out of reach even the learning of higher concepts. Therefore the have-nots progressively weaken. Thus capitalism inevitably evolves back into feudalism overtime, having different privileges for different classes.

At its most extreme stage, the state we are in now, capitalism evolves to corporatism which is a type of global fascism were the overwhelming power, wealth, and influence of the haves (now king-like) leads to their direct control over global proceedings, whether or not made public. The leaders being leaders of companies and not nations or governments, and are therefore out of the spotlight, making this modern version far more insidious and dangerous than all other previous manifestations of fascism throughout human history. The executive officers of these vast corporations become the dictators of world affairs with absolute power, mocking any nation's government. The global masses are exploited for their labor and fed that which they produce at further expense to themselves at a gain to only the haves. This exploiting system is then forced upon new countries when one host is used up, and these parasites seek out another. Any resistance to their will is met with propaganda (1. To gain support from their own nation for their actions, and 2. To "convince" the other nation that the proposed actions are "good" for it) and "terrorism" which is the creation of ambiguous and illusionary threats to either demonize any enemy or resistance to their system, granting support from allies, and giving reason to cause war. Thus increasing waste and consumption to their profit by A. the war itself and B. by new territories whose resources are added to the system of waste and consumption. Exploiting oversees workers in the name of progress. Public consent being maintained by various knowledge filters securing mass ignorance.

A way revolution is avoided is through labor unions, which act as ambassadors from the haves to the have-nots. They are emanations from, and are utterly controlled by, the haves to set wages on the borderline of happiness. The wage, no matter how large it may seem, decreases per year as the cost of living rises disproportionately to the wage increases. The system is strictly to control revolution of the massive group of exploited have-nots. However, once sufficient control is secured, the wages will rapidly drop. This can already be seen in the massive amounts of workers exploited for slave labor wages all throughout, India, Russia, China, and Mexico. As can be seen these countries make up much of the world's population, thus much of the world is already enslaved by this insidious nonsense.

The need suppliers have mercilessly merchandised everything sacred. Just look at any Christian holiday, so far removed from the sacred with plastic light up Santa clauses, and rabbits. Wasting light energy with meaningless home decorations, and buying material things instead of quietly worshiping the divine whose living body is nature not some cheap and graven plastic image which most likely is not biodegradable. No offense to the Christians (or any other religion whose sacred beliefs have been desecrated and unconsecrated by the heartless merchandising machine). It is not their fault – they have been lead into this mode of thoughtless thought and deem it acceptable because of years of their higher senses being numbed to its foul presence. It is a sacrilege, yet to the need suppliers only selfish gain is sacred and all in their way are trampled mercilessly asunder while any tactic possible will be utilized to bait their fellow man especially utilizing what is most dear to him; the sacred or the beloved.

Thus, thanks to the degenerative effects of capitalism in practice, our dying world has lost sight of any goal to its existence. Their malformed goals and ideals are now a new shiny car, or a flashy gadget that everyone else has, or robbing their fellowman. No sacred, noble, pure acts or higher goals are amongst any of them, a blaspheme to the one God worshiped by all men under various names. They reach for dust while infinite power lays just beyond. Their madness is so profound that they laugh at truth and love, peace and harmony, and feverishly rub their fingers raw digging for more gold, slaying all in their path. No higher thought exists, and if it dare appear it is quickly corrupted and turned away from harmonic solutions. Sculpting this global society to purposefully maintain waste and consumption for the continual profit of the very few.

Unrestricted Free knowledge is the key to the power and freedom of the Individualistic society. As capitalism is based on the acquisition and application of material wealth for the advancement of the minor individual self, Individualism is based on the acquisition and application of knowledge for the advancement of mankind as a whole and greater Self. This system still possesses capitalistic principles even though material wealth is no longer the priority. The Individualist counteracts the negative effects of modern capitalism while retaining its free market and private ownership by placing minor corporate limits as checks to negate the natural tendency for capitalism to bias to extreme and volatile contrasts between the haves and have-nots. The Individualists also implement self sufficiency causing many need suppliers to lose their dependent hosts and thus weaken and die, unless they be a truly useful good or service contributing to the greater good of mankind.

A final word of warning is shown in the definition of Fascism by The American Heritage Dictionary:
"A philosophy or system of government that is marked by stringent social and economic control, a strong, centralized government usually headed by a dictator, and often a policy of belligerent nationalism."
As one can see, large corporations possess all the elements of a fascist definition. Their internal hierarchy is stringently controlled and their control over economics effect global affairs. Their strong centralized leadership is their executive officers, the highest being their dictator, (one who issues commands). There nationalism is company marketing propaganda creating loyal followers who go as far as tattooing company logos upon their bodies, no different than a country's flag.

B. SOCIALISM

From Latin Socialis, (of companionship) from Socius (companion, partner) and ism, (practice, quality or system) Thus "the practice of companionship"

Defined by: Sonoma State University, Department of History
1. Adherence to the theory of social organization which believes the proprietorship and the authority of the means of production, capital, land, etc. should belong to the entire community.

Defined by: University of Manitoba, Department of Anthropology
2. Economic system centered on the belief that the means of production (such as land) should be collectively owned and that market exchange should be replaced by collectively controlled distribution based on social needs.

Defined by: Summit Ministries, Manitou Springs, CO
3. The theory or system of the ownership and operation of the means of production and distribution by society rather than by private individuals, with all members of the community coerced to share in the work and the products.

Defined by: Teachnology.com
4. A political or economic theory in which community members own all property, resources, and the means of production, and control the distribution of goods.

Defined by: WGBH educational foundation
5. Any various theories or systems of social organization in which the means of producing and distributing goods is owned collectively or by a centralized government that often plans and controls the economy.

The Individualist's method of defining socialism removes the possibility for an entity separate from the people to feign socialist practice. The Individualist defines socialism as:

An economic system where the means of production and distribution are equally owned and governed by each citizen of the union.

These definitions speak for themselves. The people are in power, not the *government*. When compared to all past governments throughout history claiming to have been socialist, on sees how far from truth they were. Yet the Individualist is not to be considered socialist by praising portions of this system, it merely takes this power of the people and merges it with capitalistic free market purged of faults, soon to be explained in detail.
There can be little comments on this system being it has yet to be implemented.

C. COMMUNISM

From old French, commun (Common) and ism (practice, quality or system) thus "common quality" or "the practice of common quality"

Communist philosophy believes that a communal life gives true freedom from limitations and contentment in one's works. By allowing people to do what they want for how long they want too. Cooperating with one's fellow man in this way eliminates the desire to exploit one's fellow man. Thus, in its ideal form it is a peaceful system of absolute equality, and subsequently practically a fantasy.
Communism is an archetypal concept. Which, contrary to popular belief, has never been implemented. All *governments* to date claiming to be communist are naught but corrupt attempts at socialism, masquerading dictatorships bringing misconception and negativity to both socialism and communism. Communism is the pinnacle of socialism. It is an Ideal state of human cooperation which has never yet

been achieved save by some small sects such as monasteries and most likely will remain a fantasy. The exact reason why communism cannot be implemented is because of the faults of man. Every man, save not one must be enlightened so that the entire society is pious and selfless in order to achieve such a degree of equality and cooperation, this epic challenge is why communism remains a fantasy.

All supposed communistic systems to date have kept a hierarchy of elite ruling and dictating to the workers, a direct contradiction of the practice of communism, as they have not established communal ownership of property and absolute equality. These dictatorships and repressive *government*s that falsely claimed to practice communism defame its name. For example China's supposed communist system has a ruling elite suppressing all workers and dealing them out to the western capitalists for slave wages, the working poor are far from in control as directly defined by communism. Where in any of these supposed socialist and communistic *government*s and economies has the working class ever ruled? Never. It is only by groups of despots separate from the people who claim to represent the working class while they direct and control them for their own ends. No different from any other controlling system, no matter what one labels it, it is simply tyranny. Socialism can only truly exist under a direct democracy, otherwise it is perverted, and thus cannot evolve into communism.

Thus far the definitions of the above governments and economies were relatively simple, summed up in a few sentences. This is how any word should be. When a word cannot be described in such a simple manner the word has become ambiguous and used for too many purposes, sometimes conflicting. It is at this time when the word needs either redefined or replaced by a newer clearly defined term. Look up fifty different definitions for communism and you will find fifty different answers. The word means so many things now because so many fools have titled *government*s as communistic when they were nothing above tyranny. It has also become a word applied to any form of evil, or suspect political practice.

Therefore, much is written below on communist definitions because of the term's dire need for disambiguation. The vast meanings of the word shall be shown to clearly distinguish from the definition to be used in this document so as to avoid being demonized when describing the few gems this system has to offer to nobility.

1. The political, social, and economic system of certain countries in which the state, governed by a single party without formal opposition, owns all property, controls the production and distribution of goods and services, and, to a great extent, controls the social and cultural life of the people. – Vincent Massey High School

-- The " governed by a single party without formal opposition" part has little to do with communistic economy and a lot to do with tyrannical *government*. Also "and, to a great extent, controls the social and cultural life of the people" would be under tyranny also, as communism by definition has no ruling class. It also fails to define "the state" which is supposed to be the people and not a separate tyrannical entity.

2. A. A term that can refer to one of several things: a social and economic system, an ideology which supports that system, or a political movement that wishes to implement that system.
    B. Communism is an ideology that seeks to establish a classless, stateless social organization based on common ownership of the means of production – Wikipedia

-- The latter, the political movement, is what has demonized the system. Too many tyrants have falsely claimed to have implemented the system, utterly defaming it.

3. An economic theory which stresses that the control of the means of producing economic goods in a society should reside in the hands of those who invest their labor for production. In its ideal form, social classes cease to exist, there is no coercive governmental structures, and everyone lives in abundance without supervision from a ruling class. – Illinios State University History Department

-- According to this definition one can see that communism has never yet been implemented.

4. An economic system in which capital is owned by private government. Contrasts with capitalism.
– Deardorff's Glossary of International Economics.

-- This definition does not describe communism, but tyranny. Capital is owned equally by the people in communism and there is no private ownership. Capitalism is where capital is owned by private forces, some larger than governments.

5. A system of government in which the state plans and controls the economy and a single, often authoritarian party holds power, claiming to make progress toward a higher social order in which all goods are equally shared by the people. – WGBH educational foundation

-- The authoritarian party is a misleading concept because once a civilization is in unity any deviation from that is not unity, thus all in agreement would consequently be all of the same belief, therefore "a party". Again the state is not defined leaving much space for the entity separate from the people to be implied which again is tyranny. Also communism is more an economic system than a governmental system. Its cooperative economic methods actually negate government in its ideal form.

6. A political theory derived from Marxism, advocating a society in which all property is publicly owned and each person is paid and works according to his or her needs and abilities. – University of Sydney, Cuban Missile Crises glossary

-- Marxism is but one branch of communist philosophy, thus this definition defines only Marxist communism, not communism itself.

All these definitions were thus shown not only to show the various definitions claiming to define a concept while either erroneously defining it, only partially defining it or defining another word in its place thus propagating misunderstanding among the masses. Therefore, for the remainder of the document only the definition below will be used.

An economic system where all property and the means of production and distribution are equally owned and governed by each citizen of the union.

Myths have become associated with communism because of the tyrants who used its label to hide their tyranny. One of them being the belief in no god. This is found in some schools of thought derived from communism but is not an ideal communistic belief. Some of the earliest communistic societies were monks sharing between each other thus the belief in God was definitely present. Communism is an economic system, to describe thoughts of divinity in the same sentence is to deviate from the scope of the core definition. When doing so one is discussing "communism as applied to God" instead of defining communism itself. The Individualist believes that only ignorant, profane and tyrannical systems would outlaw or teach no God in any government or economic system.

Unfortunately the most popular system of communism is Marxist communism which indirectly teaches violence. Violence need not be implemented to usurp corporate fascism or any other oppressor. The Marxist revolutionary solution can easily be used by evil in the guise of good to rally a powerful revolutionary force and when finished with them, enslave them. The only way this or any other type of enslavement can be avoided, and an oppressor successfully removed and a newly implemented system maintained, is by thorough education of the masses to the principles which initiate, uphold, and maintain both systems as well as the reasoning for doing so, else the system quickly devolves to tyranny.

Individualism sees communism as an extremist practice, far from practical application to the masses. Its high regard for cooperation and fellowship is recognized and the basic principle is adopted by Individualism. Its noble attempt to stop man from focusing on material things by negating private property is also acknowledged but deemed too extreme and a disregard of mans inherent desire to own. Individualism taxes excess property to achieve much the same goal while allowing as much property as one can afford. It must be said that ideally communism is a quiet, peaceful and pious system meant more for ascetics, as opposed to an entire globe, unless, of course, that globe becomes a globe of ascetics.

D. INDIVIDUALISM

There is but one definition for Individualistic economics true throughout time:

1. An economic system encouraging self production, stressing the meaningful purpose of all things created, and efficiency in that creation, where the amount of private land and size of private business is fairly regulated and a major portion of the means of production, distribution and trades are equally owned and governed by each citizen of the union whose idea of success is the attainment of the highest possible degree of perfection in mind, body and spirit in the life span allotted.

This alternate concept of economic success prioritizing intellectual gain as opposed to material gain, leads to efficiency of every industry, honing them toward the evolution of mankind. All deviations from this path are accordingly seen as wastes of time and energy, consequently rendering most of the present economic mechanisms pointless. The unnecessary complexities of which were initially formed by handing over one's personal responsibilities to others initiating a cycle of malignant growth. Self-sufficiency, the key to true freedom and growth, was lost. Education was altered to make corporate tools instead of wise individuals. Free unrestricted knowledge remedies all of these ailments creating an enlightened society, each contributing to all government and economic decisions. This is ensured by erection of the Greater Eye of the Populus (GEP), a system of notification composed of the people keeping each individual informed and relaying their opinions and desires directly to the necessary department. The result is a content, efficient society in harmony with each other and nature whose actions truly mirror the desires of its people.

The Individualist is an obvious adversary to the pointless machine of waste and consumption. Its unhealthy fixation upon "economic growth" and "creating jobs" has become a madness. A project funded by the people which creates 1000 "jobs" sends 1000 people into servitude for the machine and increases the waste and consumption proportionately. Far less money spent on teaching 1000 people self sufficiency frees them from the system and decreases its waste and consumption proportionately. Allowing their work energy to be directed toward loftier goals such as refinement of self, acquisition and assimilation of knowledge and using both to aid mankind. The old aphorism "give a man a fish and he will eat for a day, teach a man to fish and he eats for a lifetime", takes on profound meaning here. Without this knowledge of self-sustenance one's very life is in danger and one is forced to depend on another. The perfect unbreakable chain for a slave.

The Individualist therefore becomes the demise of the need suppliers because he fulfills his own needs and takes all aspects of his life into his own hands naturally dissolving the market, a loop composed of the people as end consumer as well as the exploited resource. Taxed on both ends by a middleman who does nothing. Individualism establishes regulations keeping the size and influence of surviving private businesses in check by business ownership and employee responsibility laws coupled with 'large entity' and 'excess property' taxes. These cause any private entity which grows large to yield great returns to the people, who are the society upon which its existence depends.

The native Americans had a simplistic society in harmony with creation, the Individualists recognize this important value but also recognize the power that technology has to assist mankind in evolution, if brought into the same scope. As more people begin working strictly for them selves, production would slow yet result in efficiency. Technological advances would increase in frequency and magnitude because of the great deal of time people have to peacefully think deeply coupled with their highly advanced free education system. Regularly working directly with earthly resources and waste, the society also becomes thoroughly energy conscious. Resulting in efficiently created products which have a greater purpose, last longer, and are made of more friendly materials. The Individualists establish a variety of Populus owned facilities, such as fabrication shops, mills, mines farms etc. to assist these ends, not to replace a private market, but simply to allow individuals access to something they may need. The erection, disbandment and operation of these facilities are directly controlled by an annual consensus of the people.

INDIVIDUALISTIC WEALTH

There is individual wealth and omniwealth, that is, the sum total of all wealth. A measurement of any thing changing throughout time must be taken at one moment in time, a snapshot true only for that moment. The Individualists view wealth as such a changing body. Therefore to measure it, it is analyzed at one moment in time and called Static Wealth. **Static wealth** is the degree of the quality and quantity of both material and immaterial things accumulated by an entity. It is "macrovalue". **Value** is the degree of quality and quantity of both material and immaterial wealth contained in a single thing. It is "microwealth". As can be seen, the Individualists include immaterial things as a factor of wealth also, for they too have value. Such as knowledge itself has a high value to the ascetic, and gold is worthless. The value of use is incorporated into this definition by example of a shovel. It is composed of material things organized into the specific shape for the specific task by knowledge alone, its immaterial component. The degree of quality of the materials used, such as hardened steel, and quality of knowledge applied such as a rippled cutting edge to cut through roots, would both add value as opposed to a stick with a sharp rock tied to the end.

Static Wealth possesses the following two major components which interact over time creating a compound mechanism that the Individualists call "Dynamic Wealth", which is the cause of all human actions.

1. Material wealth is the degree of quantity and quality of material things. Its foundation being natural resources, matter itself, the finest division of which is energy.

2. Immaterial wealth is the degree of quantity and quality of immaterial things. Its foundation being knowledge, the finest division of which is consciousness.

These two directly interact forming:

1. Products are the result of Knowledge applied to resources, it is static power, potential, capability

2. Dynamic Power is the result of Knowledge applied to products to fulfill a goal. Dynamic power consumes material wealth for motion. Thus a **Need** is the material wealth consumed by dynamic power creating voids, which are goals. (Omniwealth, being it is the sum total of all wealth, also has consciousness, thus it can exert dynamic power also. Such as a forest fire converting material wealth to motion, thus creating needs. If it happens to consume one's home it creates a goal for that one, a new home.)

3. Wisdom is the efficiency resultant of the frequency of the interplay of the two polarities of wealth, (material and immaterial). Or more simply: knowledge that has been practiced to the point of clear understanding of its most efficient application. Or knowledge that has been applied to the point of rectifying it to its most efficient application by identifying many negative vectors.

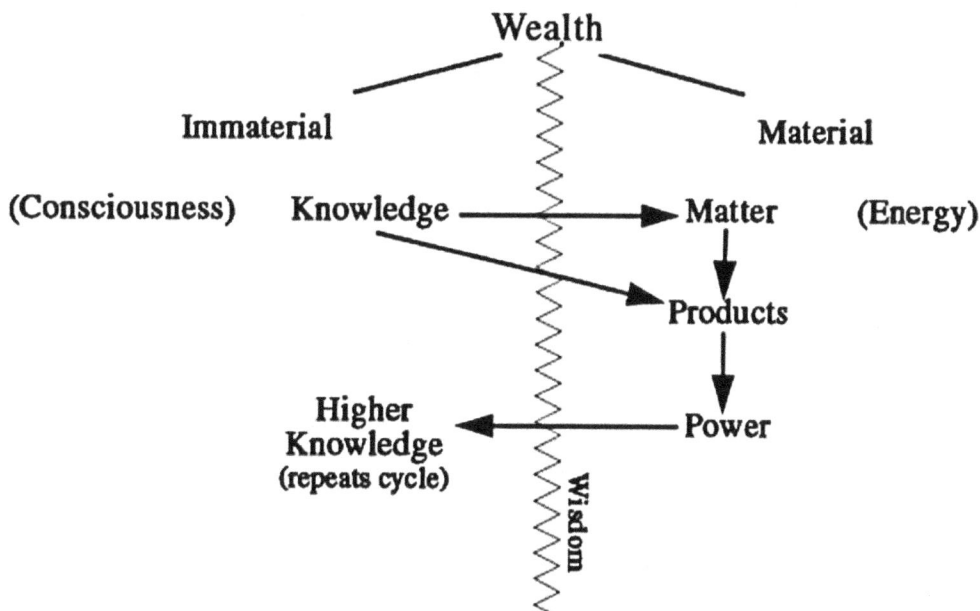

In its broadest sense Zero wealth is the Void, no thing, material or immaterial. In this massive void one has the ultimate goal. The ultimate fulfilled goal is the ultimate infinite void filled with the ultimate infinite experience, which is the ultimate wealth, all things (Omniwealth). The individual consciousness itself is the smallest portion of this wealth. Incarnation grants the initial material wealth, the physical body. The senses of the physical body begin to relay knowledge of the surrounding Omniwealth. **Knowledge** (immaterial wealth) is experience, information received by the senses.

The Individual consciousness is constantly organizing accumulated knowledge more efficiently with each new piece of knowledge acquired, this action is called Imagination. **Imagination** is speculation by analysis and synthesis of current wealth, simply the movement of things into an order. Its magnitude (number of permutations) is directly proportionate to the accumulated wealth. Thus if one has experienced only a mouse and a leaf one can imagine all combinations of just those two, such as a fury leaf or a green mouse, but one could not imagine a bird, imagination is limited to experience, which is knowledge, which is wealth. **Uncertainty** is the variable, the forever unknown quantity due to infinity. Such is the static measure of Omniwealth, thus uncertainty lay in all calculations.

In this process of analytical organization the individual wealth is also constantly compared to Omniwealth. Within this comparison degrees of harmony exist. **Harmony** is an individual wealth equal to Omniwealth yet on a smaller scale. Thus it resonates with it giving one insights into the nature of Omniwealth (All). The Void (all things not yet possessed) becomes uniform when in harmony and thus exerts a uniform pull on the individual consciousness causing distinct desire to seemingly vanish. **Desire** is a goal unaccomplished, (the force of attraction of a void). A **Goal** is a missing aspect of wealth, a negative wealth, a void. Out of harmony goals exert a pull to varying degrees based on the degree of discord.

When Individual wealth resonates with
Omniwealth, one is in Harmony

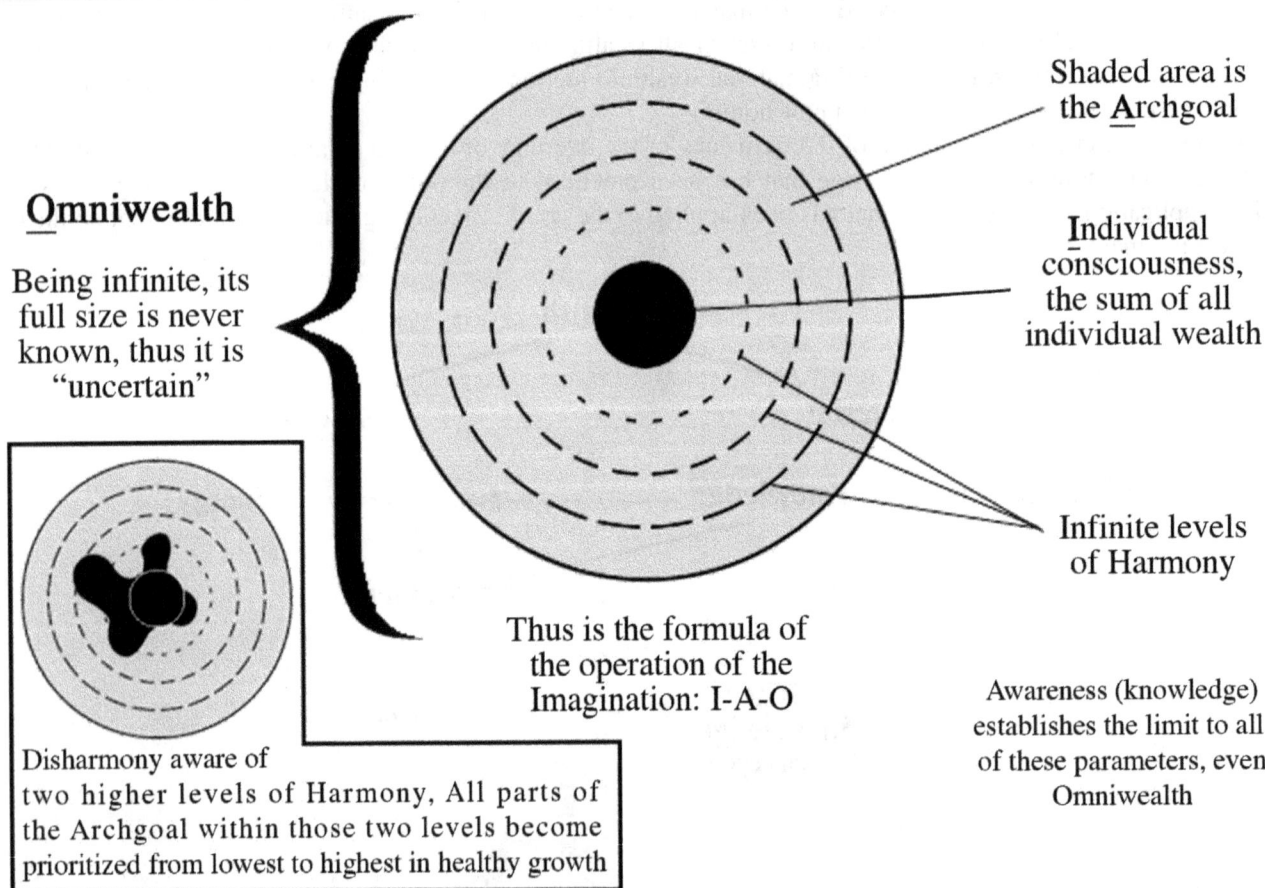

Shaded area is
the Archgoal

Omniwealth

Being infinite, its
full size is never
known, thus it is
"uncertain"

Individual
consciousness,
the sum of all
individual wealth

Infinite levels
of Harmony

Thus is the formula of
the operation of the
Imagination: I-A-O

Awareness (knowledge)
establishes the limit to all
of these parameters, even
Omniwealth

Disharmony aware of
two higher levels of Harmony, All parts of
the Archgoal within those two levels become
prioritized from lowest to highest in healthy growth

A goal is selected to fulfill because of the speculated capabilities (products) its addition to wealth would grant. Thus is manifested the relative potential power level of goals. Potential power of a goal is a measure of the current "macrovalue" (static wealth) of the individual consciousness relative to the speculated size of Omniwealth (all things). This individual macrovalue subtracted from the speculated size of Omniwealth leads to a proportionately sized goal (void), for one cannot have a goal bigger than the *known* universe. This is the Archgoal (The Void, all things not possessed). The level of its potential power is speculated by the individual static wealth multiplied by the speculated size of the Archgoal. This goal shrinks in size with the accumulation of individual wealth.

An example is the tribe living on an island for centuries, thinking it is the totality of existence, content they understand all forces "in the universe" they are omnipotent on their island. There are no goals left to fulfill, their individual wealth is equal to their speculated size of Omniwealth. Until an advanced culture comes along taking them up in a plane and showing them that they live on a vast globe, which spins around a stupendously huge sun in an incomprehensibly immense universe. Suddenly their proportionate wealth is profoundly altered, uncovering countless new goals and potential power.

The Archgoal can be divided into an infinite system of fulfillment vectors. Wisdom is what determines the efficiency of travel along vectors determined by understanding. **Understanding** is the knowledge of the nature of a thing. **Nature** is a predicable/known action of a thing under the influence of specific forces. Understanding plots the series of vectors to fulfill either one or all goals. A **Vector** is a predetermined series of applications (products and dynamic power) supposed to end in a fulfilled goal. **Reason** is a compound vector, the specific vector of sub-vectors to fulfill an over-goal orchestrated by understanding to avoid known negative vectors, (consequences, misunderstood nature). Thus the wisest reason displays the greatest understanding by fulfilling the Archgoal in an instant.

The vector(s) are organized by feasibility and priority directly related to current static wealth and strength of desire (pull of void). For without certain knowledge or resources, a vector may not be feasible until those items are accumulated, thus accumulating those objects necessary becomes a priority vector, thus all vectors together become a reason. However even if a vector is unfeasible, if the desire is sufficient the path may still be chosen, yet it is most likely inefficient (unwise) and fraught with consequences (misunderstandings, negative vectors). This assessment of the sequence of goals takes time, but its efficiency is not directly proportionate to time. The complexity of the vector and current degree of understanding and wisdom yield a minimum and maximum solving time. Thus is the origin of hastened, hesitant, and over analyzed decisions. However, time can be used to directly increase the speculated size of omniwealth simply because imaginations organizing and synthesizing task is infinite. (Basic example, pg 151)

Once the final reason is chosen the consciousness moves toward the void along the plotted vector. **Will** is the movement of consciousness along a vector causing subsequent reactions in Omniwealth. Will is what makes Omniwealth dynamic and self-interactive, creating time. If correctly plotted the movement ends in a fulfilled goal. A **Fulfilled Goal** is an intentional addition to wealth. This adds not only the goal but additional knowledge from insight into correct understanding (if a goal was not accomplished the initial vector was flawed shedding light on the flaw in understanding creating a desire to fill that void etc.)

For example of the above mechanics, let stagnation be examined. (Not to be confused with sloth, because in stagnation one may still be applying will. **Sloth** is lack of application within inharmonious wealth. It is resistant to the pull of desire. Sometimes false contentment.) A narcotics abuser spends years doing drugs all day. He is therefore now very efficient in getting and using them for the same goal accomplished years ago, the goal of physical pleasure. This particular goal yields little wealth and is an ever present void because the senses can never be filled, the instant the stimulus is removed the sense instantly becomes a void again. Thus from the initial experience little, if any, new wealth is now acquired for the consuming dynamic power exerted. Thus with no wealth accumulation there are no capabilities gained therefore there is no potential power increase, hence no growth. All these fulfilled goals, being of negligible potential power, cause a rate of growth which would take lifetimes to fulfill the Archgoal. However if this individual's static wealth was very limited, so too would be the speculated size of Omniwealth leading to a subsequently limited Archgoal. Therefore, to this individual, this tiny nearly powerless goal may be relatively huge. This is further reasoning for the Individualists' implementation of free knowledge. It increases the speculated size of Omniwealth in the minds of all, allowing them to realize larger goals and to use all their dynamic power to fulfill them. Simply the realization of a goal (void) initiates a pull (desire) on the perceiver. When the largest voids (goals) are filled, the largest gains in potential and dynamic power are subsequently achieved, creating powerful individuals and a powerful society.

The Individualists realize that the highest possible goal is the achievement of Omniwealth, which is all things and thus the infinite experience. The most efficient vector to attain this is one line that ties all individual units of wealth together in their most efficient order *effortlessly* accumulating them all in that order up to the last unit. It is Omniwisdom. In this light all other goals and vectors are "less wise" to varying degrees. This is the benchmark used by the Individualists to gauge their goals. (**Effort** is a measure of Will through resistance (inefficiency). Directly related to wealth consumed by dynamic power.)

The Individualists believe that first there was one consciousness which was all things (Omniwealth). This then divided itself into infinite individual consciousnesses. Each individual consciousness attempts to accumulate all these infinite pieces of self, each also a consciousness, and reassemble them into the original infinite whole. Time, the sequence of these accumulations, is an illusion because in infinity an infinitely long second is as long as an infinitely long day. Thus the One is still whole eternally, yet is still infinitely divided eternally. It is the divided consciousness which moves through this eternal Oneness in a specific sequence that causes the illusion of time. The more of its self it accumulates (knowledge) the more this illusion breaks down. One begins to realize that there is only one consciousness, and one goal, reunification. Thus all consciousnesses must reach this degree of recollection to reunite with each other into the original self. It is for this reason that the Individualists believe in tailoring their goals as high as possible and with the broadest benefit to mankind possible, being that it is all One self. To help another is to help one's self, this is proven by the phenomena of inspiration, when knowledge is shared, new knowledge erupts which may then assist the initial giver. To help many is to help oneself many times. This must not be confused with utter selflessness, for to properly help others one must be strong in mind, body and spirit, if one neglects oneself, there is little hope for that one to help mankind.

This Individualistic concept of wealth consolidates the individual and his goals into one by relating them as two parts of a larger whole (omniwealth), thus the very use of wealth itself is a factor of wealth, lending growth to either the individual (positive) or the void (negative). There are goals for the self at the expense of others, goals for the self which are neutral to others, and goals for the self that benefit others. Of these goals, the first has no place in a society because the net benefit to the society may be negative thus a "negative" goal, like many goals of the present world. With the second type, at least there is no negative effect to society but its contributions are minimal. For what use is knowledge and material wealth if it sits idle? It is simply potential that may be wasted (inefficient, thus unwise) because of death before its use. The third causes a dynamic interaction of individuals rapidly increasing the pace of evolution. Whether an individual is alone in nature, or with men, he is in a society, because of all things being one thing. The word "society" itself is derived from the Latin *societas* (fellowship, union) derived from *socius* (a sharing). With this understanding the Individualists always strive to be mindful of All in their calculations to fulfill any goal.

The power level of an entire society is the sum total of each individuals wealth divided by their numbers. Therefore the Individualists instill the largest possible speculated size of omniwealth in their brethren and share all knowledge so that all have the highest portion of immaterial wealth available. Then the finite material resources are fairly distributed, (not to be confused with equally distributed). A change in life style grants the time needed for imaginative assessments, realizing the highest goals, and plotting the most efficient paths thereto. This creates all the conditions for accumulation of incredible potential power in each individual causing the potential power of the entire society to become incomprehensibly vast. This is the highest power a society can have simply because of the finite nature of material wealth and its impotence without applied knowledge. Such as a mere pencil applied to mere paper used to enlighten the entire race shows that material quantity and even quality is insignificant next to applied knowledge. Thus the easiest way to increase the power of a society is to instill the highest available knowledge in each individual, it consumes negligible material resources to do so and the returns are near endless. It is very similar to how the Federal Reserve creates money out of nothing, except its power is very real.

Thus, True Individual Dynamic Power is knowledge applied with the highest attained wisdom to material wealth to accumulate the most units of consciousness (knowledge/awareness) for each unit of consciousness as a whole. More simply, it is knowledge applied with the highest attained wisdom to material wealth to achieve the highest benefit to Omniwealth as a whole (the self is obviously included within Omniwealth, therefore this does not imply utter selflessness). Or loosely as knowledge applied with highest attained wisdom to material wealth to achieve the highest benefit to mankind (or society) as a whole. Therefore the True dynamic power of a Society is their collective knowledge applied with collective wisdom to their collective material wealth to accumulate the most units of consciousness for each unit of consciousness as a whole. Thus achieving the highest benefit for the individual, the society, the globe etc.

This is the Infinite Work of the Individualist leading to True Wealth and True Success on infinite levels. Due to the nature of uncertainty, it is uncertain when the Individualists will be truly content. **Contentment** is the cessation of fulfilling goals. Various factors cause contentment, lack of resources will cause contentment because dynamic power consumes resources. The achievement of harmony will cause a *seeming* lack of desire due to its uniformity. Or simply descent into sloth negating positive growth. At very least, the Individualists are assured contentment at each new level of harmony.

Energy Theory of Value

Value is in the eye of the beholder. A ton of gold, or the world's fastest computer, each "worth" millions to many, mean very little to the ascetic. However the book printed upon 3 dollars of paper may be worth millions to him and nothing to others. Knowledge could be said to be more valuable because unlike gold, it is never lost unless it is *not* shared. It is the wealth that can be distributed without loss to he who gives. However in a material world one must deal with finite material things thus a system to fairly achieve that distribution must be wrought. The Individualists believe that simplicity is the strongest system, thus all value, use-value, exchange-value, worth, price must be reduced to a simple system.

Apart from **Price,** which is desire of profit and even feelings of entitlement, (what one feels like one deserves for the effort applied) there exists True Value. True Value is beyond the feelings and desires of man. It is in the realm of pure energy. For any one item, X amount of energy was applied to extract, refine and transport the resources. Y amount of energy was applied to design it, Z amount was applied to create it and distribute it to the end user. Thus the **True Value** is the sum total of the exact time and energy utilized to manifest that item in its present form, composition, and location. The True Value does not compensate for inefficiency of the crafter, or any inefficiency along the system. Thus something completely useless could have a tremendous True Value, like many present day products. Gasoline being one of them, if the costs of war over oil was added into the price, we would most likely be paying over ten dollars per gallon.

True Worth unveils the True level of mastery of the craftsman (or production method). True worth is a comparison between the True Value of two (or more) things over their respective times. The lowest true value is considered "one" and the higher becomes a percentage of that. These two values are then divided by their times to yield true worth. For example:

Two souls, both create the exact same object of exact quality etc. save the one took twice the energy and twice the time to produce it. Soul A's energy efficiency would be one while soul B's use of twice the energy would be 1/2. Thus soul A's True Worth is: $1e/1t = 1$. Compared to soul B's True Worth of $0.5e/2t = 0.25$. Thus soul B's item is truly worth only a quarter of soul A's item even though the items are exactly the same.

True Worth reflects the degree of wisdom as efficiency. Yet it will never determine practical worth to an individual which is a judgement solely in the mind of that individual. Furthermore, it does not reflect the emotion which the item was wrought in be it Love, Fear, War, Peace etc.

To build a system of this nature from scratch would not be so challenging. To implement the system into another system already working is slightly more challenging. Adhering strictly to the above definitions one must first know all energy consumption beginning at the raw resources. Each human and machine used to mine uses X amount of energy over Y amount of time per volume of resources produced. The machine itself was built from raw materials which were refined, shaped into the machine and shipped, thus its True Value must also be divided amongst the volume it produces. Even the train transporting these goods has very high true value that must be considered.

If implemented from scratch the energy of extraction of resources would be divided by the produced volume. Thus different iron ore mines would have different true values for their products simply because of differences in digging difficulty through different rock hardness, let alone different choices in equipment, even though the end product is simply iron in both cases. The product's total energy of creation would be stamped upon it and registered.

When transported, an additional stamp would be placed adding a calculated portion of the true value of the transporting vehicle and amount of fuel used upon arriving at its destination. When fashioned into a shape an additional stamp is added recording the amount of the plant's consumption of time and energy used in shaping the item along with a portion of the plant's true vale. A final stamp is placed recording fuel consumption and a portion of the true value of the final distribution vehicle upon arrival at its final destination.

The end result is a time and energy breakdown on the side of a product that is no different than the nutritional breakdown on the side of food packages and just as simple to implement. It would label the raw ingredients, and the time and energy consumption of each stage, the total being its True Value. All the plants, farms, mines and mills etc. would have to include their registered number so that consumers can look into them if desired, assisting consumers to be aware of the relative efficiency of each plant, farm, mill, mine etc. This system would allow consumers to make wiser comparisons of items clearly seeing their True Worth.

The initial challenge is the assessment taken to implement the system. Once it is implemented it gets progressively more accurate as each manufacturer beings purchasing machines that already have an accurate True Value stamped upon them making its division amongst the products created by or with it that much easier. The division of the True Value of a machine into the production must be exactly the same throughout the society. The suggested time is 365 days. For a simple example: If a machine has a true value of fifty units divided over fifty years its addition to a product which took a year to build was 1 unit. If a machine with a true value of one unit builds the same product in the same year its added value is also one. But if the standard division was one year (365 days) the first machine would have to add fifty units to the product clearly showing its possible inefficiency allowing the customers to then research this machine by following the plant registration number and determining if there is some valid reason. In short it eliminates concealing inefficiency.

This system of True Value and Worth does nothing directly to the price which a manufacture can place. It simply allows greater energy consciousness to the entire society permitting clearer discernment as to what are wise alternatives. This would eventually cause inefficient systems to either evolve or die out. This system is made stronger by the implementation of the GEP, which would constantly evaluate manufacturers for accurate energy assessments.

To keep fools from raising prices because they know an energy conscious society will purchase their energy efficient product, another standardization is made. It is the minimum hourly wage converted to an estimated consumption of energy. This value is created and updated yearly by the GEP. It also has nothing to do with price, but simply gives consumers another benchmark to judge price on the basis of energy converted to average man hours. For example, if one was told that a product took 8 average man-hours to build, he would immediately have an idea of the worth of the product in relation to his own individual output per hour and his own personal judgement of himself as average, above or below. Normally, expended human work energy is an ambiguous and rough determination. With the mechanism described below it becomes a much more "real" value.

This Minimum wage value is determined as the average amount of calories burned by the average worker in the average occupation plus all daily needs.

1. At rest the average body burns about 11 calories per pound per day so that a 155 lb. man burns 1,705 kcal. During light work the same will burn roughly an additional 245 calories per hour or 1960 calories per 8 hr day, plus the 1,705 just to keep the body running, yields 3,665 kcalories or 14,535 BTU just to repay the man the work energy he expended.
2. The average distance traveled per day is 30 miles, most of this is in commute to work. Thus an additional 2 gallons of gas at 15m/gal yields 227,000 BTU
3. The average daily electricity he will use is 9.6kWh or 32,757 BTU
4. The average daily heat is 75 kWh or 255,911 BTU
5. Depending on the various systems for water retrieval and wastes removal it is assumed an addition $1.11/day to accomplish these tasks or 42,252 BTU*
6. His communication with phone and Internet are $3/day or 113,738 BTU*
7. A 100,000 dollar home over 30 years approximately $33.33/day or 1,263,629 BTU* (A mere 346,143 BTU without interest)
* Based on $0.09 per kWh
** Does not include a vehicle payment

Thus 1,949,822 BTU per day or **243,728 BTU per hour** is the minimum wage. This is the bare minimum energy an average individual utilizes daily, therefore needs to be compensated this amount to maintain equilibrium. For additional perspective this value is shown below converted into the equal amount in other energy forms and the price in that form: (note: federal minimum wage is 5.85 now, to increase to 6.55 7/24/08)

1. Electricity: 71.43kWh @ $0.09kWh or $6.43 2. Corn (&cob): 614 lbs {$20.83} 3. Soy: 33.88 lbs {$4.23} 4. Sunflower seeds: 24.41 lbs. {$2.93} 5. Ethanol: 3.17 gal {$8.70} 6. Gas: 2.15 gal, {$6.42} 7. Soy derived diesel: 1.86 gal {$5.77} 8. Sunflower derived diesel: 1.87 gal {$4.62}

Without any system to convert a True Value amount of energy into a relative price, a consumer is simply left with a true worth comparison as described above. Thus the individual who creates an energy efficient product with a capitalizing mindset realizes this society will magnetize to his product because its true worth is far better than similar items. He uses this to his advantage and raises the price. This is not to say that there is anything wrong with this. It is simply saying that the consumer is at a disadvantage because there are no further benchmarks to judge the final price and gain insight into the demeanor of the manufacturer, such as if he is over charging or fair. With this minimum wage value the energy value of the product can be directly converted into a dollar figure thus exposing the approximate markup of the manufacture. Assisting the consumer in his final decision.

This breakdown also shows where efficiency can be increased in society as a whole as it reflects the average individual consumption. One can see above that simply the removal of mortgage interest alone eliminates 917,486 BTU per day per individual. The implementation of self-sufficiency will further decrease this consumption. Furthermore this value allows the labor of men to be converted into an approximate True Vale to be divided over their products produced enhancing the accuracy of True Worth.

As can be seen in all of the above prices for the exact same amount of energy in different forms, they all have a different price. One would expect differences due to the application of energies such as Food Energy, Motive Energy, or Raw Electrical Energy, but each of these groupings should be similar, yet they are not. This allows it to be clearly seen which type of energy is cumbersome to produce and which system of conversion to energy is less efficient than another clearly delineating to the people what systems need to be improved.

With the energy efficiencies of fuel production able to be compared to price, people will begin to question why should they pay more for the exact same amount of energy, causing expensive fuels to either refine their efficiency methods or phase out. The prices of all fuels will reflect a True Worth value in addition to their Fuel Energy value both in addition to price. This is where waste will clearly be seen. It is possible that the true worth (the amount of energy taken to create and move the product) will be far greater than the energy contained in the product. Simply, it will be like spending two dollars to buy a dollar. With an energy conscious society, even if the price is low, negative products as these will soon be abandoned or forced to increase efficiency.

The Individualists implement one final system to galvanize the energy awareness of their society: The implementation of the Energy standard. No different than what the gold standard was, the energy standard allows one at any time to trade in issued certificates for real energy, either Food Energy, Motive Energy, or Raw Electrical Energy at a Populus Resource Reserve or use them as currency at any Populus facility. This allows the self-sufficient to trade in crops, self made fuels, surplus electric from wind and water turbines and even labor to fill the voids in their environment. With bills/notes as Energy Certificates, the society becomes further energy conscious being that its bills and trade constantly refer the mind back to energy efficiency.

The Individualists do not arbitrarily print their certificates like the hollow systems of today. Aside from the energy created by Populus facilities and stored as reserves. They issue one registered certificate for each real trade. The entire transaction recorded in detail and added to the reserve. For instance, if a man trades in a fifty-five gallon drum of diesel containing approximately X Btu of energy, he is issued a certificate(s) for Y, and the amount of diesel is sent to the reserves and duly recorded. When certificates are used at a Populus facility they are then registered as "expended" and may be destroyed to prevent human temptation to corrupt the system if seen fit. For simple example, the above man's diesel had 4 units of energy (e). After the conversion he was issued a certificate for 3e. Therefore the reserve now has 4e. This man then uses a Populus fabrication shop spending his 3e there. The fabrication shop physically used 3e of electricity to power his activity. Thus the 3e is registered as expended. The reserve now has 1e and 3e of disbanded currency.

Populus issued certificates are accepted as hard currency at any Populus facility. As the system gains in use, individuals and private businesses will also begin to use them and the old hollow currency will phase out. The certificates issued are based on raw electrical energy. Any item traded for a certificate is reduced to it simplest form by the functions listed below and issued a certificate for that amount in energy. For example:

A man wishes to trade 1 lb of soy for certificates. 1 lb of soy is know to contain V amount of Vital energy and yield W amount of fuel with the loss of X amount in conversion, that fuel yields Z amount in raw electric at the cost of Y amount in conversion. Therefore $W - X - Y = Z$ the energy value of the certificate issued. The GEP will establish an old market conversion value for raw energy until the old market is phased out. This is the Standard Energy Value (SEV), this value links the Individualistic system to the old market. For example $0.09/kWh, a common price of electricity. This value will be assessed each year and as efficiency increases this figure will drop. Assisting the phasing out of the old system and increasing the accuracy and fairness of the functions below, as some only exist because the old market still exists. As ideally the Populus reserve attempts to see only energy and efficiency not human desire of entitlement for expended effort (price).

The Populus Reserve recognizes three tiers of energy, Vital (food), Fuel and Raw. Food being the most complex and raw being pure electricity. When trading, one does not have to trade for a certificate, one can trade for real items by following the functions below, such as corn for soy, diesel for corn etc. Below are examples of the Energy tier conversions.

1. Food to food = 1a: (the lesser of Va/Vb and Fa/Fb) b where 'a' is the food to be traded to the reserve and 'b' is the food received. V is the registered food energy value per amount and F being the registered fuel yield of that particular food. The reason why it is the lesser of the two is so that one cannot trade a food that has a low fuel energy yield for a food with a higher one thus profiting even if they have identical food energy values. For example, 1lb of corn has 397 Food BTUs and yields 4,125 Fuel BTUs (0.05 gal of ethanol). 1lb of soy has 7,194 Food BTUs and yields 3,054 Fuel BTUs (0.02 gallon of biodiesel). If one came in with a pound of soy and traded it for an equal food energy amount with corn, one would get 18.12 pounds of corn which could yield 74,745 BTUs in fuel energy (nearly a gallon of ethanol), which is nearly 25 times the fuel yield of the pound of soy traded.

2. Food to Fuel = The registered fuel yield of that particular food less the registered Conversion Efficiency Coefficient (CEC) of that conversion (such as soy to diesel, there is energy lost in conversion)

3. Fuel to Food = simply Btu value to Btu value

4. Fuel to Fuel = ideally this would be simply Btu value to Btu value, for one type of fuel Btu generates no more electricity or motive energy than another does. Some simply take up more or less space per Btu which is actually an inefficiency, such as ethanol which takes up nearly twice the space as biodiesel for the exact same amount of energy and is twice as expensive. One would think that for such an inefficiency it would be half as expensive. Therefore to keep the Populus reserve free from illogical corruption of this sort until the old market dies out the conversion must be 1a: (the lesser of Fa/Fb and Ma/Mb) b where 'a' is the fuel to be traded to the reserve and 'b' is the fuel received. F is the registered fuel energy value per amount and M being the registered current market value of that particular fuel. The reason why it is the lesser of the two is so that one cannot trade a fuel that has a low market price for a fuel with a higher one thus profiting even if they have identical fuel energy values. For example one could trade 1 gal of gas worth $2.99 for 1.47 gal of ethanol which commands a price of $4.05 for the exact same amount of energy (113,500 Btu).

5. Raw to fuel = ideally this would be Btu for Btu. But, until phase out this function is used: 1a: (the lesser of Ra/Fb and Ma/Mb) b where 'a' is the raw energy to be traded to the reserve and 'b' is the fuel received. R is the Standard Energy Value of raw electricity (SEV) F is the registered fuel energy value per amount and M being the registered current market values. The reason why it is the lesser of the two is so that one cannot trade electricity that has a low market price for a fuel with a higher one thus profiting even if they have identical energy values.

6. Fuel to Raw = registered Btu content of fuel less standard fuel CEC.

At first glance at these conversions, all trade seems to be had at a loss to the individual, as with any pawn shop, but the loss is illusory because the gain goes to the reserve which is the people which includes that individual. One gives up some energy in the trade for the convenience, to the benefit of society.

The old market system charges others for the amount of difficulty they experience creating their product. Effort, by the Individualist definition, is simply inefficiency. One should not be charged for the inefficiency of others, thus rewarding the most inefficient. By phasing this old market out all energy will have the same value, the currency then becomes energy itself. Therefore profit becomes a function of efficiency. For example if one makes a gallon of diesel containing X Btu, it will only trade for that amount regardless of the time and energy one put into it. The man making that same gallon in half the time and resources therefore profits. A further example is the homebuilder. Each piece used to build the home, down to the simplest nail will have a true value. All his men will work an exact time, the house would have a true value equal to the sum total of all these values. Ideally the home is only worth this amount, thus the faster this homebuilder builds these homes, therein lies his profit. This system allows for no making of profit out of nothing. Only efficiency of technique will afford profit. Soon profit will be found in growing energy, gathering it from wind and water, and efficient conversion of that energy. Many fuels and fuel using devises will phase out along with the old hollow market system, as fully electric devises are found most efficient.

Below are the forms taken by the Populus Reserve Certificates and their comparisons to present currency. The SEV value used as example in the below certificate comparisons will be 0.09/kWh.

Hnote = 1 hectoWatt-hour or 341 Btu Similar to a penny
H5   = 5 hectoWatt-hours or 1,705 Btu Similar to a Nickel
Mnote = 1 megacalorie (3,965 Btu) Similar to a dime
M10   = 10 megacalories (39,656 Btu) Similar to a $1
M20   = 20 megacalories (79,312 Btu) Similar to a $2
M50   = 50 megacalories (198,250 Btu) Similar to a $5
M100 = 100 megacalories (396,566 Btu) Similar to a $10
M200 = 200 megacalories (793,132 Btu) Similar to a $20
M500 = 500 megacalories (1,982,500 Btu) Similar to a $50
Gnote = 1 gigacalorie or 3,965,666 Btu Similar $100 (actually $104.60)

The Individualists believe that this system allows the populace to clearly see the flow of energy, in single items, entire procedures and the whole of society. Quickly exposing each and every inefficiency as well as their remedies with endless insights. Causing the noise of the friction of this current market, its effort, to be alleviated. The pace of life consequently will slow and relax as the race in waste and haste to nowhere is stopped, plummeting consumption to less than half of its present value and returning peace, harmony, reason and sanity to man.

Some Rough Figures

- Corn: $1.90/ bushel at 56 Pounds yields 3 gallons of ethanol.
- Ethanol yields 77,000 BTUs/gal sells at $2.75 / gal or 28,000 Btu/dollar.
- As food one bushel (70 ears) corn yields 22,232 food Btu (5606kcal) Less than 3 days of food energy.
  (Due to inedible cob, about 45% of total ear mass.)
- Gasoline yields 113,500 BTUs/gal sells at $2.99 / gal or 37,960 Btu/dollar.
- Peanuts: $4.00 for 1/100th ton (20lbs) yields 9.6 lbs. oil 7.7 lbs. gal (1.25 gal)
- PeaDesiel yields 130,900 Btu/gal sells at $3.43 / gal or 38,163 Btu/dollar
- As food 20lbs yields 207,065 food Btu (52,210 kcal) about 26 days of food energy.
- Soy: $7.50/ bushel at 60lbs yields 10.8 lbs. oil (1.40 gal)
- SoyDiesel yields 130,900 Btu/gal sells at $3.10 / gal or 42,226 Btu/dollar.
- As food one bushel soy yields 431,640 food Btu (108,840kcal) About 54 days of food energy
- Sunflower: $3.36/ bushel at 28lbs yields 7.6 lbs. of oil (1gal)
- SunDiesel yields 129,200 Btu/gal sells at $2.47 / gal or 52,308 Btu/dollar.
- As food one bushel sunflower yields 291,564 food Btu (74,396kcal) About 37 days of food energy.

* The above biodiesel prices were figured using $0.0925/lb for the value of meal remaining after extraction. Plus an additional dollar per gallon as $0.80/gal for processing and $0.20/gal profit.

Natural oils that may be used as base oils for fuels include canola oil, castor oil, corn oil, cottonseed oil, crambe oil, hemp oil, jojoba oil, linseed oil, meadowfoam oil, oiticica oil, olive oil, peanut oil, rapeseed oil, sesame oil, soybean oil, sunflower oil, safflower oil, tung oil etc. Allowing many diverse region types to be cultivated for renewable fuels.
1 kWh = 3412.14 Btu // 3.966 Btu =1 kilocalorie

III. The Individualistic Understanding of Divinity

The Individualist believes that all men and women are of divine hereditary right being that they are all the sons and daughters of God.

First shall be defined the Individualists understanding of divinity and secondly how The Individualist applies this understanding to existence. The Individualist believes in the Unity of energy understood using reason and direct experience. It is proven that no matter how far you break down an atom, or no matter how far one looks into the heavens, that no definitive end has of yet been found in either of them and therefore to date they remain infinite in breadth, from the microscopic to macroscopic. Thus this entire collection of infinity can be called – the universe, in other words, one complete whole, or literally the "One Song" (*uni* - one, *verse* - song). One massive machine whose parts work together in harmony and perfection to One end. The Individualist remembers this truth as:
Infinity is equal to One, or: $\infty = 1$

Also the Individualist recognizes the fact that each individual has a consciousness whose exact location cannot be found within the body, and whose exact nature cannot be agreed upon. Whether it is the result of numerous biochemical interactions or in fact a "spirit" from some realm unprovable it matters not. The fact is that there is a consciousness. It is also fact that animals posses one, plants to a lesser degree and even particles themselves to a very basic degree as quantum mechanics is now unveiling. Thus all things are conscious. Therefore, if All is equal to one then the sum total of all consciousness is one gigantic consciousness.

It is a fact that all matter is composed of energy and the smaller it is broken down, the simpler and more like pure energy it becomes. Using the above reasoning that all things are conscious to a lesser degree, and as one begins to divide them, they become a purer form of energy of increasing simplicity, one can conclude that the smallest division will be simultaneously the purest energy and the most basic form of consciousness. Earning the title "Pure Consciousness" by the Individualists. It is the smallest building block upon which all more complex and less pure energy assembles. Therefore all things are composed of the pure consciousness, thus the sum total of Infinity is One specific consciousness.

Using the above reasoning and the fact that consciousness is what makes one a "being", we elaborate by stating that the above One consciousness is therefore One being. The Individualists therefore believe that there is only One being and this being has divided itself infinitely to experience itself through itself. Therefore, two individuals speaking to each other are merely the same being communicating to itself. This One being can be given any label you desire, "the One", "The Infinite", "Cosmic Consciousness", "The Source", "The Great Spirit", "God" or any other name you desire for no matter what you label the limitless infinite, it remains the limitless infinite. For familiar purposes the word "God" shall be used in this document hereafter.

It must be realized that the above reasoning deals with strictly the material world and the findings therein. However, Individualist further believes in the likelihood of many other, "worlds", "planes" "realms", "dimensions" etc. in higher and lower vibratory frequencies than the model above. Yet, if ever proven, it is certain that they will overlap this same model being only further aspects of the One Being simply with different rates of vibration. These "dimensions" will likewise be infinite in number, frequency, and individual breadth just as the above model, all super imposed over the One thus creating an infinity of mind numbing proportions and utterly inconceivable by the waking consciousness. This immensity undoubtedly creates a feeling of insignificance and alienation. The Individualist quickly realizes that God is all things and therefore is all around them and within them permeating all things at all times. Therefore one is never alone. Accompanied by the fact that God is all knowing, one then realizes one is meant to be wherever one may be, successfully annihilating the feeling of being lost and the feeling of insignificance.

The nature of infinity is simultaneously simple and complex, this generates all the philosophical arguments throughout time. By the above reasoning one can see that the atheist is right (god is naught), the monotheist is right (god is One), and the pantheist is right (God is Multiplicity) etc. Simply All beliefs are right because God is ALL, even nothing, even man, even an atom and all atoms. Yet its complete form is the immense, complex, sum total of infinity, which is simply One. There is not enough deep contemplation of this Infinity in these sad times to pull man away from their debased material obsessions. Most modern religions either directly or indirectly confound their followers by telling them what to believe instead of encouraging them to find out for themselves the truths of nature by deep contemplation of infinity which is God. This leads to all the religious problems we have today – The "I am right and you are wrong" syndrome of the sadly blind people unaware of the simple meaning of Infinity which God is. It is this simple: God has created all things, and loves all things unconditionally, and IS all things, God is not separate from the creation, God IS the creation, and there is only one thing and that one thing is God (otherwise God is not infinite). Human beings are blinded by this incomprehensibly huge yet simple truth and see only the *Illusion* of separation.

This lack of understanding of the all-inclusive nature of infinity has lead to the ignorant religious wars of today. People who fight over their own belief are seeing an incomplete picture of infinity and are insulting the colossal and all encompassing nature of their God with their small closed minds. They are blinded by ignorance which the Individualist calls "The Illusion of Separation" being that they cannot see the unity of all things described above. This sparks arguments and the desire to be "correct" within argument which is a fear of the unknown, because no one but God knows truly what is correct. This fear creates the need for one to surround oneself with those who think alike thus gaining a feeling of security in being "correct". Thus are formed large opposing groups whose collective fear now reverberates repulsively against each other, because Unity attracts and separation repels. War of various degrees erupts. Thus the Individualists believe that there is only One universal system, all else is a limited, profane bastardization, dividing mankind. For these reasons the Individualist is wary of those of faint praise. They who simply believe a God exists but think no further into it, allowing themselves to be told what it is and how to act by others of the above nature, pulling them into one group or another, poised to pounce into war.

The only instruction the Individualist obeys is one's own consciousness and not any others. The voice which speaks to the heart is the voice of God and the most important Holy Book to study is the infinite book of the universe where The Creator of All has presented all the details of Its handy work directly to the observer; from the hearts of men to the hearts of suns. To be studied with unceasing fervor and diligence by every Individualist. By this method the devout Individualist is assured that he will in fact not only believe in God, but personally communicate with It as its worthy instrument upon Earth. Experiencing God, not being hollowly told about It second, third or fourth hand.

This is the flaw of many modern religions, the lack of education on how to truly commune with their Creator. They teach little or nothing of the sacred languages or meditation techniques to bring one closer to God, to know first hand their Creator, and to achieve True Illumination. Instead all of that is veiled and the people are *told* what to believe, this is a controlling devise and a blaspheme. The Individualist is strongly encouraged to study all religions and discern for oneself the same fundamental message underlying all of them, by listening only to one's heart and not to any other. For from there speaketh the unconditional love and wisdom of the Infinite, which will serve only to guide one to illumination and not to confusion, ignorance or bias.

Humans spend their lives reading over these documents written by man attempting to interpret ink and paper, while neglecting study of the most ancient text written in light and life, which is the very natural world they live in, the creation itself and the human temple in which they dwell, both written and created by God not man. Each prophet interpreted the creation for themselves and encouraged man to interpret for himself, yet man worshipped the prophet and *his* personal records of interpretation instead of interpreting all things for themselves. Even Buddha, recognized in various religions as a prophet, rejected the infallibility of accepted scripture and said: "Teachings should not be accepted unless they are borne out by our experience and are praised by the wise."

The Individualist believes that within this pan of the infinite, this Unity, in comparison to it, one has no significant power or will whatsoever. Everything that happens is because of God. You, the consciousness, are merely a witness to the works of God. The sum total of all the witnesses is the complete consciousness of God. Thus each consciousness is a tiny spark of God, an exact reflection of the creator but on an infinitely smaller scale. Thus the Individualists believe that no "idea" is generated by the human mind. It is received from the Divine. The ideas already existed in the mind of God, who is the timeless All, by that very statement it is clearly seen that the idea is God's alone. The idea itself is simply energy, light from/of God, it is God because there is only God, thus all things are made of the fabric of Its body, even an idea. The reception of the idea is an experience, an awareness of a certain aspect, no matter how brief, of the infinite. This is why no idea can be owned. One may deceive oneself into thinking how strong one is in mind or body or the bright idea one had, when it was all given to that one, for one can create nothing on one's own. Only by cooperation does God bestows Its gifts upon one the more one tries to act as It, a balanced infinite creator. By attempting to perfect oneself, one will be granted perfection to the degree equal to one's work expended towards that goal.

The lack of thoroughly taught and understood practical spiritualism applicable to every hour of life which yields real results, coupled with the aimless, monotonous materialistic world, has contributed greatly the present and growing lack of direction, purpose, incentive and true contentment of mankind. What separates man from animal is not the ability to reason or the possession of intellectual faculties, it is the ability to contemplate the divine. By taking away spiritualism man is reduced to an animal. No true fulfillment, satisfaction, contentment, or Love can be had. Man then uses lusts, drugs and other hollow physical pleasure as a substitute to fill this void to no avail. This is the very reason for much of this modern worlds misery, drug use, lustful relationships lacking any true love, divorce, and many sad lost souls engaged in countless other practices of depravity. These activities only serve to increase the thickening black shroud encloaking the Earth. Submerged in lusts man does not think clearly or at any degree beyond the animal mind. Materialism benefits three fold by this condition: One, man breeds like the beasts and creates many children raised unintelligently, thus they become feeble hosts for the machine to feed upon, incapable of deducing their escape. Two, with the higher mind blotted out, man is unable to contemplate the nature and reason of his situation or any method of escape therefrom, and is easily convinced into acceptance. Three, the lusts of the animal mind are unquenchable desires which spawn countless niche markets and black markets eagerly run and harvested by aspiring materialists.

Therefore, the Individualists clearly define their purpose for living so as to never be misled into ignoble practices. They believe that the soul has come to this beautiful world to experience it and learn from it, not to be enslaved within it. The Individualist believes that existence is about perfecting one's self in mind body and spirit to the highest degree possible in the life span allotted so as to be an efficient conduit for the Pure consciousness an assist mankind to do the same, thus perfecting the human race as a whole. This is the great work of the Individualist leading to true wealth and true success.

Work energy directed only at the material world, such as a materialistic goal, leaving little or none for the spiritual (immaterial) world, upon which the material world is based, causes the energy to remain in matter as opposed to diffusing through all planes. Therefore by ignoring the foundation, the building collapses. It is for this reason that today's materialistic society is destined to crumble regardless if the reader adopts the practice Individualism or not, either way they will be forced to rely on themselves when the machine collapses. Therefore Individualism is not a just a belief system to practice, it is an inevitable force of nature.

In contrast, work energy directed towards the acquisition of knowledge leads to strength in mind body and spirit, resulting in an overflowing of health, wisdom and intelligence, which combined properly yields illumination – a deep understanding of the highest, be it "God", "The One", whatever one chooses to label the infinite. The Individualist perfects oneself in this manner not only in order to benefit oneself, but one's brethren, one's planet, one's cosmos and one's God. Along this path is much wisdom to be recorded and shared, by sharing knowledge and experiences of this type the Individualist helps all of one's fellows mature and evolve faster, with the force of inspiration.

The very act of withholding knowledge is selfish, and selfishness is evil which is darkness and separation, the division of the void. Good is Selflessness, light and unity, these two are comparable to involution and evolution. By withholding information an individual may gain considerable power but his fellow brethren are restricted and thus the totality of mankind as one organism is restricted in evolution because a part of itself is withholding the light of God, which is knowledge, which is unity. When knowledge is shared other knowledge erupts, this force is Inspiration. Upon receiving an idea, the Individualist rejoices that God has given him this light and hurries to share it with his brethren. Because not only has it empowered him, but by sharing it, it empowers the entirety of humanity thus accelerating its evolution enabling other men to receive light earlier and thus have new insights earlier than without. They in turn share these newer insights with the initial individual and also their fellow brethren and thus the cycle continues and they evolve at an infinitely more rapid pace. So by sharing knowledge the Individualist helps himself exponentially as opposed to just keeping the one idea for himself. Thus is further reasoning for the Individualists' implementation of a system of free unrestricted shared knowledge, the most important element to the success of the Individualistic society.

Any hope for individual illumination is impeded by the old market system by taking away time itself. Time to have restful awareness is how humanity evolved in the first place. With a surplus of food there was a surplus of time. This time allowed our ancestors to deepen their thoughts which caused their animal mind to recede as the higher mind began to exercise its imagination and ability to contemplate the divine. Time is required for deep thought, and assimilating knowledge and communicating with the divine to receive ideas (light) which is the very wellspring which allows evolution to continue. Time is required to thoroughly rest and exercise the body and mind thus ensuring the peace and health of each. Time is required to work on constructive projects aiming at the evolution and advancement of the self and of the brotherhood of mankind. Time is required to evaluate the present technologies and develop those in harmony with nature and the universe which is God. Without time, none of this happens and mans evolution recedes into darkness.

Suppose then that one achieves some degree of enlightenment, what is the next task, the next priority in personal evolution? The Individualist clearly knows it is to assist all others to achieve the same if not a higher state of awareness, thus accelerating the evolution of mankind as a whole. Rescuing those who worship dust, and dirt such as material goods, lust, money, debauchery, deceit, degradation, immorality, dishonor, disrespect and any other corruption of a weak and rotted soul. They then continue their work, for their work is endless, as there is always a higher degree.

The Individualist is not a religious fanatic yet has an unbreakable belief in God, they look up to more evolved beings as their role model and attempt to reach that degree of refinement. The Infinite God is the ultimate role model. The Individualist attempts in all actions and all times to act as close as possible to God. Knowing that God is a balanced infinite creator, so too the Individualist attempts to be an infinite creator on Earth while assisting one's fellow brethren, the other children of God. This social philosophy creates an unfavorable environment for weakness to spawn or grow uncaught, thereby empowering the household, the community, and the Nation.

Yet still there will be those arguing whether the concept of "God" is real or illusory because of their misunderstanding of the above principles of infinity. Neglecting all mentioned studies and doubting that God can be experienced or truly known whether by study, meditation or some metaphysical technique, asserting that it is merely faith only to be proven upon death. However even without these practices or experience, with faith alone one's life is still enhanced simply by the logic of believing vs. non-believing. First off if one believes in an eternal spirit and then dies discovering verily that there is no eternal spirit . . . One would not know anyway. Yet if one lives life disbelieving and then dies, discovering in dismay that one's belief system was terribly wrong, there will most likely be great regret to deal with when one awakens instantly to "spiritual" awareness and recapitulates on how restricted a life one has lead. Clearly then, the only logical choice is to believe. Thus the Individualist must add that the man who doubts God without employing techniques to experience It, is like a man who denies mathematics without ever practicing it.

Lastly, it is fact that energy cannot be destroyed. And by reasonable hypothesis it is reasoned that the smallest breakdown of energy is pure consciousness. Thus whatever happens upon death, the Individualist believes that the consciousness continues by the above principles. Armed with this entire unified concept of divinity the Individualist fills his soul completely, leaving no voids, freeing him from the lusts of the animal mind and all of the darkness and pitfalls which accompany it. It is not enough to be a believer in this logic, but a practitioner, for one could believe, and yet commit terrible acts of injustice to one's fellow man. One could also not believe and be a very noble citizen, it is here shown that virtue holds precedence to the Individualists, but it is stressed that the belief of unity will only enhance virtue's integrity.

Thou believest that there is one God; thou doest well: the devils also believe, and tremble. But wilt thou know,
O vain man, that faith without works is dead?
James 2:19-20 King James Bible

--- PART TWO ---

Applying Individualism to the Present World
The Operating Methods of the Populus

"The liberty of a democracy is not safe if the people tolerate the growth of private power to the point where it becomes stronger than the democratic state itself. That in its essence is fascism --ownership of government by an individual, by a group or any controlling private power." -- Franklin Delano Roosevelt

The Individualists believe that simplicity in a system is more efficient, more powerful and more difficult to corrupt, complexity being a proportionate veil for corruption. All governments posses complexity to varying degrees. The Individualistic Populus minimizes this to an extreme extent. Unlike modern *governments* which have endless departments, divisions and sub division, mimicking only chaos and nonsense, two elements that do not exist in the healthy human psyche, Individualism has consolidated and refined its system into four major heads. Each representing a major function of the human consciousness, the desire, the intellect, the memory, and the will, seated respectfully in the body, mind, spirit and soul. They are attributed as such to make them more natural, easily remembered and clearly understood by each member of the union. They remind the people of the harmonic reflection of Individualism, that is, that the greater body of the union is an exact reflection of its composite parts, which are all of the people, and that it functions in much the same way.

As it has always been, but lately forgotten, the employer of these new departments is the people not the president. Their role is to strictly represent the people and govern the president, not vise versa. These departments take priority to listen and react to the people, and the presidency second, if at all. In Individualism the permanent ruler will be the people, all of them, they have become the executive branch. Ideally the position of the president becomes obsolete, as it merely exists similar to, but even less so, to what it is now, merely a figure head, with no real power unto itself. If it remains, it simply communicates to the group the collective will, but instead of it being the collective will of the corporations, such as the present day, it will be the collective will of the people.

These departments in no way represent authority, they are simply collective organizing forces of the Populus' mind and will into a single refined force of a specific nature, a constructive force, not a controlling force. They act upon items only by direction of the Populus as a whole for they have no powers in themselves. Theses four departments are titled 1. The Greater Eye of the Populus (GEP) 2. The Hall of Vital Records (HVR) 3. The Library of Accredited Free Knowledge and Instruction (LAFKI) 4. The Populus Homestead Management Center (PHMC).

There are fifteen executive departments in the executive branch of the present US *government*. They are assimilated into the refined Individualist system in varying degrees, their names are:

1. Department of Agriculture (USDA) 2. Department of Commerce (DOC) 3. Department of Defense (DOD) 4. Department of Education (ED) 5. Department of Energy (DOE) 6. Department of Health and Human Services (HHS) 7. Department of Homeland Security (DHS) 8. Department of Housing and Urban Development (HUD) 9. Department of Justice (DOJ) 10. Department of Labor (DOL) 11. Department of State (DOS) 12. Department of the Interior (DOI) 13. Department of the Treasury 14. Department of Transportation (DOT) 15. Department of Veterans Affairs (VA)

With the assimilation of each department comes a disbanding of a near countless group of administrations, agencies, authorities, boards, bureaus, centers, commissions, committees, divisions, and offices, amongst other names given to these wasteful and impotent vacuums to taxpayer money. Each subdivision shall be examined and given clear reason as to its disbandment, therefore certain subdivisions will require extensive detail to make clear the reason of the disband and shed light on often obscured points. Be it known that these suggested changes and new checks and balances proposed are to maintain the constitution of the United States, any proposed disbandment is deemed necessary to revert the union back to constitutionality.

In the coming sections which detail the Individualistic departments it will be discussed whether they maintain, disband or assimilate certain activities of the old world. The implications of these three phrases are as follows:

<u>MAINTAINED</u>

Generally assimilated into the Individualistic system with little alteration.

<u>DISBANDED</u>

Found to be either irreparable, obsolete, wasteful, corrupt, or a combination of these. All records and patents etc. of all dismantled *government* divisions and subdivisions etc. are now the property of the people and in the care of LAFKI.

<u>ASSIMILATED</u>

These departments also have faults to varying degrees. All in all they are dismantled but whose general functions could be said to continue under the action of one of the four limbs of the Individualistic society.

* Any subdivision not listed is to be assumed that it was rendered obsolete by the functions of the four offices of the Individualistic Populus and subsequently dissolved.

"Whether it is nobler in the minds of men to suffer the slings and arrows of outrageous fortune or to take arms against a sea of troubles and thus by opposing, end them." -- William Shakespeare

I. GREATER EYE OF THE POPULUS (GEP)

"We, the People, are the rightful masters of both the Congress and the Courts. Not to overthrow the Constitution, but to overthrow the men who have perverted it." - Abraham Lincoln

The operation and affairs of the present day *government* have drifted too far from the control, understanding and awareness of the people. The "Greater Eye of the Populus", representing the collective active will of the people, is created to reverse these effects by regularly informing the people of every action of the (ideally) *four* government departments. To perform this duty it acts as the eyes and ears of the Populus gathering detailed information from every place to which it is directed. The information it provides allows the people to wisely choose where to direct their collective energy. It then gathers their views, concerns, and votes, and presents them to the proper department. In the Individualistic system, that department would then take immediate action upon that end command. However, until that true system is realized, the present world *government* is too often opposed to the people's will. Therefore, the GEP immediately reports the government's reaction to these presented concerns to the people so that they can see exactly to what degree the government is acting contrary to their will. Thus allowing the people to take action, assisted the entire way by the GEP. All of this is accomplished by a monthly document mailed to every adult citizen entitled "The Populus Informer".

A. STRUCTURE AND DUTIES OF GEP

1. THE POPULUS INFORMER

Modern reporting agencies are limited and passive in their approach to informing the public of the activities of their *government*. The GEP will be very active, ensuring the monthly delivery of The Populus Informer. The Populus informer is a document compiled by the GEP and mailed out once a month, either as a digital email or a hard copy*. It contains a detailed report on each of the four branches of government. The local GEP is responsible for its final distribution being that they must combine the Federal and state reports with their local report into one final document. This final document gives a detailed account on 1. Each branches' current activities (as directed by previous Populus consensus) 2. Their individual items up for consensus (items are ideas produced by the populace) 3. The pros and cons of projects and systems initiated, and 4. Any other important or specifically requested information. Any issues of lesser significance are not placed into the Informer simply because of space limitations. They are cataloged and archived each month at LAFKI as "The extended Informer" for the inquiring citizen and remain active issues.

The Populus Informer furthermore includes a form, the "consensus form", which is a mandatory reply. It commands reply on each of the four branches, the GEP, HVR, LAFKI, and PHMC. The reply should include; opinions, ideas, comments, suggestions, concerns etc. The minimum reply is 1,200 words, the maximum is 3,600 words distributed in any way amongst the four departments and their three levels, local, state and federal. Therefore if one comments equally on all, one would have a small 300 word reply for each. Else one could spend all 3,600 words on just one level of one branch, either way, one is expected to make some significant comment on something. The Populus Informers are written completely opinion neutral, they are detailed yet clear and rapidly readable with no wasted words. The estimated reading time is one average eight-hour working day, (40min per section). The estimated time for response writing is also a maximum of eight hours. Therefore, for one day per month the entire adult population reads and responds to the Populus Informer for less than sixteen hours. They must do this within three days of receiving it, and then send it to the address of their designated Populus Consolidant. Each of these forms has a source number to identify the original writer, this information is not viewable until the following month so that the entirety of the consensus remains anonymous. This allows the opinions of congressmen, scientists, doctors and the common man an equal consideration, as those consolidating the consensus are also of random social class. This results in an authentic public opinion nearly impervious to corruption. Any suspected tainting can be pinpointed by following the source numbers available to the entire population after one month.

* For those doubting the feasibility of this many hard copies see page 83 for junk mail statistics)

2. RESEARCH BODIES

The information found in the Populus informer is the largest duty of the GEP. It compiles this information by four independent investigative and research bodies each related to the four departments. These bodies are composed of elected officials and employees, not temporarily summoned citizens such as in the voting process. The officials are elected on a yearly basis for a maximum of two consecutive years or four years total to minimize bias in the information presented. Any of them can be brought under review at any time by the vote of the people. No aspect of government, be it elected official or employee, may withhold information from the GEP unless in defensive war, defending its soil as a neutral nation (see the '6M law' pg 74).

The GEP's directives come directly from the people. It obeys these directives by percentage of consensus, not by simple majority. Thus, if 55% of the votes say to move in one direction, 55% of the GEP force does so while the remaining portion follows the other votes, the end result ensures an exact representation of the will of the Populus. To illustrate, if only one percent of the people want to look into an official, one percent of the GEP will independently conduct that research and list it on LAFKI if the findings are too small to place into the Informer. However, it just may be found that the one percent was correct, and the individual was, in fact, corrupt. Such would never have been discovered in a simple majority system. This is practiced even to the point of conflicting interests where it then researches the pros and cons presented proportionately and attempts a synthesis which is reported the following month. For example, 60% of the people want a facility dismantled. 40% want an addition added to it. After research (60-40), it is found that an addition of those qualities could be added to a similar facility thereby allowing dismantlement the proposed structure pleasing both parties. This synthesis and supporting research is then presented to the people the following month for a second vote. This may cause many opinions to change, and gain majority vote for the synthesis. If the results still conflict after three months the most feasible synthesis is then acted upon.

The four departments are:

a. Populus Monitor

Stationed within the GEP, the Populus monitor is responsible for writing the monthly reports on the present state of the union and the current activities of all four departments at the federal state and local levels. It keeps a close eye on all department activities and their elected officials, and can not be made to monitor private individuals. Each month it collects the final consensus synopses of each level (federal, state, local) and incorporates them into the Populus Informer which is then immediately sent to the people.

b. Populus Investigator

The Populus Investigator operates out of the HVR, it is an investigative body representing justice. Unlike the CIA or FBI, it cannot enforce law, it can only release a report on its findings which must then be acted upon by the local militia at the will of the Populus. The Populus Investigator may also monitor private individuals at the direction of the people, if suspected to be breaking laws.

c. Populus Researcher

Operating out of LAFKI, The Populus Researcher is directed by the people in all of its activities. It is a scientific body researching all natural phenomena. It breaks down the 'knowledge filters' which capitalism and separate government cause by withholding research. It further breaks them down by presenting all that is discovered, even if controversial, unlike many schools of thought who throw out or bury findings which do not fit into their accepted paradigm. This ever growing body of free knowledge assists science to progress unimpeded.

d. Populus Inspector

Operating out of the PHMC and representing each individual concerned for their tax dollars, this branch regularly audits the other three departments, all Populus facilities, and assets for efficiency of operation and corruption. It also enforces and ensures accuracy of the reported True Values of all systems, products and facilities public or private. It absorbs the present PCIE and ECIE (The President's Council on Integrity and Efficiency and the Executive Council on Integrity and Efficiency) causing all inspector generals to become employed and appointed directly by the people. This eliminates the common bias of presidential appointment to such powerful positions. A position of this nature allowed to be chosen by one man with personal interests, possibly leading to the act of appointing one's friends to bias inspection of invested corporations and bring heat down upon one's competitors, is completely absurd. The interest of one man thus perverts all democracy, twisting the forces designed to protect the people into forces to protect himself. No thing affecting the Populus will ever be chosen by one man in the Individualistic society. Furthermore, no inspector general may use apprehensive force unless warranted. This warrant will be given solely at the discretion of the Populus.

3. THE MECHANICS OF INDIVIDUALISTIC DIRECT DEMOCRACY

Every adult citizen actively contributes to the GEP one day per year. Before explaining why, it must first be touched upon, "why society at all?" Briefly, because nature is harsh when confronted one on one, and society makes life very simple. For this simplicity, and for the truest direct democracy, is one day per year too much to ask? This day is simply less than eight hours of reading and less than 16 hours of writing. Most likely it will all be achieved in less than ten hours. Therefore it is considered a mandatory duty in the Individualistic society. No different than mandatory jury duty save one does not have to leave one's home.

Each month 1/12th of the population is selected and divided into a number of tiers depending on the size of the population (See Diagram below) so that in one year each citizen is active. The duty to be done is to receive 12 consensus forms from citizens in one's general area, read them, and then write one synopsis less than 3600 words consolidating the twelve documents into one. This must be done within three days from receipt of the forms, and is then sent to the next higher tier, each of which is conducting the exact same procedure. The end result is a perfect consensus of the entire population.

Each tier, a power of twelve, is described briefly below.

0. President
There is one president, he must have previously served as a Vanguard. Merely a speech giver to the people, he draws up a final synopsis of the work given to him by the Vanguards, and his alterations to it are closely watched by the GEP and the Vanguards. His is the final consensus synopsis for the Federal Level.

1. Vanguards

The Vanguards are an elected group of twelve elders (over 45 years old) divided into four groups of three each representing one of the four departments. Upon reading their consensus forms they create their synopses, then exchange each division to its proper group, so that those representing the GEP have 12 final reports pertaining only to the GEP likewise with the other departments. Each group then prepares a final synopsis (by each group member consolidating 4 into 1, the final three merged into the final document) for that specific department. These four documents are then given to the president to make his address.

2. Arch Heralds

The senate cooperates as part of this tier, therefore only 44 civilians need summoned and each titled Arch Heralds. They must have been a Herald previously in life to hold the position. Ideally the Senate would be reduced to 96 and the heralds would be increased to 48 keeping even powers of 12 and creating an even $1/3 - 2/3$ ratio. This $1/3$ random variable helps dilute any acts of bias reports within the senate. This tier is also responsible for the final consensus synopsis of the State level.

3. Heralds

There are 1,293 random Heralds in addition to the 435 House of Representative members. They must have been Intelligencers previously in life, and they are not physically present in the House. As all of the randomly summoned civilians, they work from home. Ideally the House would be reduced to 432 members and the heralds raised to 1,296 members to maintain a power of 12 and an even 3/4 to 1/4 ratio. This would thoroughly dilute any favored idea within the House.

4. Populus Intelligencers

There are 20,736 (12^4) Intelligencers per month. They must have previously been a Lesser Intelligencers in life. In addition to the general synopsis, they also create the final consensus synopsis for the Local level.

5. Lesser Intelligencers

There are 248,832 (12^5) Lesser Intelligencers. They must have previously been a Lesser Consolidant.

6. Lesser Consolidants

There are 2,985,984 (12^6) Lesser Consolidants. Due to the heavy drudgery of the Populus Consolidants, sometimes having to read more than 12 documents, the burden lies on the Lesser Consolidants to take these rough records and refine them into a more concise and proper report.

7. Populus Consolidants

There are ideally 35,831,808 (12^7) Populus Consolidants. This tier only becomes necessary when a country's population reaches 47,775,744. Then the tier slowly grows in size with the population. Its monthly summons is determined by: (The entire adult Population / 12) − (1 + 12 + 100 + 435) − (44 + 1,293 + 12^4 + 12^5 + 12^6), up to the maximum of the tier (12^7). When the population reaches 573,308,928 (which is 1/3 over 12^8) this tier will be reading 16 documents a piece. The moment the population surpasses this, this tier goes back to reading only 12 documents and the base tier then becomes active as a growing group of Consolidants and begins reading the portion of excess documents.

8. Base Tier

With a maximum of 12^8 readers, it is a growing sub tier that helps relieve the workload upon the Consolidants until it gains significantly in size. Its size is determined by:

(The entire adult Population / 12) − (1 + 12 + 100 + 435) − (44 + 1,293 + 12^4 + 12^5 + 12^6 + 12^7) = monthly summons to base tier (M)

The amount of documents they read is determined by:

{The entire adult population − (12^8)} / (M) = number of documents read by base tier.

When the population reaches 2,149,908,480 a change occurs, because the 7th tier, the Consolidants, are now reading 16 documents again. 12 from the general population and 4 synopses from base tier whose monthly size has grown to 143,327,232. Therefore, the Populus Consolidants stop reading all general documents and switch to reading strictly base tier synopses while the base tier adopts a new name, "The Greater Consolidants", granting the Populus Consolidants a light work load of 4 synopses. (With this light load they are expected to make very clear reports.)

Being that base tier is then the only reader of the general Populus, the amount of documents they then read is determined simply by:

The entire adult population   /   (M) = number of documents read.

Keep in mind that this entire operation is only costing the individuals involved a maximum of 24 hours and most likely a mere 10 hrs, ten hours *per year*. Each month approximately 8.33% of the adult population is summoned for a maximum of 24 hours of their year. Easier than jury duty, and much more important. This system truly involves all of the people and due to its constant changing nature, very short time span for each writer, and the amount of people involved, it dilutes nearly all attempts to bias affairs by small groups of people. All synopsis are registered and cataloged in LAFKI along with their source numbers, so that all original documents can be viewed by anyone at any time should something become suspect.

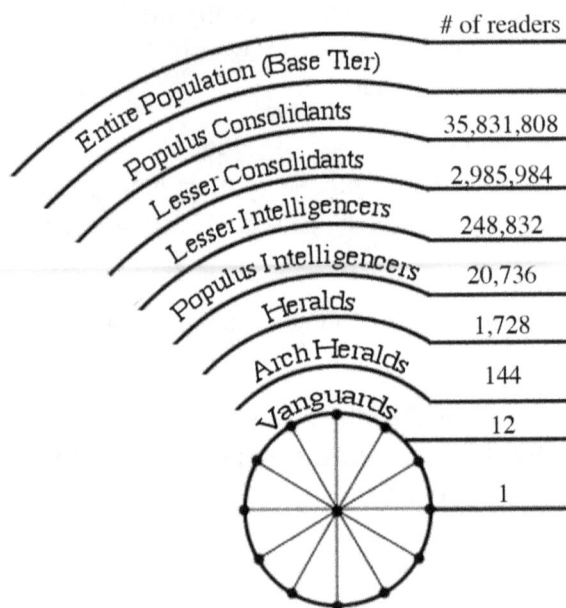

Tier	# of readers
Entire Population (Base Tier)	
Populus Consolidants	35,831,808
Lesser Consolidants	2,985,984
Lesser Intelligencers	248,832
Populus Intelligencers	20,736
Heralds	1,728
Arch Heralds	144
Vanguards	12
	1

With Individualistic direct democracy, representatives represent much smaller local groups (12 per person) small enough that they can be independently monitored by any member of that group thus ensuring to generate and hold fast to an authentic consensus of the people. Therefore the Individualistic government is truly of the people and not a separate entity. This system eliminates the function of the Electoral College and practically the presidency being that all decisions are made by the people. In the distant future it may even eliminate the need for the senate and the house for the same reasons. In its ideal state the GEP contains the entire legislative branch of the present government. The total cost to each individual to initiate this system is a mere 13 days per year of their lives to achieve true and equal representation and a truly free society.

To implement this system into the already present *government*, congress requires some minor alteration. The senate having only two members per state was a trustworthy system when the population was much smaller and the corporate dollar much lower. But today, with companies profiting hundreds of billions of dollars per year, 100 people (the entire senate) is far too easy to compromise entirely. Further more if the entire senate was compromised and only one third of the seats are cycled every two years, (as is the present case) it means nothing because it only takes two thirds to prevail over any issue. Thus if the senate remains in the Individualist society, *two thirds* of the seats will be cycled every two years and the maximum senate term reduced to four years. This is in addition to the 44 random arch-heralds which will further assists to dilute a compromised senate.

For the seats to cycle at these parameters one seat must cycle every two years. These seats are called green seats, with the four-year seats being called past elder and elder seats. To be an elder one must be 45 years of age or older, to be a green the age is 26 to 44 years of age. The reason for the green seat that is youth is a well spring of imagination and creativity, and also usually in closer touch with newer things. They add unique perspective into the Populus' will, and keep the elders in touch with the latest. Their seats cycle every two years because of youth's nature to get carried away, however, they can return after a two year leave; or when 45 and sit as an elder. The elder seats become past elder seats in the third year. It is the past elders duties to teach the ways of the house to the new elders and the greens.

The salaries of congress will then be reduced. From 1789 to 1815 Congress members were paid $6.00 per day. In 1815 they were paid $1,500 per year. Today their lowest salary is $165,200. Thus, the lowest paid politician makes approximately 4.5 times more than the average man. The salary of all elected officials should be capped at the average national salary so that the individual is operating on the same level as the people he is supposed to represent, thus instilling within him the same hardships and concerns. This makes aspiring representatives not hunger for the official position simply because of money, but because of desire and love, resulting in a very effective representative. Furthermore, Congress can no longer make their own salary adjustments, they can only request it from the people. Salaries of all political positions are determined solely by Populus vote, as it is their personal tax money. Finally, no politician may take any contribution from a private entity for any reason at any time. For even when federal laws limit the amount of money one entity can contribute, it is often circumnavigated by "bundling political contributions" where numerous subsidiaries of one company will give large contributions. "Contributions" only cause intentional oversight in regulatory processes.

B. EXECUTIVE DEPARTMENTS ASSIMILATED

a. Mine Safety and Health Administration
ASSIMILATED as part of the GEP, specifically, in the Populus Inspector department.

b. Occupational Safety & Health Administration (OSHA)
ASSIMILATED as part of the GEP, specifically, in the Populus Inspector department.

C. OTHER DEPARTMENTS ASSIMILATED

a. CIA
DISBANDED The Individualists believe this department should be restricted from any covert activities. Secretiveness in any form causes ignorance to the public and without all knowledge the public cannot make informed decisions. Secretiveness to the public means operations in the hands of the few. Secretiveness by a federal *government* implies that *government* has interests separate from the people. The only purpose and interest of a federal *government* is to peacefully act as an uniting force for the separate cells composing it. Thus secretiveness is a threat to the people who are supposed to control that *government*. How can something be called a friend and ally when it withholds information from its master? If some thing is suspect, there is no reason to be covert, the actual knowledge of being suspected is a deterrent in itself. A suspect is informed he is being watched. All covert activities, such as bugs, computer spyware, etc can easily be turned against the public, like a guard dog biting its master. Also it is recommended that an investigative body as this be simply an entity of intelligence collection and have no powers to enforce or detain. This gives an agency too much power and takes the people out of the loop. Therefore if all of these changes are made to the CIA it becomes no more than the GEP. Thus, it is disbanded.

b. GAO
DISBANDED (The Government Accountability Office) If one wants to know where all of the taxpayers' money is disappearing to, do not inquire with the GAO. Little truth flows from their quill. Nothing they say can be proven without taking years of time and millions of dollars to conduct the necessary independent research. Thus, their lies are fireproof. All money going into political pockets will be shown going into useless programs such as poverty abstinence education, losing over 100 million dollars per year to something a parent should teach.

II. THE HALL OF VITAL RECORDS (HVR)

The Hall of Vital Records acts as the collective memory of the people as well as its energy reserves. It holds all information on all civilians, such as finances, taxes and personal records etc. It is a storehouse of static information, including law. The dispenser of justice, it is divided into federal, state and local levels, and in its ideal state it will contain the entire judicial branch of the government. It consists of many fortified structures, similar to banks. In fact, many will be converted banks of the old world (after their dismantlement). Some will be home to courthouses and/or local militia barracks. This phenomenon happens today, many times the police station is built close to the courthouse, then the banker builds next to the police station. Thus the natural evolution is the HVR facility. The ideal structure is a fortified courthouse, home to the local militia and storehouse of the local reserves and Populus finances in its center. A place of safety and justice owned and controlled by the people, there are few safer places to keep all Populus records and resources.

A. THE STRUCTURE OF THE HVR

1. POPULUS COMMON WEALTH

The Populus common wealth is the pool of all collected money, from taxes, Populus facility overages, and the savings of the people. The money from taxes is put to distinct uses, the overages from Populus programs and facilities is divided equally among the people of that level, (local, state, or federal) and deposited into their account in the common wealth. This savings of the people and their profits from the system, can then be lent as no interest loans.

Usury is made illegal in the Individualistic society, as well as privatized banking. The reason is because combined they are simply an exponential power generating machine turning the people's work energy into the privatized fortunes of others (see diagram pg 13). They exist only because people give them money. All corporations place their capital into banks including income and payroll. Citizens, as employees and customers, also place their savings into the bank. Thus with this massive influx of funds, the bank increasingly gains in "loaning" power by fractional reserve, which requires the bank to only have a percentage, such as 10%, of the amount it loans in actual funds available. The bank actually never pays out any significant amount:

1. When the bank is required to pay employees "X" for their paycheck, many of these people place a large portion of that amount right back into the bank as their personal checking or savings, thus the bank has little net loss to its loaning power. 2. The bank supposedly makes money off of investments into corporations. When this money is given to the corporation it goes right back into the bank, by it being deposited as working capital or by the corporation purchasing something, wherein the selling corporation takes this profit and places it in their bank. Again, little initial loss to the banking industry, which then receives profit from the investment because of usury (a loan based on fractional reserve, thus profit is being made on 90% of non existent money). 3. When a customer wants to buy from a corporation and gets a bank loan, the loan given to the corporation goes right back into the bank as that corporation deposits it as profit. Thus again, little loss to the bank. The bank then profits by usury on the loan to the customer (another hollow fractional reserve based loan), often at absurd degrees.

Thus the bank is the only one in the loop who profits and that profit is on 90% non-existent funds. The employees, who are also the customers (buying the products which they created), give hard work energy on both ends. The corporations are an intrinsic part of the banking system with a symbiotic relationship, and at times are the creators of the bank to initiate this cycle (such as GMAC, General Motors Acceptance Corporation, a subsidiary of GM, if independent it would be the 8th largest US bank. Ford Motor Credit would be the 10th largest US bank). Viewed in this light, generalized, the people are working to create a product, and then paying a middleman to have the product which they created. It is a pointless stumbling block. Exploitation of man to the scandalous profit of the few by demanding more work energy than that which was given, and furthermore that which was given, upon which they make their demands, was only 10% real. Therefore they demand re-payment on 90% of nothing.

To present a clearer idea on this pointless waste created by usury:

1. $211 Billion (and growing) of US tax money goes towards just interest on the national debt every year.

2. The national average mortgage payment is about $1600 per month with roughly 22 million US mortgages (now, possibly 44 million) at 6% interest over 22.5 years (the average of 30 year and 15 year mortgages), totaling 35.2 billion dollars per month, of which 42% is purely interest (the average interest of 30 year and 15 year mortgages). This equals over 14.8 billion dollars *per month* in interest alone for just the mortgage industry. In light of the Individualistic energy values, this would be 164.4 million megawatt-hours of electricity *per month*. This is over forty one times the electricity produced by the Hoover dam *all year*. Now imagine all the other areas where usury applies, personal loans, business loans, automobile loans, credit cards etc. All loaned on fractional reserve making profit on non-existent money at the hard labor expense of the greater population. The amount of monthly energy wasted for the greed of a few is simply maniacal, and will be stopped immediately by the Individualists.

Being that all individual and corporate money is already in some banking system, little will apparently change with the implementation of the Individualistic common wealth system, save that all funds will be backed 100%. The common wealth is a massive pool of the entire wealth of each level, local, state and federal, owned equally by all the people and functioning similar to a credit union. It is the only legal pool of money, and its actions are directed monthly on the local, state, and federal levels, directly by the people. It charges no money to hold money and pays no interest. Its operating costs are paid by specifically allocated tax dollars which are also a part of the pool. It is no different than the tremendous pool of the people's money held today by the various privatized banks generating a privatized profit, save that this common wealth is strictly controlled by the people to the benefit of the people. A single centralized financial system such as this can only be implemented in a true direct democracy such as the Individualistic society, all else will become a dangerous controlling devise, even if deviating in the smallest degree.

2. LENDING

With the removal of usury the people will have more personal money, what is rightfully theirs. To take a loan is another emanation of giving up one's own responsibility and depending on another. The only valid reason to take a loan is if one *needs* something immediately, which is rare. Too often this is confused with *want* something immediately. Modern banks exploit this human weakness and ignorance, by orchestrating loan agreements so that the borrower buys the product two to three times over its value due to interest. This leads to far less money for that individual, and far more expended work energy for only that one item, to the greater profit of the bank. Currently over 75% of the entire US population holds some type of debt adding up to over 12.8 Trillion dollars, (9.7 Trillion of which is just mortgages, 735 Billion is credit card debt) each with varying degrees of usury. This is larger than the 8.3 Trillion dollar national debt. This amounts to a national picture of 75% of the population expending at least twice as much energy as is needed for the objects which they desire. Thus, usury is not but waste, it is a solid figure which represents the degree of impatience, irresponsibility, dependence, servitude and vanity of the population, the root causes of astronomical amounts of wasted energy.

For the needs that everyone has such as food, shelter, and basic transportation, the Individualistic society has programs fulfilling those needs. Self-sustenance is taught in detail, volunteer labor co-ops exist for those in need, to build one's own home and even basic transportation at cost, etc. Housing and transportation alone amount to over $10.2 Trillion of the total $12.8 trillion household debt (over 500 billion in outstanding auto loans carrying approximately 45 billion in interest (interest not included)). Thus, by two simple Individualistic programs, nearly 80% of all civilian loans are rendered obsolete. The remaining 20% ($2.6 Trillion) are credit cards, store credit, personal loans and similar debt. This portion is most likely not need, it is most likely non-essential material goods.

The very existence of loaning builds up a society and mindset around it. By this very element it creates excess work, and combined with usury this waste is magnified, add fractional reserve and it reaches shameful proportions. For example, if one knows that loans are available for all that one may desire, one is more prone to take a loan for non-essential reasons. One now has to work harder than without, thus one requires more work. A surplus of workers causes businesses to see an opportunity to take on more labor, for which they also need a loan to meet the higher payroll. Nevertheless, they take it because the surplus of workers will increase their production output. They therefore have to sell more product to pay back the loan and its interest. Armed with the latest marketing techniques they convince the people to buy their product, regardless of its use value or true worth, who then also take a loan, continuing the cycle. Thus the existence of lending generates a false "need" for lending, it becomes a crutch to depend on, a common place practice of the masses, many of whom are ignorant to its inherent waste. This is not entirely harmful if usury and fractional reserve are removed. Without these there is no wasted energy, one repays exactly what was given. With them still in the system, the dependence created is leveraged and it becomes servitude. For, the "tax" on that which is lent, not only generates unnecessary expended energy, but also the loss of time to that individual which is directly related to lack of peace and enlightenment in mind, body and spirit as already discussed.

Furthermore, Loaning encourages overproduction because the end price becomes nearly insignificant. The manufacturers are aware that few can afford their product on their own, but with the banks involved that is no longer an obstacle. So without fear countless products are produced. Entire Lots are filled with boats, cars, RVs, mobile homes etc. and their prices are high, maximizing profit as price is of little concern. The corporations enter into a symbiotic relationship with the bank installing quasi bank representatives at their facilities, loan officers, who are paid bonuses by the bank for the number and types of loans they rake in for the bank. All roping in the people to the servitude of usury, feeding wants instead of needs, causing endless waste.

Accordingly, people lose track of essentials and get caught in vanity – vain action, irresponsible and impatient motives whose collective end result is a massive waste of energy which only taxes society and eventually the globe. But this is not the extent of the waste of usury. Of the 5.3 million outstanding mortgages, 1.7 Million of them now face foreclosure, that is about one out of every three mortgage loans ending in a homeless individual or family, who most likely spent many years making payments. All of that money is lost, wasted, or as the Individualists describe it, "stolen". Same with the 1.3 Million auto repossessions on average auto loans of $23,800, or about 6% of every auto loan. Entire markets of need suppliers spring up around foreclosure and repossession, which themselves use energy, thus are an energy cost on wasted energy – this is utterly intolerable to the Individualist and is still not the full extent of the waste. To illustrate:

A bank loans to a buyer on fractional reserve for a $100,000 house for 30 years at 6%. Because of 10% fractional reserve, the bank owns this house for a mere $10,000. The buyer spends 10 years paying $1,000 monthly payments adding up to $120,000. This is $20,000 more than the cost of the home, and 12 times more than what the bank paid for it. However on paper it will show the buyer still owing around $52,000. His employing corporation happens to cut jobs to utilize exploited oversea labor, unemployed, and without knowledge of self sustenance, the buyer can no longer make the payment on the house which should already be his. The bank gleefully forecloses, taking the house and leaving the man with nothing, but a loss of ten years of his life and $120,000, an enormous waste of energy (at least 1,300 megawatt hours, enough electricity for over 300 people for an entire year). The bank has gained $110,000 plus a $100,000 home to use again in the same scam. Thus is the case for 1 out of every 3 mortgages and one origin of the tremendous profits written off as "loss" by the banking industry. Fractional reserve, usury and privatized banking are therefore cast out with great contempt from the Individualistic society.

50

With out this predatory lending the people can clearly discern between a want and a need. If one needs transportation, and wants a full size SUV, with no system to support this unwarranted desire but one's own net worth, one might see that a small electric vehicle is not only all that one can afford, but actually more economical. In such a system, their is no usury, no waste, no excess work for usury, no excess work for naught (loan foreclosure) no excess work on unfair demands (fractional reserve claiming to pay "X" and charge interest and repayment upon "X" when having only invested 1/10th of "X"). Thus is saved incredible amounts of energy and time to be directed towards needs, such as the refinement of mind, body and spirit of the greater population.

As can be seen the Individualists see very little reason for loans. As such there are no loans given for:

1. Non essential material items
2. Major transportation (Minor can be had from Populus conversion centers. (see pg 121, 122)
3. Houses (Populus Laborhood programs help one build one's own home (see pg 109)
4. Education (education is free)
5. To company owners of over 100 men, or any owner or member of a company that creates a sin taxed product.

The majority of loans will therefore be given for true needs and innovative projects. True needs will be determined by the Populus, such as a machine to till ground, a press, a kiln, electric turbines, water detention tanks etc. Innovative projects may be simply a prototype or possibly a business. Any prototype funded must have accurate plans supplied to the Populus who is allowed, at any time, to utilize the designs for any reason. Any private business started on Populus funds pays 1% of its annual net profit to the Populus common wealth for the life of the business.

Large companies are not eligible for common wealth lending therefore must solicit the private public for funding. The present debt in the American private sector business is 9 Trillion dollars (also larger than the national debt) the three largest borrowers being General Motors, General Electric, and Ford With debts of 300, 195 and 175 Billion dollars respectively. Their common practice of selling bonds which generate interest is made illegal as a result of illegal usury. This is not to say that a private entity cannot lend money, it simply cannot charge interest for it. However no private entity can collect pools of money from multiple individuals without giving proportionate ownership in return, otherwise one would then be a bank. Thus, stock can be had in private companies save that the dividends paid to share-holders must be of the *total* post-tax profit of the company divided proportionately, not a portion of it. Furthermore the recipients no longer have to pay capital gains tax upon this money being that it was already taxed as corporation profit.

The way common wealth lending works is very similar to the present procedure except the time frame may be longer and more carefully scrutinized. Being that it is the people's money, the people will have the final approval of any significant loans. All personal information of the applicant is listed as well as a brief synopsis of the reason for desiring the loan including a reference number directing readers to the detailed information stored in LAFKI. This is then included in the HVR section of the monthly Populus Informer. The amount of people who will be approving the loan depends on the level of use of the loan be it local, state, or federal. The applicant must have existing assets valued higher than the loan desired, this is proven by field documentation conducted by the GEP. The applicant must also have a annual productivity rating higher than 30% of the loan amount desired, as all repayment must be accomplished within five years.

This system maintains a healthy level of production because high priced products are now within the reach of the common man, such as a 100,000 dollar hydraulic excavator. An individual proving a prosperous and beneficial application for this machine, and making only $37,000 per year, the average US salary, is granted the loan. The individual repays twenty thousand per year at $1667 per month (a mere $67 over the present average Mortgage payment). Thus many individuals who once would never consider such products, are now a substantial market. With this access, coupled with the time induced by self-sufficiency, the number of well thought out innovative projects, checked by society, will soar. The aspiring scientist suddenly has an entire lab, the starving artist now owns a studio, the backyard mechanic now has a garage, the tinkering metalworker now has a shop, the hobby biodiesel maker becomes the local refinery, dreams become reality, innovation and inspiration reach record heights, the breakthroughs in all science and arts propel the society into a new level of understanding. This is the Individualistic vision.

The loan obligation in the Individualistic society is much more serious. There is no repossession nor is there default. If these existed one could easily abuse such a generous system. By agreeing to the loan one locks oneself into fulfillment. If one's own method of acquiring the funds to pay the amount fails, that one is placed into a Laborforce at an allotted rate until the loan is paid. One can also volunteer for the Laborforce and list that as the initial method of loan repayment. Either way this fact will be a significant deterrent for exploitation of the system and greatly increase the forethought of taking loans initially. One should feel great guilt for late payments on money that was lent without usury or fractional reserve for it is pure generosity of the fellow man. In such a case the lender is actually lending 100% of the amount and not 10%, as do the present day lenders who use the guilt of good souls to get their unwarranted usury figured upon 10 times the value of what they actually lent.

3. POPULUS PROJECT FUNDS

The Populus project funds are the portion of money within the common wealth from the collected taxes of the people whose use is allocated proportionately to the desire of the entire Populus at each level, local to federal, as ascertained by the final consensus synopsis of each month's Populus Informer. The projects can be anything the people desire such as a park, a mine, a solar farm, a factory, a bridge, a dam etc. These desires are generated by the past months' major opinions, ideas and concerns discussed by the populace as topics of the Informer, and voted thereupon, at times in various stages for many months, such as a bridge. First, the general idea is to have a bridge, all agree. Next the details begin to be discussed, such as where is the best place to build it and why, and then what type of bridge, etc., right down to the final paint. Thus the entire community takes part in the discussion and the project, from the community engineers, to the ironworkers, farmers, tradesmen, businessmen etc. all giving their unique perspective. A closer bond is formed between the people and the projects accomplished by their society. A greater care and feeling that they have helped in some way is formed. Each month between Informer issues the latest topics will be discussed throughout the population increasing the depth and detail of responses for the following month leading to a final project that pleases all, and incorporates the thought energy of an entire people who funded it. Thus their works will be spectacular, and not rushed and dull like so many present day projects. Buildings built in weeks with no intelligent placement, altering land with little thought of the consequences, utilizing cheap and environmentally harmful materials with no portion of artistic quality throughout. Each developing idea in its entirety will be available for all to view at any time within LAFKI.

This Individualistic system already exists in a corrupted form. For example, banks only exist because the people give them money, and the profit that they have, made on the people's money by fractional reserve, now makes them an independent entity with its "own" money even if it was had by unarmed theft. To keep this example simple, the banks get their money from the people. The corporations also get their money from the people in three ways, 1. Buy selling a product to them 2. By having them invest or 3. By borrowing off a bank who is a pool of the people's money. Therefore the people completely fund every entire operation as well as build it, just as in the Individualistic system. The difference is that the "profit" and privileges goes to the top management of the corporations and the banks, instead of going to the countless amounts of people whose collective nickels, pennies and hard labor, built the entire fortune and whatever systems were initiated along with it, be it a factory, to a car, to a bridge. Furthermore, the actions of the top management and the proceedings of the projects initiated are not directly controlled by *all* of the people involved, beside the share holders or product purchasers, there are the huge bank loans drawn which symbolize countless numbers of investors entirely not represented (all people with checking or savings etc.).

The Individualistic system equally represents each individual and their will throughout the entire procedure because their money is equally funding the project. Therefore, the profits of whatever systems become initiated by their will are returned to all the people in the form of reduced prices on products, special benefits or quarterly lump sums returned to the Populus common wealth to be allocated toward additional projects, or divided equally among the people as they desire.

4. THE POPULUS RESOURCE RESERVE

The Populus Resource Reserve is the storehouse of energy for the respective level of the Populus, from the local to the federal level. The detailed operation of which has already been discussed beginning on page 30. They are the issuers of currency as energy certificates and will be the translator of the present hollow money system to the new fully backed energy certificate system until the old currency is phased out. They accumulate their reserves through trade with individuals and through the operation of Populus facilities such as food crops, wind and solar farms, hydroelectric plants, fuel crops etc. The system allows utterly self-reliant individuals to trade in produced goods for currency to utilize other Populus systems such as various facilities, lending or to pay their taxes.

5. POPULUS ACCIDENT FUND

Being that no private entity may collect a pool of money without giving proportionate ownership in return, all insurance establishments are made illegal. The Populus accident fund takes the place of all accident insurance such as auto, worker compensation, homeowner's etc. It is a portion of the collected taxes whose amount is determined annually by its activity. For simple example, if the base premium was X for every individual, and at the end of the year a substantial amount was left over, that amount would be returned to the populace and the following year the premium would be adequately reduced. Upon the reverse the premium is increased the following year. This way any major accident is absorbed and truly felt by the entire population.

All individuals have the exact same policy, each is responsible for the first 500 dollars, the amount owed is dependent upon the amount of property one desires covered over the base fee (based on average property value and amounts). If the accident involves one at fault, this one must repay the fund in part or in full as determined by the people. Such as if one was blatantly negligent, such as DUI, the full amount must be repaid (on top of fines and Laborforce time). This system increases the level of responsibility for one's actions and deters negligence.

For permanent injuries there will be no long-term payments. All accidents happen from some degree of negligence and are accordingly harsh lessons thereof. Society cannot be taxed for the misfortune, or negligence of individuals. The Individualists will list all such claims in the Populus Informer and have the people judge to what extent one's self-sufficiency has been effected, as well as the exact size of the monetary award, if any, (such as in the case of an individual losing an arm) and furthermore, to what extent some may be willing to volunteer help. This deters the countless numbers of leeches who claim phantom pains and chronic illness, and tax the rest of society for their lies and weakness. The society as a whole will clearly judge such things. Such as a little girl caught in a flaming car and the middle aged man claiming chronic back pain from a common collision. It is assured that society will shower the child with assistance, and merely encourage the other to stand up and act like a man.

Accident payments cover property loss, and provide basic assistance until one is back on one's feet, as well as any additional assistance the people see fit to add. It provides no monetary award to pain and suffering bar none. It provides no funds for medicine, being that that is covered by The Populus Health System. Therefore as part of the people's responsibility, they must list all their property with the HVR in case of loss. Unlisted property will not be covered.

Private businesses must repay the entire amount regardless of fault, because they are not considered essential to the owner's existence. They are assisted by an entirely different aspect of the fund dedicated solely to private business. This portion of the fund is generated by a portion of each companies' annual collected taxes allocated into the Private Business Accident Fund. This keeps the potential massive losses of businesses from effecting the people, and keeps the assistance money strictly a pool of money from private businesses. Every three years the unused portions of this fund, if any, are distributed into the common wealth as the people see fit.

6. POPULUS HEALTH SYSTEM

The Populus Health System is a pool of funds collected from a voluntary, non income based flat fee divided equally per capita of $4090 (about $341 per month). Adults are responsible to pay this fee for their children. (The detailed discussion of this fee begins on page 86). Anyone may opt out of this plan, but if they happen to receive care, they will be ordered to repay the amount within one year or sentenced to time as a Laborforce member until paid. Thus, some may see it as a risk to opt out. Any overage in the fund at the end of each year is returned to the people and the following year's fee is accordingly reduced. The practice of Individualistic philosophy of refinement of body, mind and spirit with the excess time available to each citizen will create a stress free environment of powerful and healthy individuals. Each individual will be healthier longer into old age, and also less careless then the present day average citizens. Thus, the amount of health care needed will progressively diminish. In the distant future, this program may be completely obsolete.

7. POPULUS MILITIA

In the Individualistic society the entire population is required to serve mandatory military time, (the detailed discussion of why this is so is found on page 132). With this surplus of soldiers, the police are rendered obsolete. The position is then filled by the people as citizen police, upon completing their military training. Each citizen will be schooled in law, the defense of their neutral nation, and the protection of their fellows. With each citizen as a previous militiaman or woman, a strong comradery is formed and the frequent "power trip" of authority figures is negated. The policing militia is seen as fellow brothers and sisters, taking their turn at the duty of protection and peace keeping, rather than being seen as alien authority figures. They watch over their fellows as opposed to watching their fellows. Their duties will be much the same as present day police, save that their training is more extensive being that they are firstly soldiers capable of defending a nation.

However, it must be stressed that this system cannot be implemented until absolute neutrality is achieved and the *government* is downsized and back in the solid control of the people in a complete direct democracy. Any deviation will be perverted into a terrible war machine, with internal military revolt against the controlling forces the only escape.

B. EXECUTIVE DEPARTMENTS ASSIMILATED

1. DEPARTMENT OF HEALTH AND HUMAN SERVICES (HHS)

The department of Health and Human services should be entitled the department of Human Injustices. This department along with its sub agencies creates any drama to justify the presence of their unnecessary departments only to sustain their own existence, not the well being of the citizens. They are simply outlets for corrupt officials to lend money to organizations who will in turn return a "contribution" to them. This money is none other than the people's money, and little of it benefits them. Of all of the executive departments this one will be examined most extensively.

a. ACF - Administration for Children & Families

Wrongly titled federal aid, (taxpayer's aid being a more precise term), Individual Welfare is a crutch which perpetuates weakness. (This subject is discussed in detail on page 104)

The Individualists shall examine in detail the mission statements of this department and weigh them against reality.

"The Administration for Children and Families (ACF), within the United States Department of Health and Human Services (HHS), provides national leadership and creates opportunities for families to lead economically and socially productive lives. ACF's programs are designed to help children to develop into healthy adults and communities to become more prosperous and supportive of their members."

Major Goals

"ACF is responsible for federal programs that promote the economic and social well-being of families, children, individuals and communities. ACF programs aim to achieve the following:"

The ACF succeeded in only creating dependency, the opposite of Independence, a cornerstone of democracy.

"Families and individuals empowered to increase their own economic independence and productivity";

They succeed in the exact opposite, thus they fail their mission statement and need disbanded to prevent further waste and incompetent failure.

"Strong, healthy, supportive communities that have a positive impact on the quality of life and the development of children;"

Every welfare community is weak and rife with drugs, thievery and prostitution, causing all businesses to close. This decreases available jobs and increases the dependency upon handouts. Thus the children they claim to develop are only developed into better criminals who better understand the system of taxpayer handouts. Again, great success in the exact opposite of what they claim.

"Partnerships with individuals, front-line service providers, communities, American Indian tribes, Native communities, states, and Congress that enable solutions which transcend traditional agency boundaries;"

These partnerships are had because the dependency of their vast army of welfare recipients causes these recipients to vote in the favor of any politician or group declaring to assist welfare. Thus this dependency is purposefully maintained as a guaranteed block of votes.

"Services planned, reformed, and integrated to improve needed access;"

Which increases dependency and all of the above mentioned forces by making the dispensation of handouts more efficient.

"A strong commitment to working with people with developmental disabilities, refugees, and migrants to address their needs, strengths, and abilities."

Assisting in this manner weakens individual strengths, and abilities by not having individuals acquire their own needs thus exercising their own latent abilities and strengths.

SUMMARY: This backward and blind department does exactly the opposite of what it claims. It is disbanded without delay to engender recovery and healing of the communities it has corrupted with Individualistic self-sustenance knowledge and teaching. Which will accordingly cut off voting assistance to those who support weakness in mankind to exercise control.
Simply by opening one's eyes can one see that the level of poverty and number of destitute neighborhoods is rapidly increasing. This establishment is obviously ineffective.

b. AoA - Administration on Aging

DISBANDED This establishment is a smiling face of the venomous pharmaceutical industry. It longs to convince as many people as possible that they are weak, and then lead them away from natural health care, such as proper diet and exercise. It persuades them that there is a magic pill for every ailment, and gets them to take as much as possible. The Medicare and grants they offer go directly to the pharmaceutical industry and their heinous associates, most of which are supplying unnecessary "health care" which taxes insurance and Medicare.

Programs supporting age are not needed in the Individualistic society. The Individualistic elders are the icons of society. They are the wisest, strong in mind, body and spirit. They have honed themselves continually to ever increasing perfection, not allowing themselves to waste away into decrepit invalids unable to remember what they had for breakfast.

c. AHRQ - Agency for Healthcare Research & Quality

DISBANDED It is in this department where data reports, which may have been initially truthful and honest, are edited, tainted and finally released. The information is skewed to make one favor and rely on products or services from specific providers in bed with government officials. Competing health care providers are deemed low quality thereby directing the flow of business toward the corrupt.

d. CDC - Centers for Disease Control & Prevention

DISBANDED This department is a collection of paralyzed individuals who report only what is impossible to cover up any longer. It is persistent and determined citizens, not the CDC, who eventually bring an end to the practice of using under tested chemicals in mass quantities. These chemicals grant to the public the strange diseases like MS, Lou Gehrig's disease and the endless types of "cancer", the ambiguous name describing all unexplained mutation. When this department is forced into a study its pace is slow and hindered by the industry who is known to be responsible yet is too influential to circumnavigate.

e. CMS - Centers for Medicare & Medicaid Services

DISBANDED Rendered obsolete by national health care. The Medicare Prescription Drug, Improvement, and Modernization Act (or Medicare Modernization Act, MMA) signed by President George W. Bush on December 8, 2003, is a massive overhaul to Medicare, and was enacted with hardly any public debate. It was created by and for the drug, health care and insurance Industries, with the executives of these companies being on the advisory committee drafting the bill. In just the preceding year the pharmaceutical and health industries made political contributions amounting to roughly $27 million, and hired 675 lobbyists, over half with federal ties, (26 former congress members) spending over $91 million in lobbying efforts.

Many supporters were given campaign contributions including G.W. Bush receiving $466,000 in 1999, whose administration had ties to the pharmaceutical industry, such as Bush senior, and Mitch Daniels being directors of Eli Lilly and Gail Wilensky holding 10.5 million in health industry stock.

This bill was a blatant manipulation of the government for private interests at the expense of the people. Nonsense as this stands in the way of simplistic healthcare, not raped by thieves in the guise of representatives, healers and lawyers. This manipulation shows that they have profitable reasons (not logical ones) for demonizing national health care, showing that without their profits and control, health care would be simple and affordable for all.

f. FDA - Food & Drug Administration

DISBANDED Employing some 12,000 individuals, the FDA oversees products totaling $1.5 trillion in annual sales, approximately ten percent of the US market. The FDA is an arm of the food, chemical and pharmaceutical industry, not an arm or ally of the people. It exists only to protect its masters and curb, skew, and slow justice, court proceedings and the facts. (Such as the approval of Monsanto's genetically engineered hormones and covering up evidence of cancerous mutations.) It is operated by public money yet it poisons the people and defends private corporations. At times it receives much corporate funding, and often its officials are appointed with special interests. (See pg 95 aspartame)

The FDA is influenced by synthetic chemical and pharmaceutical manufacturers to look the other way, insufficiently test synthetics, give bias articles, or make hasty decisions based on too little information. Contrarily, at times, they slow decisions of safety while holding overwhelming evidence of hazards, worried more about the multi billion dollar profit of those funding them than the myriad of adverse effects caused in the human organism. Often specific officials are "funded by" or benefiting from investments in the companies they regulate. Regulation policy thus becomes riddled with loopholes, such as the known mutagen BHT not having to be listed on products which contain it, if its amount is under 5% of an ingredient.

g. HRSA - Health Resources & Services Administration

DISBANDED This is a data center of information which funnels business towards the healthcare providers, services and products which support this department and in turn are supported by it by receiving grants from it. It is a data bank of disinformation and corrupt resources. It holds no information encouraging self health care or natural herbs etc, nor are any grants awarded to such applications. It is simply a funnel to steer the ignorant to the slaughterhouse, where they will receive their very own parasite to drain their life and money from them.

h. IHS - Indian Health Service

DISBANDED An insult to a nation which never had disease or the need for a "health service". This stands as a testimony to the natural Individualistic way of life. To live unnatural and inharmonious is to have unnatural and inharmonious aliments manifest in the body. A strong spiritual belief overshadowing the material nature of existence is a foundation of strong health. This department does nothing to educate the masses of the abject poverty these people have been subjected to by crushing their culture and forcing them into materialism, the opposite of the spiritual life they once enjoyed. Their people raped and enslaved by the "heroic" Columbus, and forced to learn the language and teachings of dependency, while theirs of true independence was erased and forgotten. For this the native Americans will receive free health care in the Individualistic society.

i. NIH - National Institutes of Health

DISBANDED The NIH is a medical research agency. It receives millions of dollars per year from biotech and pharmaceutical companies to either falsify research data, or let it go undocumented. The funds are either formal contributions or monies paid in various forms to specific officers and scientists who neglect to report such incomes. The grants they dispense are often given to contributors or companies invested in by officers. They recruit large amounts of people to literally conduct experiments upon, in exchange for free drugs or upgraded health care. These worldwide "clinical trials" are a huge profiting industry for the doctors, blockbuster pharmaceutical manufactures, and all in between, on the taxpayers' dollars.

j. NCI - National Cancer Institute:

DISBANDED The main cause of cancer is the myriad of synthetics humanity ingests, rubs upon their bodies, and is forced to breath because of the fumes of all of the unnatural products created every day on a preposterous scale. The same pollutes the waters and then pollutants are added to remove those pollutants. Man has made the entire Earth unclean. The reversal of this shall see the cure for cancer. It is very simple, unnatural things create unnatural things. Impure things will cause impure results, faulty building blocks create a faulty building. Giving the body unnatural substances allows the body unnatural building blocks with which it builds unnatural substances. There is no mystery where cancer comes from, it is the filth and unnatural manipulation of the pure earth which man has thoroughly poisoned. Nowhere in this department will one find this simple truth, or any action against the true source of these diseases, because it is a half a trillion-dollar industry. When this establishment conducts "research" it never looks at the cause, only the malignant effect before them, thus it is perpetually doomed to failure.

k. SAMHSA - Substance Abuse & Mental Health Services Administration

DISBANDED This department gives grants to pharmaceutical and other "health care" providers for mental health, addiction, and other natural phenomena which they label as disease so as to create a market. For example:

1. Mental Health

Mental heath has two general types,
A. Physical Deformation
   The Individualists believe that most mental conditions resulting from deformation at birth can almost certainly be traced back to the parent's food or environment containing one or many unnatural chemicals, as well as a lack of parental physical fitness. Mental health because of severe trauma during life is the result of some degree of negligence on someone's part. These will be among the severe disabilities cared for by the Individualistic system.
B. Learned
   The present society creates insanity in various forms because the society itself is rapidly becoming less and less logical, and its terrible schooling program is geared towards dependence as opposed to wisdom. This creates parents who cannot properly rear and guide a child and often neglect them. These children then look to the schools for guidance, and finding none, the cycle continues, worsening at each revolution.

2. Addiction

   Addiction can only be cured by will power, testified by any junky or cigarette smoker who has succeeded. The word "addiction" is pushed and pushed upon subjects until they accept weakness as a natural human characteristic, thus it encourages them to be weak and rely on the pharmaceutical industries' magic drugs to "wean" them off. This is simply a heartless marketing ploy for their toxic drugs and services, many times keeping these individuals on their drugs for years.

3. Natural Phenomena

   It appears that this department is actually administering mental health to the entire United States. Such as "Child Stress", a ridiculous phrase, which the myriad of fools produced by this insane world, buy into with ruthless conviction, broadcasting their profound ignorance. Children feel things such as this and ADD because the nonsense of this materialistic society in no way assists the soul, which came to this world to learn, not to be sucked into a philosophy of materialism. Modern schools teach nothing of value to the soul, nothing of its divine heritage. Thus forced into nonsense the soul revolts as the world demands acceptance of the insanity, and so are formed the children's "disorders". They are perfectly understandable results of this dying society, yet appear as complete and total mysteries to the "doctors" and "psychologists" of the world of ignorance we live in, described by them as "disorders". They then proceed to give these children Adderall and Riddlin which are amphetamines, having very little difference from the illicit drug meth-amphetamine, the same drug fed to the front lines of the nazi war machine.

All of the above three things (save for physical deformation, which could be slowed by eliminating all unnatural substances) can easily be cured by the will coupled with proper education and Individualistic philosophy. They are instead maintained and exploited by this corrupt department in the guise of a healer to market billions in unnecessary drugs and health care service, wasting energy and taxpayer funds nursing effects instead eliminating causes.

l. ATSDR - Agency for Toxic Substances & Disease Registry

ASSIMILATED This department is suspected of watered down and corrupted information. Its basic operations are absorbed by the Populus Research.

2. DEPARTMENT OF JUSTICE (DOJ)

a. ATFE Alcohol, Tobacco, Firearms and Explosives

DISBANDED This is an organization operating almost totally without supervision. It murders men for tax reasons and is used as a militia for the need suppliers to rout out any individual opposed to their insidious and tyrannical views. In the Individualistic society individuals will pay these taxes upon purchase and may own as much of any of these items as they wish. But the instant they misuse them they will be summoned to court, not murdered at their homestead. (The August 21, 1992, Ruby Ridge incident in Idaho, and the February 28, 1993 Branch Davidian incident in Waco, Texas.)

All guns are registered. Anyone found with unregistered firearm receives a mandatory six-month Laborforce assignment. Mass sale of liquor must be reported, minor sale of liquor by home brewers permitted but the Individualist are aware that carelessness in processing can yield a poisonous and lethal product, and proceed at their own risk. There are no laws against minor tobacco production for personal use and hobby sale, major tobacco production is monitored and taxed very similar to the modern methods. Encouraging tobacco users to grow their own and alcohol users to make their own will assist in reducing the size and power of these two industries. Finally, anyone hoarding explosives is obviously suspect of some kind of wrong doing, unless in commercial demolition. Therefore all explosives are registered.

b. DEA Drug enforcement administration

DISBANDED This department does exactly what its name implies, the enforced administration of drugs. The sole creators of the "war on drugs" they play both sides, the criminal and the administer of justice. They are the watchdogs of the drug producers, legal and illegal. Dominating all territories and confiscating the drugs of 'unauthorized' dealers, they secure the market for their masters. The Individualistic society does away with this entire racket by its simple drug laws outlined on page 78.

c. U.S. National Central Bureau of Interpol

DISBANDED This department is disbanded as it is obsolete in a neutral nation. If need be the People's Militia will handle an affair within its own boarders.

d. Federal Bureau of Prisons

DISBANDED and obsolete because the Laborforces have replaced the prison system.

e. Federal Bureau of Investigation (FBI)

DISBANDED The Individualists believe this department should be restricted from any covert activities. Secretiveness in any form causes ignorance to the public and without all knowledge the public cannot make informed decisions. If someone is suspect, there is no reason to be covert, the actual knowledge of an investigating presence is a deterrent in itself. A suspect is informed he is being watched. All covert activities, such as bugs, computer spyware, etc can be easily turned against the public, like a guard dog biting its master. Also it is recommended that an investigative body as this be simply an entity of intelligence collection and have no powers of enforcement. This gives an agency too much power and takes the people out of the loop. Therefore if all of these changes are made to the FBI it becomes no more than the GEP. Thus it is disbanded and assimilated into the GEP.

f. Foreign Claims Settlement Commission

DISBANDED This small department is disbanded after total neutrality is achieved and all claims completed.

g. Drug Intelligence Center

DISBANDED Rendered obsolete as drugs are legal controlled substances of the Individualistic society.

h. U.S. Trustee Program

DISBANDED With the dismantlement of private banks and usury, all debt becomes valid. With usury it is understandable how one may get buried beneath debt. Without it, all debt is valid. Therefore there is no bankruptcy in the Individualist society making this department obsolete.

i. 1. Community Oriented Policing Services (COPS), and 2. U.S. Marshals Service

DISBANDED These two subdivisions are disbanded as they are made obsolete by the People's Militia

j. Office of Justice Programs

ASSIMILATED This office is assimilated into the general operation of the HVR. Its myriad of bureaus and subdivisions will be scrutinized, overhauled and refined.

k. Office of the Pardon Attorney

MAINTAINED This small office is maintained, however the final decision is decided by the people, not the president.

l. 1. U.S. Parole Commission, 2. Executive Office for Immigration Review, 3. Executive Office for U.S. Attorneys

MAINTAINED These three offices are maintained as part of the HVR.

3. DEPARTMENT OF LABOR (DOL)

a. Bureau of International Labor Affairs

DISBANDED This department is disbanded as it sends far to much taxpayer money out of the nation and likewise has too many interests outside the nation which are all easily compromised. A neutral nation worries not about the problems of other countries, and does not accept their goods if their manufacturing process breaks any US law. The Individualistic society would not simply place them on a list, which no one sees, and allow them into the nation. Also, if a private US business owner has companies outside of the US he is subject to their law, and will be taxed accordingly to bring goods back into the Individualistic US.

b. Employee Benefits Security Administration

DISBANDED Due to the elimination of usury, money no longer gains interest thus pensions are obsolete. Each individual must be responsible for one's own future and prepare accordingly through saving. Furthermore the only health plan there is, is the Populus health system, all private health companies are responsible for their own affairs, therefore one takes responsibility upon one's self when having private health. When all those grandfathered into the Individualist conversion have been paid in full, this department is disbanded.

c. Employment Standards Administration

DISBANDED Federal contracts are no longer given to private entities. The people will decide what to build, where to build it, how much to spend for it and the PHMC will act upon their wish. No profit or interest is anywhere in the loop of the construction. Profit is had only by the people when the facility begins to operate. Furthermore, too many manufactures favor War because of the profits they can obtain by it. There also shall be no involvement of Populus funded agencies in private organizations, such as unions. Federal involvement with labor unions is a known source of corruption. Lastly, workman's compensation shall be handled by the PAF.

d. Women's Bureau

DISBANDED any agency, policy, etc. that affects or benefits one group and not another is bias and not unified. Therefore to maintain Individualistic true equality, this department is disbanded but its spirit, the desire to educate, lives on in the unrestricted knowledge and teachings of LAFKI

e. 1. Veterans' Employment and Training Service (VETS), 2. Bureau of Labor Statistics (BLS), 3. Employment and Training Administration (ETA)

ASSIMILATED These three departments are assimilated into LAFKI

f. 1. Mine Safety and Health Administration, 2. Occupational Safety & Health Administration (OSHA)

ASSIMILATED as part of the GEP

g. Office of Disability Employment Policy

MAINTAINED as part of HVR, yet overhauled and refined.

4. DEPARTMENT OF STATE (DOS)

a. Arms Control and International Security

DISBANDED This subdivision is far too foreign oriented for a neutral nation, the study of other nations actions, can be performed by the GEP. Internal security will be handled by the Populus militia.

b. Economic, Energy, and Business Affairs

DISBANDED This department encourages and solicits merchandising which only serves to addict others to the elite manufactures' practice of waste and consumption. A self sufficient neutral nation does not need this peddling within its own borders let alone within exterior foreign nations, especially at the tax payers expense to the benefit of only large private corporations.

c. Democracy and Global Affairs

DISBANDED The Individualistic neutral nation cultivates mind body and spirit to perfection in each of its individuals so that the nation as a whole evolves to perfection. It does not enforce its ways upon any other but leads by example so that others beholding it can be inspired by its actions and choose for themselves whether or not to adopt its methods. To enforce one's own system upon others is force, regardless of one's good intent or not. To quote President Bush: "The survival of liberty in our land increasingly depends on the success of liberty in other lands. The best hope for peace in our world is the expansion of freedom in all the world." This is a phrase to justify entering another's nation and applying one's own will to another's way of life 'for their own good'. Arrogantly asserting that one knows what is best for humanity, or to feign kindness so as to set up a new nation of consumption and waste to the profit of the few. Similar nonsense is the phrase "freedom isn't free", for which, some agency needs to be started with the people's tax dollars to inform every fish in the sea, every bird in the sky, and every other animal free from their birth, that they have been believing in error that they are free for the last hundreds of millions of years. It is comical how only the supposed smartest animals, the humans, are deceived into such idiocy.

d. Public Diplomacy and Public Affairs

DISBANDED All that this department does is performed much better by the GEP with the people as priority. The Individualistic society has no interest in soliciting the American image outside its own borders for it has no desire in propaganda of any type.

e. 1. Management, 2. Political Affairs

ASSIMILATED into HVR operations. These two departments are refined and thinned. The Individualistic US maintains strict neutrality and its presence in foreign nations shall be lessened and its activities within them stopped. In the future when full neutrality is realized these departments may be disbanded at the direction of the Populus.

5. DEPARTMENT OF HOMELAND SECURITY (DHS)

a. Federal Emergency Management Agency (FEMA)

DISBANDED This ridiculous division has unchecked power and authority, encourages construction in disaster prone areas it is an outlet for Populus money to be dumped into unverified claims. A mockery of order in even the most primitive of eras.

b. Computer Emergency Readiness Team (US CERT)

ASSIMILATED this division becomes fully Populus owned, there will be no public/private partnerships.

c. Federal Law Enforcement Training Center

ASSIMILATED into the HVR

d. Management Under Secretary

ASSIMILATED into general functions of PHMC

e. Operations Coordination Office

ASSIMILATED into the HVR. The US monitoring of this division is conducted by GEP and enforced by the HVR.

f. Policy Office

ASSIMILATED into the general operation of HVR

g. Preparedness Directorate

ASSIMILATED refined as general procedures of HVR

h. Science and Technology Directorate

ASSIMILATED into the GEP

i. Transportation Security Administration

ASSIMILATED in the general operations of the HVR

j. U.S. Citizenship and Immigration Services

ASSIMILATED into the general functions of HVR (see immigration page 73)

k. U.S. Coast Guard

ASSIMILATED in the general operations of the HVR

l. U.S. Customs and Border Protection

ASSIMILATED into the HVR as a special Populus militia unit, its present size and training doubled.

m. U.S. Immigration and Customs Enforcement

ASSIMILATED into the GEP

n. U.S. Secret Service

ASSIMILATED into the HVR

o. Domestic Nuclear Detection Office

MAINTAINED

6. DEPARTMENT OF THE TREASURY

a. Bureau of Public Debt

DISBANDED This is the division that keeps America in debt, as its name asserts. "Borrowing money to run the federal *government*" obviously means that the *government* is too big. Some estimate that this department borrows over 5 Trillion dollars per year and hands the interest over to the American people to pay. The interest is over 3/4 of a Billion dollars per day. Thus the people pay for expenses of *government* actions beyond their vote and control, which benefit only the few.

b. Internal Revenue Service (IRS)

DISBANDED The IRS is not an agency of the federal government. None of its employees are employees of the federal government, they are employees of a private corporation, called the IRS run by the Secretary of the treasury of PUERTO RICO and that is exactly how it is listed in US Code and federal regulations Titles 5, 26, 27. The IRS, a private entity, can legally seize assets without obtaining judgment in court and cannot be sued. An invulnerable private entity which does not obey the people is not an element of a just society.

c. Office of Terrorism and Financial Intelligence

DISBANDED These two topics shouldn't even be in the same office of control, unless, one is laundering money through Clearstream International to Bahrain International Bank, owned by Osama bin Laden. There are already too many "intelligence" agencies, the GEP shall be the only one, and it shall report to the people, not to the *government*. The list of suspect subdivisions in this department is as follows: 1. The Office of Terrorist Financing and Financial Crimes (TFFC) yes they probably do finance these things with the American taxpayers' dollar 2. The Office of Intelligence and Analysis (OIA) 3. The Office of Foreign Assets Control (OFAC), control is the key word 4. Financial Crime Enforcement Network (FinCEN), surely they conduct many, making Enron and Worldcom look like child's play 5. The Treasury Executive Office for Asset Forfeiture (TEOAF), These are merely thieves with law on their side 6. IRS Criminal Investigation, It is frightening how this department needs not the judgement of the courts. Its existence is unconstitutional, as are its actions. (See IRS above)

d. Alcohol and Tobacco Tax and Trade Bureau

ASSIMILATED into the general tax collecting operations of the HVR

e. Financial Management Service (FMS)

ASSIMILATED "conducts services for the federal government" It will be downsized along with the *government* and report directly to the people, as the *government* is not an entity to have anything answer to.

f. 1. Office of the Comptroller of the Currency 2. Office of Thrift Supervision (OTS)

ASSIMILATED There are no banks to monitor in the Individualist society. These offices are merged into the GEP and will only monitor the Populus funds, all other activities especially in foreign nations, are ceased. This less complex arrangement allows the departments to be significantly downsized.

g. 1. U.S. Mint 2. Bureau of Engraving and Printing

MAINTAINED within HVR

7. DEPARTMENT OF VETERANS AFFAIRS (VA)

a. 1. Veterans Benefits Administration, 2. Veterans Health Administration

ASSIMILATED into the HVR. All current recipients are grandfathered into their current plans. However it is closed to any new beneficiaries as all US citizens become members of the Populus Militia, therefore are veterans and are covered under the Populus Health System. With a budget of over 69 billion dollars, the VA lags and delays veteran claims, ignoring veterans who had their life on the line, it often loses and falsifies data and cannot be held accountable. The Individualist society will recognize all grandfather veterans with free health care for each veteran holding them exempt from the common health tax, this is the least they deserve for being used by spineless corporations and banks who sent them to fight their unnecessary battles of greed. With the death of the last recipient these departments will be disbanded.

b. National Cemetery Administration

MAINTAINED in the HVR in honor and respect of those who fought for freedom, even if some were deceived and fought for corporate interests. Their courage and sacrifice will be remembered.

C. OTHER DEPARTMENTS ASSIMILATED

a. FDIC

DISBANDED The Federal deposit insurance corporation is a organization composed of shells within shells which practices fraud, inside trading, and issuing bank charters to money launderers. Its executives are nearly all working for underworld forces. Any institution with significant complexity is a web for redundancy and refraction of light. Thus it is darkness granting the ability to work concealed within it. Furthermore, it insures the money of private banks with public funds of the taxpayers, or the hollow fund printed by the Federal Reserve.

b. Federal Reserve

DISBANDED Operating unconstitutionally, the Federal Reserve is a synthesis of private and *government* control, an intimacy which should never be. The government is the people, there should be no involvement of the people's funds in any private affair to any degree. The Fed controls the people's currency and operates in extreme secrecy, keeping the public in the dark, who constitutionally, are the only ones who should be controlling currency in the first place. Thus there is great private control of the funds and credit of the people, and all the rules; fractional reserve, usury, debt collectors and reporting agencies, bankruptcy laws, debt repayment laws, are all in their favor. They can issue credits based on nothing to banks, which can then lend out 9 times the amount. Thus the banks, the private few, control the people, the masses, the government, by controlling currency, forcing them into slavery. Claiming ownership over all facilities, all land, and all property. They control the currency by buying and selling bonds, thereby inserting or removing funds into the system at their will. This power to take money in and out of circulation was used to purposely cause the great depression, amongst other suspected diabolical acts. The Individualists shall inform the people of this blatant thievery and deception, and teach them that the only validity to the Fed dollar, or to any ownership claimed by a bank, is as far as one believes it to be true, and the degree to which the authorities obey the banks instead of the people. Thus the authorities and the people must be one in the same.

D. HVR IMMEDIATE REFORMS

1. SOCIAL SECURITY INSURANCE

Social security is nothing but a massive pyramid scheme paying its beneficiaries directly from the Social Security Insurance contributors (the people), not from the accrued interest of a "trust fund" as some believe. The "trust Fund" is filled with US Treasury debt securities, debt obligations taken by the *government* whose interest is paid by the taxpayers, who are supposed to be accruing interest not paying it. Thus the people are paying the people with an unnecessary middleman siphoning off their funds. This ambiguous debt covers up what these supposed representatives actually do with the taxpayers' money, much of the money is indeed invested and substantial interest received, but it is by *government* officials and their private interests, not the common man.

For selfish intentions, the *government* has made itself appear as an entity more responsible than those it is supposed to represent. The caretaker of the people and their money while it gets fat from the interest. It is simply another system of dependence, where the people have allowed their responsibility to be handed over to another. A deliberate deception to make people accept the *government* constantly dipping into their pockets in hopes of receiving something in return. Unfortunately most people die before getting back just what they put into it let alone making a profit, a blatant thievery in the guise of benevolence.

Being that the people are paying the people, thus exchanging money for no reason but the benefit of the middleman, they shall stop exchanging at all. In the Individualistic society the people are responsible for their own future as is their right and duty, none of their money is taken from them, assuming them to be incompetent and unable to plan their own financial strategy. The people shall decide what they want to do with their own money and invest it (or not) in any way they chose. If they make bad decisions and have no money in the future they will have the Individualists knowledge of self-sustenance and the Populus Laborhoods to fall back on. If they are crippled and abandoned by family, the Laborhoods have light tasks and open arms for them. In the Individualistic society the old are the wisest, unlike today where the lies and withholding of knowledge progressively stupefies the public with age so that the toddlers are now the wisest. The Individualist elder will not have made foolish mistakes regarding his or her own private future. The wisest Individualist will need no money. The Individualistic society abolishes SSI and pays those who paid into it all of their money back and distributes the remainder (if any) equally.

2. INDIVIDUALISTIC LAW

NOTE: this is not intended to be a document on law, therefore the following points are only briefly discussed, in so far as to impress the Individualist philosophy of the subject reasonably upon the mind.

Law Defined:

Defined by The cognitive science laboratory at Princeton University

1. Legal document setting forth rules governing a particular kind of activity;
2. The collection of rules imposed by authority;

Defined by Wikipedia

Law (a loanword from Old Norse lag), in politics and jurisprudence, is a set of rules or norms of conduct which mandate, proscribe or permit specified relationships among people and organizations, provide methods for ensuring the impartial treatment of such people, and provide punishments for those who do not follow the established rules of conduct.

Defined by the American Heritage Dictionary

1. A rule established by authority, society or custom
2. The body of rules governing the affairs of man within a community or among states; social order
3. A set of rules or customs governing a discrete field or activity

All the above definitions use the word "rule" to define law, therefore rule must be defined:

Rule Defined:

1. A principle or condition that customarily governs behavior;
2. Prescribed guide for conduct or action
– The cognitive science laboratory at Princeton university

1. An authoritative direction for conduct or procedure, specifically:
a. One of the regulations governing procedure in a legislative body
b. A principle of conduct observed by the members of a group
– The American Heritage Dictionary

The above definitions describe principles of conduct agreed to and followed by a group. The question that comes into play is who creates the principles. Sticking strictly to the above definitions we see that either custom or authority creates them. As far as custom goes the reasoning for some customs is not always clear, so it is not worth while to argue customs here. However, "authority", is the alarming word. If the authority is the masses of a non corrupt direct democracy of the people, than the laws reflect exactly what the people believe and are therefore noble. But if the authority is an entity separate from the people and removed from their true wishes, then the principles erected thereby are not noble. They become simply mechanisms of control.

Mechanisms of control can be successfully undermined with simplicity. Complexity in law is directly proportionate to its corruption, ineffectiveness and use as a controlling mechanism. From antiquity the systems of law were very simple until relatively recently. Only in the last 2000 years has law compounded rapidly to its ridiculous modern form. Egypt survived thousands of years with a mere 42 principles which could easily be memorized by all citizens. As time progressed laws became more complex, and it is NOT because society became more complex as will be described.

Has the vast amount of species of animals living in harmony for millions of years across the globe required countless weighty books of endless stipulations? Complexity in law is only due to deceit and/or ignorance. The fact that such a civilization as Egypt lasted for thousands of years on 42 simple principles is further proof that complexity and sophistication are unnecessary elements for harmony and longevity of a civilization. The basic underlying principles of the Egyptian laws below are Waste and Harm, and waste could be viewed as a further emanation of Harm, the source of all social problems. As history progressed laws developed to describe the various ways one can harm another and the degree or severity of that harm, thereby moving away from describing the *source* of these problems. This is where a madness began to develop, because there is an infinite range of manifestations of Harm and degrees of the same which man can inflict upon his fellow. Man could not create enough paper and ink to record each type of incident let alone their respective punishments. This madness causes law to compound and become increasingly complex at a recursive rate, confounding all those beneath it while benefiting the few who are aware of its proliferating nonsense yet consciously allow its continuance and alter it to their benefit, a practice which becomes increasingly easy with its increasing complexity. The root of this madness is none other than the act of describing the misdeed instead of describing the source of the problem, which is the flaw in character that has initially produced the misdeed.

By comparing the Egyptians "source" oriented code to those "misdeed" oriented codes which come later, one will clearly see how the understanding of the source of the problems becomes lost, and maniacal focus upon the infinite manifestation of misdeeds becomes the dominate mode of thought persisting to this day. This misunderstanding was handed down generation after generation and the systems, like a cancer, grow at an exponential rate towards future systems of infinite madness. The older, simpler systems of law had long life spans while the modern more complex systems, have shorter life spans, thus complexity also correlates to shortened life span and instability as opposed to simplicity having a longer life span, and stability.

Even though they begin to deviate from 'source' oriented thinking and descend into the psychosis of infinite misdeeds, the Code of Hammurabi (1700BC) and the Twelve Tables of Rome (449BC – 201BC) were both displayed publicly so that every citizen knew the law. They were both small enough to commit to memory, in fact the twelve tables were written in rhyming verse to facilitate memorization. It was authoritarian powers who hid the laws from the people thus making the law unknown and causing inequality of punishments such as with the early patricians to the plebeians, a section of history repeating itself at this moment. Any code of law with more laws than can be memorized easily by each person is unnecessarily complex for the shear purpose of controlling individuals with false freedoms and leveraging other individuals with legislature. The growth rate of this madness has become so fast that today, new laws are made each day and change so fast that few can keep track, that is if they even knew of their existence in the first place. This is Absurd. Most Laws of today are merely designed by one corporation's lawyer to bind up the competition until they can either find a loophole, amend the law or get a new one passed. This is a blatant attempt at binding one's brethren, and creating a psychotic compounding complexity impossible for any one man to keep track of without making it a life's practice. It is a direct impediment to the simple and rapid evolution of mankind. Modern Law has become naught but a playground of inequity, smothering any noble ideal of Truth and Justice.

For these reasons the Individualist focuses only on the concept of Harm, the very root of all misdeed. How then does one deter this? The Individualists find the simple solution in their concept of divinity. If there is only One being, and all are but subdivisions of this one consciousness, than to do harm to anything is to do harm to the only self, the One, thus oneself. This concept is taught from birth repeatedly to assist the uprooting of the source of Harm. When the unity of all creatures is fully taught and understood, few will initially do wrong because they realize to harm another is to simply harm themselves. The remaining misdeeds committed will be the acts of either the desperate or the deliberate.

This concept of Harm, as any concept, can be twisted by the depraved. Balance must be maintained throughout the material life. To harm nothing is ideal, yet this world is not yet ideal. Therefore, in such a case as an invading army, one of this nature might say that the precept is broken by causing harm in defense. Or a plague of animals comes to the point of disrupting harmony, thus eliminating them for protection is also considered harm, but it too is in defense. The Individualist observes nature and sees that animals attack to either to defend themselves or in desperation (hunger). Mans mind should be sufficient to keep himself from desperation leaving only defense as a means of Harm (beside deliberate). Defense from humans in an ideal world would never be needed for all would be practicing the same principle. But again this world is not ideal, therefore the Individualists master self-defense and simultaneously pray it will never need to be used. By this method it is ensured that this concept of harm will never be used to pacify a nation leaving them weak and defenseless for any invading army to easily crush.

There also must be mentioned the incident of abstract harm, the stuff in the minds of weaklings. These are such things as insults, and offence taken from another's actions. Again, ideally the Individualist is beyond these trivial things and does not engage in this conduct nor consider them a form of harm. One's personal actions or comments, while possibly offensive to others, simply displays one's level of evolution and one's grasp of Individualistic thought. Thus the one who purposely sets out to offend, succeeds in only being recognized as an ignorant fool. There can be no punishments or monetary rewards for such childish actions or complaints.

a. The 42 Principles

The Individualists understand that simplicity is the watchword and uphold 42 simple self-governing principles. They are aware that the ancients knew Truth, and how simple it is to love each other and live in peace and harmony. They are ever watchful for the twofold enemy who attacks this light: the learned evil, and the ignorant deceived by the learned evil, they who attempt to convince man that it is foolishness to believe that life is in fact simple and easy to live.

These 42 principles are arguably as old as dynastic Egypt, 3150-31bc or possibly far older. Scholars agree they can definitely be found in texts dated 2600-2000bc or older, and are found compiled neatly in the papyrus of Ani dating to1240bc. Egypt and its antiquity have always been subjects of great debate. For sound reasons the Individualists believe that these moral laws were followed by the Egyptians prior to dynastic Egypt, but settle on the date of 3150bc as being the date at which these principles were actually organized into a formal belief (law) system.

Therefore these 42 Principles of Ma'at (Justice) predate the Code of Hammurabi by about 1,450 years, the Ten Commandments by about 1,850 years, and the twelve tables by 2,700 years and were practiced while all these other systems were practiced until about 31 bc. The 42 principles are displayed below so all can see the simple yet powerful beliefs of the Individualists.

In the original code, the 42 affirmations are written in past tense as "I have not", because they are declared to judges after one dies and enters into the afterlife. They are written here as affirmations of one's present incarnation. For over three thousand years this very simple code of laws upheld arguably the long lasting human civilization ever known, with India, and China, following. Contrast this with the "modern" United States law composed of hundreds of pages, in a society a mere 231 years old already on the verge of collapse from corruption and materialism. It seems to show a great error in thought, even an insanity.

Note: Some new evidence may date Egypt much further back in antiquity making it even much more successful and undisputedly the longest lived civilization.

1. I will not do misdeed.
2. I will not steal.
3. I will not act unjustly.
4. I will not murder.
5. I will not waste food.
6. I will not cheat the scales.
7. I will not defraud temple offerings.
8. I will not lie.
9. I will not waste the day.
10. I will not abuse my sexuality.
11. I will not cause the shedding of tears.
12. I will not act with guile.
13. I will not break the Law.
14. I will not commit fraud.
15. I will not hoard land.
16. I will not keep knowledge secret.
17. I will not bring dishonor to anyone.
18. I will not argue.
19. I will not commit adultery.
20. I will not wrongly copulate.
21. I will not cause terror.
22. I will not cause destruction.
23. I will not be an aggressor.
24. I will not turn from words of right and truth.
25. I will not utter curses.
26. I will not act with violence.
27. I will not bear false witness.
28. I will not prejudge.
29. I will not judge.
30. I will not exaggerate.
31. I will not cause harm.
32. I will not do evil.
33. I will not commit treason against my ancestors.
34. I will not waste water.
35. I will not speak in anger.
36. I will not blaspheme the One Most High.
37. I will not be arrogant.
38. I will not desecrate holy places.
39. I will not plunder the dead.
40. I will not mistreat children.
41. I will not hinder the worship of God.
42. I will not mistreat animals.

The Individualists believe that the teaching of these moral principles with Individualistic philosophy in the school and at home up to adulthood will drastically reduce the number of harmful actions perpetrated in society. Knowledge becomes the deterrent, not the fear of punishment. In addition to these 42 principles, the Individualist adds "The Twelve Preventative Concepts" which shut forever the doors which lead to the madness of the present world. They constitute an understanding of the forces to be kept in check and kept in mind. They overlap and condense the 42 principles, clearing up the ambiguous areas which could be exploited, and they are more serious in their implications.

1. I will not lose sight of the source of problems, harm against the One, thus I shall honor Its every piece.
2. I will not withhold knowledge
3. I will not hand over my responsibility to another
4. I will not cause harm to any man, beast, or environment save for subsistence or defense and then, minimally.
5. I will not impede the will of another so long as that other violates not the 54 principles
6. I will not make additional laws which do not apply equally to the entire populace.
7. I will not act upon any decision that affects another individual without that others consent
8. I will not waste anything
9. I will not govern any other than myself
10. I will not make a private bank
11. I will not make currency that cannot be redeemed at any time for real energy.
12. I will not practice usury or the sale of currency for a gain higher than the value of that currency, directly or indirectly.

c. Punishments

There are no punishments for breaking the above fifty-four principles directly, as they are mostly moral laws to prevent the misdeed initially. The punishment is issued to the misdeed, which is inevitably caused by breaking the above precepts. The Individualists do not attempt to describe every misdeed and various punishments, they recognize only three basic misdeeds, Assault, Murder, and Theft, each having eight major manifestations, totaling 24 misdeeds. (See table) They are listed in a points system granting them punishment levels of 4 to 8 points, thus there are a total of five basic punishment levels. Each of these levels is then multiplied by an offence multiplier of one to three degrees. The degrees represent 1. A first time offender 2. A past offender and 3. A multiple offender. Therefore there are 13 punishments. (actually 15, but the products 8 and 12 repeat) The punishments are all time sentences based in Laborforce assignments. They are as follows:
1. (4pts) 3 Months 2. (5pts) 6 Months 3. (6pts) 1 year 4. (7pts) 1.5 years 5. (8pts) 2 years 6. (10pts) 2.5 years 7. (12pts) 3 years 8. (14pts) 4 years 9. (15pts) 5 years 10. (16pts) 6 years 11. (18pts) 7 years
12. (21pts) 8 years 13. (24pts) 9 years
(There is only one exception to these times and that is with the premeditated murder of a person. This act adds an additional five years onto the calculated sentence.)

Category		Subcategory		Type		Form		Examples
Assault	1	Personal	2	Actual	2	Physical	2	Battery, Rape, kidnapping, sexual assault, animal cruelty etc
						Mental	1	Harassment, Intimidation, threat, blackmail, stalking, indecent exposure etc
				Potential	1	Active	2	Reckless endangerment, (vehicle or otherwise) etc
						Passive	1	Disorderly conduct, possession of weapons, etc
		Impersonal	1	Private (property)	2	Active	2	Arson, Bombing, Break & Entering, etc
						Passive	1	Accidental destruction of Property, etc
				Common (property)	1	Active	2	Arson, Bombing, Break & Entering, etc
						Passive	1	Destruction of Property, etc
Murder	2	Human	2	Intended	2	Premeditated	2	Attempted Murder, Murder 1
						Post-meditated	1	Murder 2
				Unintended	1	Negligent	2	Manslaughter
						Accident	1	Homicide (possibly justified)
Theft	1	Material	2	Force	2	Physical	2	Robbery, looting, piracy, burglary, etc
						Mental	1	Extortion, etc
				Forceless	1	Physical	2	Larceny, shoplifting, etc
						Mental	1	Embezzlement, etc
		Immaterial	1	Rights	2	Material Property	2	Trespassing, squatting, operation without license etc
						Immaterial Property	1	Fraud, forgery, counterfeiting, laundering, perjury, tax evasion, etc
				Attributes	2	Personal	2	ID Theft, Impersonation, etc
						Impersonal	1	Smuggling, Concealing, etc

This is not intended to be exhaustive. It is merely an example of a possible method to achieve a higher degree of simplicity.

i. Defense Multipliers

There are only three major reasons to do Harm: Defense, Desperation, and Deliberation. These three words are the lawyers only weapon against the 13 sentences listed above. They too are multipliers, Defense (0), Desperation (0.5), and Deliberate (2) A lawyer can plead for one of these multipliers to be added to the base system, and at the discretion of the judge and jury they will either be added or left as a "neutral act". A neutral act is when it is found that the base punishment is fit for the circumstances.

Deliberate perpetrators are the most severely punished, their multiplier actually signifies a higher degree of deliberation, pointing more toward a conscious evil, as any act in itself represented by the base punishments are nearly all deliberate to some degree. Acts of Desperation can be understood to an extent, but they are still punished because the individual in question neglected to use his knowledge to prevent himself from entering into a situation of desperation in the first place. Defense is the least of the three, and if found to be true the case is forgiven completely as its multiplier is zero.

There exists one final multiplier which may be used at the judge and jury's discretion. It is a multiplier of 0.25 and when used by the jury it is called "the mercy of the court", and when used by the judge is simply called mercy. They can be used simultaneously, and in cases where a jury is not present, the judge may apply it twice if so desired. This will be found used in many of the lesser cases to break the three-month minimum sentence into 22 days, or coupled with a desperation plea, possibly down to 11 days. At the extreme extent, a ruling of double mercy makes the minimum possible sentence 3 days or 155 dollars, the lowest possible fine.

ii. Reparations

In addition to the time sentences, reparations may be due. They are payments strictly for damages to the victim and property. Additional abstract damages for pain and suffering or mental trauma may be added but are capped at 15% of the total immaterial property damages, and 100% of bodily injury expenses incurred (calculated by PHS). However in the case of premeditated murder, there shall be no cap for the victim's immediate family.

The reparation amount can be paid by the criminal in personal capital or property, paid voluntarily or seized by the victim. If the criminal has no capital, reparations will be paid by half* of the criminals Laborforce wages being sent to the victim. If when free and still owing reparations, the criminal has no capital producing project in one week, producing an amount greater than the weekly Laborforce wages, he is to remain in the Laborforce until the reparations are paid in full.

* The other half of the wages pays a criminal's room and board.

iii. Fines

For any crime of 4 or 5 points the time can be traded as a fine payment equal to the amount of wages that would be paid in that allotted time by the Laborforce. For example if one was convicted of a four-point crime, which is a three-month sentence, this would equal about 3,086 dollars at minimum wage, which is the wage paid by the Laborforce. Having fines of these higher amounts acts as a deterrent in themselves, and also acts as an incentive for one to enter into a Laborforce assignment, where despite its name, is a great place of learning. Choosing this avenue, as opposed to paying a fine, the criminal actually keeps half of the minimum wage earned (if no reparations are involved) while learning and helping the community.

Any crime above 5 points *must* be served as time. This eliminates the ability of individuals with wealth to escape penalization. To the intelligent or wealthy criminal the Laborforce is a humbling experience that reminds them of the foundations of a society and the great ease which a society makes out of the harshness of nature. For the ignorant criminal it is a place of learning, rehabilitation and encouragement.

Until full conversion to the Individualistic system, fines and time are applied by the statues of the "Model Penal Code" compiled by the American Law Institute, save that instead of going to prison the perpetrators enter into the Laborforce. All modern judgments for fines may be converted into Laborforce time by dividing them by the current minimum wage. Unlike the present fines, which are only a part of the bill and then there is a myriad of additional administration fees, the Individualists fines are the bottom line and cover all costs.

iv. Exile

Being that this world is far from ideal, there exist certain souls within it who are also far from ideal. These individuals repeatedly harm their fellow man or take advantage of any social structure erected by the people for their use to get along. Regardless of even the noble Individualistic attempts at education and reform, some souls, for whatever their reasons, will not agree to a code which the masses believe to be just and fair. Such a revolt is understandable in a tyrannical society, but it is illogical in a true direct democracy.

On a planet that has a finite amount of space all must get along to some degree, and all must compromise their visions of an ideal world to that same degree. If humankind had conquered space, then any who were displeased with the chosen rules or social structure, could simply leave, or be made to leave, praying for their success in setting up their ideal world on another planet. Unfortunately this is not the case. Therefore the society and the dissenter must reach an agreement. Other societies would simply invoke the death penalty and be done with it. However, the Individualist does not believe in the death penalty for two reasons: One, God gave life and God shall take it away. Two, any trial can be corrupted and a person masterfully framed, and the Individualists will not have wrongful deaths on their hands. Therefore, the Individualists summon the practice of Exiling from antiquity.

This is as close as one can come to having their own planet but with benefits. When it is realized how difficult it actually is to survive on one's own, let alone create a society, one may gain a new appreciation for society and wish to return to it with open arms. Also in the case of a "wrongful exile" the individual is most likely unharmed.

The exile can be given by a judge for any crime above 21 points. Partial exiles (expulsions with set time limits) may be given for any crime above 14 points. An exile is resorted to when the society has made a reasonable attempt at reform and education, and the individual still offends against the society. Temporary expulsions can last from a few days, to a few weeks, months, or years, all at the court's discretion according to the crime. The exile is not a punishment, and is far less cruel and unusual than the death penalty. Self-subsistence is taught in detail to all Individualists, therefore they will not be confronted with nature unarmed.

The exile zones are remote Populus land reserves such as in Alaska (for partial exiles) or remote islands (for those considered dangerous or fully exiled). To some, exile will be a death penalty, to others a college education, and to others a paradise. The Individualists are certain that most will learn to appreciate society and its safety and ease, as the entire nation of Australia is a testimony to this.

The banished will be dropped off with only their clothes and three days rations, and affixed with a GPS bracelet, which will be used to locate them when their sentence has expired. They must then fend for themselves and survive on what nature supplies while making their best attempt at sculpting their ideal world which they so desire.

By reinstating exile, coupled with the Laborforce, there are no longer institutions which simply house prisoners on the taxpayers dollar returning no benefit to the society. These "homes" are not feared by many, and are seen as a free ride to some. The exile becomes a more serious deterrent to misdeed, as one will not simply be locked in a room and fed. Exile will show that the society is a great privilege which at any time can be taken away, causing one to respect it that much more. The same respect then develops for the wisdom of self-subsistence and the independence it grants, as well as it being the cornerstone to building any society from nothing. Also because unlike the death penalty where one has a great length of time in between and one's fate is certain, one is immediately exiled and one's mode of death within exile may be starvation, food poisoning, parasites, or being slain by a predator etc. Also one can be faced with this serious dilemma for even lesser crimes. This causes one to appreciate and understand better what a society is, and to do their best to be a part of it and not to get kicked out. Not because of the fear of exile itself, but because of the fear of the lack of a society and the fear of one's own lack of capability. However, for those rare individuals, one can request to be exiled at any time, for no one is a prisoner of the Individualistic society.

Lastly, there are those who condone the exile as well as death penalty and favor a life imprisonment. Life imprisonment simply wastes tax dollars and gives one individual a life time to focus one's contempt in some masterful maleficent act in return for the theft of one's life. To the most terrible of criminals, offending repeatedly and attempting escapes, they who have gained infamy amongst the people, they are inexpensively set free into the most remote exile zone accessible. They are free as they wish and away from the society which they so hate. If they have learned well Individualistic self-sustenance they should live a very happy free life. Thus exile is a gift to both the criminal and to the taxpayers, as they no longer have a fee for such an individual.

v. Prisons

Prisons have become nothing but schools of darkness and colleges of corruption. Collections of underworld lords where their activities become refined and even practiced there. They are naught but dark capitals, with corruption as blatant as outside criminals with family members as prison employees to work interior connections. It is a mockery of reform where some individuals actually purposely commit crime for the free food and shelter prison provides. This entire free ride is paid for by the taxpayers. Thus, it is the taxpayers who are punished for each crime committed.

The US has over 2 million prisoners at an average cost of $25,000 per prisoner per year. This amounts to 50 Billion dollars per year which gives a free ride and dark education to people who need the opposite; work and ethics by practicing Individualistic self subsistence knowledge, trades, higher education and a philosophy of unity. The Individualists realize that most criminal activity is the result of improper rearing by parents and/or a flaw in logic and reasoning due to either missing information or disorganized comprehension of acquired information. Thus, these Penal Laborers will be taught not only basic values and skills, but the reasoning behind those values and skills, namely, the Unity of All, and the harshness of nature without the benefits of a society.

As it stands now, the taxpayer is paying for these criminals to be non-productive. The Individualist finds this waste of money unacceptable. The same money will be taken and used to build all needed Populus facilities with these criminals as a fairly paid labor force. Effectively turning a stagnating waste of human life and tax money into a productive force benefiting the community and simultaneously rehabilitating the Penal Laborers.

All Individualistic sentences shall be Laborforce assignments. Therefore, without delay the Individualists dismantle the entire prison system. The facilities will be converted into community colleges and similar facilities for rehabilitation of certain inmates at night and civilian free education in the day. There may be minor housing of some staffing criminals as most will be on site at their Laborforce assignment. There will be no danger to civilians because only lesser deviants will be present. It is fact that there is a 7% crime increase in individuals after imprisonment with an additional 3% increase for those who have served long sentences. Only when rehabilitation and community service work is actively incorporated do the criminals not offend again, thus proving the ineffectiveness of prisons and the virtue of the Laborforce.

Upon committing any crime and before sentencing, each criminal is asked if they like the society in which they live, and reminded that they are not forced to be a part of it and that they may choose exile at any time. This is to remind the criminal that society is about mutual respect and that nature is very harsh if not deadly when left alone within it. It also then brings to mind the importance of the Individualistic self-sufficiency knowledge. This simple but powerful realization coupled with a philosophy of unity will make many deviants capable, independent individuals willing to contribute to the society, whose existence is imperative to their welfare.

vi. Laborforce

The philosophy behind the Laborforce is efficiency. To have taxpayers pay for large institutions and the free ride and dark schooling of criminals is absurd. The Laborforce dismantles the expense of the prison system and builds community projects while simultaneously reforming the criminals. Within the Laborforce all will earn their keep, and will be made to work, not severely with whips and scourges as a slave, and not passively like today which allows inmates to sit and do nothing all day on the taxpayers dollar, but fairly balanced in between them. The criminals will be made to work in the day and study Individualistic self-sustenance knowledge and philosophy in the evening, as opposed to stagnating. They will be paid fair wage but from that wage will be extracted their room and board and any reparations owed. The remaining amount is placed into the commonwealth until the criminal completes the required sentence. This is to remind one of the value and freedom of a society, and that on one's own in nature life is much harsher than in any Laborforce assignment.

Upon conviction the criminal takes a practical aptitude test which will reveal the convict's self sufficiency skills and the degree of learning attained. The test score determines the individual's placement within the Laborforce. For example if one was a master carpenter one would be able to work as a master carpenter if that position was available. The civilian workers on site will usually act as the foremen of the Penal Laborers in cooperation with the site warden. However, if a Penal Laborer has notably high scores, and proven advanced skills, as well as a cooperative mind set and sufficient incentive, this individual could be placed as high as a project manager and remain as such so long as all the daily reports prove productive and harmonious results.

The facilities housing the Penal Laborers will be reinforced mobile trailers moved on to the site of the project. In the proper season, where possible, they will rear onsite windmills and gardens to assist the generation of food and energy for the site Penal Laborers as well as practicing a valuable skill, a reform in itself. Defection will be discouraged not only by the humane treatment and interesting knowledge being gained, but also by site wardens who also act as protection for the civilian workers. Wardens are armed with non-lethal but powerful weapons such as beanbag shot, rubber bullets, high voltage tasers and tranquilizers.

The wardens shall be scolding fathers to those not meeting at least average production. This is no different than that of the young laborer of a free man's brick layers union, scolded and hollered at for 8 hrs a day, yet this boy is free, and the harshness will turn him into a man. The Individualist will not stand for any weaklings claiming that this more than fair system, with lighter authority than most free unions, is in anyway inhumane. People supporting this claim are those who desire, 1. A nation of weaklings so that they can be easily controlled, and 2. To erect a colossal system supporting millions of criminals wasting the tax dollars of the people only so that an infinite series of markets can be set up around it wasting additional funds, time and energy to the benefit of the few.

Moreover, to appease this type of mind set, any who decide that the conditions are too harsh may always choose exile to discover how much more kind mother nature will treat them. These same fools will declare that it is also inhumane to throw individuals out of a society. With these conditions what penalty shall become established? What becomes established is what exists today, a system wherein one commits a crime and gets a free ride, courtesy of the taxpayers. As one of sound mind can clearly see, such fools favor crime and the industry around it, therefore encourage it, and are hence an accessory to multiple crimes.

The Laborforce is the labor reserves for all Populus projects. However, they can be hired out by private businesses of any size for any type of work. This will impede the presently growing practice of supporting and utilizing illegal immigration for low pay and exploiting legal immigrants for the same purpose. Private business can pay Penal Labors higher than base minimum wage if so desired, either way the Populus is not paying for their wage.

The project managers of any size site and the Penal Labors must both fill out a daily questionnaire and have it signed by the site warden. This questionnaire involves, what was learned, taught, activities of the day, and performance of self and others and if pleased or displeased and why. Frequent complaints from either side will be alleviated by the warden, if not the penal worker is moved to another part of the site, or to another site all together.

It is natural to assume that these Laborforces will be of low work ethic and knowledge and therefore low production and quality. However, incentive is offered by early release, pay bonuses, and raises for good work awarded by the warden at his discretion with court authorization granted according to the daily reports.

When the project is completed and/or the inmate is freed, he subsequently now has contacts in the working world, new skills, as well as knowledge of self-sustenance to support himself, and possibly profit. Thus if not able or willing to go right back to the company or department he was contracted to, now as a freeman, he has all this new knowledge to either find new employment, start his own business, or make a prosperous homestead profiting either by food or energy.

There are 4 degrees of the Laborforce, to describe them in terms of modern law:

Infraction: allowed to work unchained as normal employees monitored by an unarmed warden
Misdemeanor: allowed to work unchained as normal employees monitored by a lightly armed warden
Felony (non or mildly violent): allowed to work unchained as normal employees monitored by heavily armedwardens, no close contact allowed with civilians or operation of any large mobile machinery, unless proven to display positive, constructive behavior.
Felony2: (High risk): only allowed in chain gang type settings within mills, mines, mass cultivating etc., any attempted escape results in instant exile.

Ideally, the Individualistic society will produce few criminals, thus in the future there will be no criminals within the Laborforce, and possibly no Laborforce at all. The Individualists major obstacle resides in reforming the 2 million criminals inherited from the dying world. This is approximately 40,000 extra workers per state (even though not evenly distributed in such a manner). The US civilian work force has about 141 million workers, and grows about 1.6% each year. Therefore, by introducing the Laborforce the growth rate will jump an additional 1.42% for the first year, nearly doubling the average labor growth. This initial flooding of an additional 40,000 Laborforce workers per state will equilibrate to normal growth rate within five years as many of these souls will be rapidly rehabilitated, while more individuals will become self sufficient and drop out of the workforce all together. Furthermore, fewer criminals will be initially entering the penal system due to the Individualistic teachings.

Some will argue that this is a form of slave labor, far from it. These laborers have a fair wage, are assisting the community, and require such a work ethic because humans only subsist by working. To prove this fact, throw any individual naked into a jungle and observe how much work is needed to survive each day. It will be found that a very great deal of very harsh and challenging work needs to be done to survive nature, thus in contrast, the Laborforce is a paradise. It rebuilds the character by teaching knowledge and practical skills, unlike the useless specialized labors taught to the majority of the "first world" countries. Furthermore, the Laborforce is open to any and all civilians who need income or desire a specific skill, and they may come and go as they please, thus it is not composed of strictly penal labor.

d. Police

The police of the Individualistic society are replaced with a division of the Populus Militia, which is composed of the citizens of that locality. Too often modern police watch the people instead of watching over them, not feeling the proper affinity towards their fellow man. With the citizens watching over themselves, and all being militia members, a high degree of comradery is present between the police and the "policed", not to mention a higher degree of combat expertise.

Each citizen is required to know everyone in a ten-acre radius. This awareness has many safety and preventative benefits. The initial introduction is organized each year by the captain of that locality. The small orientation takes place as a public gathering wherein each citizen is informed of the local geography and his neighbors. These ten-acre sections (in some cases larger) then practice drills together on a regular scheduled basis thereby generating a higher degree of comradery. Members of the practice drills each residing at different geographical points will thereby all know a different group of people, together forming a network of comradery and high awareness, increasing the difficulty of suspect and criminal activity to go uncaught. This topic is explained in further detail on page 132 in the discussion of the military.

Wardens

Wardens are senior active duty militiamen or women assigned or volunteered for the position. The wardens are the supervisors of the Populus Laborforces and represent the people's on site interest in their tax dollars. The size of the Laborforce and the type of criminals composing it, will determine the number of wardens assigned. The wardens are responsible for ensuring an acceptable level of performance by utilizing incentives and disciplinary measures no more severe than would be expected in military boot camp. They are responsible for recording and reporting individual performance as well and issuing rewards to excelling laborers with court approval. The warden is a demanding position encompassing all the duties of military labor management and legal administration, while having to be constantly alert and on guard for protection of the citizen workers against any unsuspected uprising.

e. Common Laws

i. Alimony

Divorce happens because many people do not know what love is, and their lust too often produces children that must be cared for. Often it is true that either one or both of the parents are irresponsible, which caused the situation in the first place, and now threatens the livelihood of the children involved. It is then understandable for the society to get involved and oversee care of the children in the form of court ordered alimony payments, so that the children do not end up on the streets or become prone to criminal behavior.

However presently there is a terrible flaw in the alimony system. It does not take into account which parent is irresponsible. For to give an individual money and assume it will all go to the children without a *second* court order defeats the entire purpose of the system. For this individual could be taking this money, meant for the children, and spending it on personal luxury or drugs while the children remain neglected.

The first court order shall be the order of the parent with least custody to pay a calculated amount whose minimum is based on the Laborforce minimum wage. For if the individual does not have a job or profiting homestead to pay at least this minimum amount this one will be placed into the Laborforce until a higher paying occupation is found. The second court order applies to the receiving parent, which orders that every cent be spent on the children for necessities, allotting only 15% for non essentials such as toys, or designer cloths etc. These purchases must be proved by itemized receipts which will be reviewed by a court representative every sixty days or at the request of the other parent.

Furthermore, too often the existence of alimony, spousal support, splitting of assets etc. actually encourages divorce. Especially in situations where one parent has a high paying occupation and the other is unemployed. By divorce the unemployed can gain court ordered access to the "loved one's" money and or possessions. Thus, the Individualists make one final alteration to the system. The individual who initiates the divorce or separation, forfeits their right to sue for any monetary or material gain unless it is proven they are in a hostile relationship. This will hinder the temptation to forfeit love and children for the glistening embrace of cash, which the current structure of the system encourages.

ii. Bankruptcy

The Individualists dismantle private banks, fractional reserve and usury. With usury it is understandable how one may get buried beneath debt. And with fractional reserve it is understandable how one may dispute a debt being that a bank can demand repayment of ten times the amount it actually lent. Without these practices all debt becomes valid. Therefore there is no bankruptcy in the Individualistic society. This makes one think deeply before borrowing money. Any debt can be made forcibly payable if delinquent for 90 days. If the debtor has no material or energy reserves, the debtor must enter the Laborforce until the debt is repaid. This acts as further deterrent for not repaying a debt and encourages additional forethought before initially taking a debt.

iii. Environmental

1. Biodegradability:

Until phased out, all synthetic materials must be fully biodegradable within ten years when subjected to weather (such as wood, it can keep indefinitely when cared for but will quickly rot when left to the weather). They also must be able to be easily recycled by on site devises. (Consumers will be recycling at their homesteads more often see pg. 148)
All liquid chemicals must have a complete unambiguous disclosure of their ingredients.
Obviously these regulations hinder the use of such things as vinyl siding, plastic piping, and paints, and encourage the research into natural coatings, sealants etc.

2. Waste

All unnatural products and materials will be phased out of the Individualistic society. Until then, there will be no burning of unnatural, processed, or otherwise toxic materials such as, plastic, rubber, paint, treated wood, treated paper etc. There will be no burying or stockpiling such wastes on one's own property nor any waste of any kind expelled into the waters.

3. Forestry

For any tree cut down, one must plant the same tree twice the age of the tree cut. For example, if one cuts down a 10 year old oak, one must plant 20 one-year-old oak saplings or 2 ten-year-old oaks, or any like combination that meets the total age requirement. (This does not apply to renewable timberlands where the cut trees are always replanted. Those practicing such activities must apply for a permit.)

iv. Foods

1. The use of fertilizers must be disclosed on all foods identifying the type of fertilizer(s) and method applied.
2. The use of artificial scents and flavors shall be banned
3. All foods must have a complete unambiguous disclosure of their ingredients.

v. Immigration

Being that the Individualistic society believes that a high degree of knowledge and comradery discourages all criminal behavior and makes each individual an efficient contributor to the society, the immigration requirements are altered. The immigrants must be duly prepared to enter into this society, for the lame, inept and unprepared will find a most embarrassing challenge awaiting them.

The entry requirements are 1. One must have enough money to purchase one acre and enough money to pay for the two-year entrance course. 2. Due to the Individualistic high value of knowledge, the immigrant must take a two year course which is a compressed version of all the knowledge taught to each citizen in the advanced public schools of the Individualists. 3. Upon passing these tests, the immigrant must serve two years in the Populus military just as every other Individualistic citizen has done. If one can complete this four year challenge, one becomes a worthy citizen of the Individualistic society, and understands well their values.

vi. The 6M Law

The Individualistic society does not restrict knowledge except only in one condition, war. Being that the Individualistic nation is utterly neutral, this means that the war has come to Individualist's soil. Only at this time does LAFKI place a six-month lag on pertinent military intelligence. Any other time the citizens are fully informed of the bleeding edge of all technology.

Some officials who disagree with such free information, even though such information was fully paid for by the citizens, will use the argument that the information will leak out to the enemy. This implies a fear in one's own capabilities. If one is confident in one's strategy, and application of will, numbers and advanced technology will not matter, the US Marines will testify to this fact. Furthermore, even in average societies, the one who invented the technology is already ahead of the one who is just now reading it second hand. By the time full understanding and practical application of the new information is achieved, the ones who invented it have already moved on to the next level. Therefore, withholding information from one's own people implies an entity, separate from the people, who desires an upper hand over the people as well as over exterior entities.

Furthermore, with a doctrine of unrestricted knowledge the rate of technology growth will be far faster than any other society who practices a system of knowledge restriction. Thus, even if an enemy receives the cutting edge technology, by the time it is able to use it, an Individualistic society will be far beyond that point, much farther than an average society mentioned above.

vii. Voting

The act of electing a representative was because 1. People were deemed not educated enough to make proper decisions for themselves and 2. People were assumed to not have enough time on their hands to properly assist in government affairs. Today, people have even less time, and cannot even suitably research the Individuals who are campaigning. The often limited number of candidates limits the possibility of choice, creating a scenario where no candidate may accurately represents a new direction the people wish to turn. Furthermore, the price of campaigning removes the common man from campaigning to represent his people causing all representation to bias one class.

For all these reasons the Individualists erect the GEP and its Populus Informer. With this system representatives, as well as all the above mentioned restrictions are practically made obsolete. All laws, bills, acts, etc will be voted on by the entire nation. Voting on all law by all classes saves the law from perversion into a leveraging devise to be used for the profit of corporations and benefit of the few. Ideally there will never be any new laws passed in the Individualistic society, as their simple doctrine should remain stable and unchanging for thousands of years.

To ensure this check on corruption it is made law that each citizen must read the Populus informer and fill out the consensus form else be fined $155. The reasoning, value, and importance of this action is taught in detail in their education system.

Lastly, any representative position incorporated into the Individualistic system, or any significant position of the four departments, is elected for specific term maximums. The full length of their terms is governed by the percentage of votes won, for example, a four-year term. If the individual receives only 51% of the votes (the minimum term) the term is only 2 years long, but if the individual receives 100% of the votes the term is then the full 4 years. This division can be calculated down to the day, and accurately reflects the people's wishes of who they desire to represent them.

viii. Exemptions

There are no exemptions of any kind in tax, government, law etc. in the Individualistic society. Equality means equality, there are no partial definitions. All individuals will be subject, equally, to the exact same forces.

f. Company Laws

i. Corporate Liabilities

In the Individualistic society companies will be judged for what they are, a collection of individuals. A company is no longer an entity in itself. All individuals of a company will be proportionately responsible for the actions of that company. Proportion will be determined by the current salary and amount of shares possessed by each member of the company. Thus, a great wrong committed by a company will be proportionately absorbed by all of its members. This makes each employee, and each investor, much more apt to become fully conscious of their company's actions and risks in great detail, judging whether it is worth while to be employed there, or invest there.

This will cause the extinction of many suspect, irresponsible, and deviant corporations, unless they alter their methods of operation. This will also cause companies to adopt a policy of heightened responsibility, as a company and as individuals, as well as announce more detailed information of their practices, which will assist the over all awareness of the society, and take it another step closer to Individualistic unrestricted knowledge. This in turn will cause doubt to vanish in the minds of potential employees and investors causing companies who do great good for mankind, and are open about all of their practices, to naturally receive an influx of employees and investors.

Reducing corporate law down to just the individuals who compose it, lessens the irrational complexity of modern law and brings it closer to Individualistic legal simplicity. As an extreme example, one can envision an entire company serving Laborforce assignments for a corporate act of negligence which happened to cost the lives of a handful of people. Conversely, one could see hundreds of investors dumping money into a battery manufacturer who released the details of its cutting edge technology and proposed methods of operation.

ii. Corporate Relations

All Populus employees and paid representatives must publicly disclose all of their investments and any addition or subtraction thereto throughout their entire term. They are excluded from any decisions involving companies in which they are invested. The personal investments of individuals in positions of these natures too often encourages favoritism and corruption. For example, FDA officials approving drugs from companies in which they own stock in, or shareholders of a drug company seeking employment at the FDA for that same reason.

iii. Populus Purchasing

If there comes a time when the Populus must purchase from private companies it will do so only by public approval and vote on submitted contracts. The contracts will be clear and concise and the amount purchased from the contractors shall be proportionate to the Populus votes. For example: four companies submit contracts for 100 electric engines. 60% of Populus chooses company A, 20% chooses company B, 15% company C, and 5% company D. Thus, 5 engines will be purchased from company D, 15 from company C, 20 from company B etc.

iv. Small Business Taxing

The Individualistic society turns the power to the small business by lifting all business profit tax on any businesses under 100 people. All members of the company, from the employees to the owners pay only the national flat tax of 12.46% plus their applicable state and local taxes. Thus the entire company acts as one individual paying the same tax applied to every individual. All earnings not declared as profit by some individual in the company must be reinvested back into the company. This will assist small businesses in growing and competing with larger entities. Upon sale of the business or any of its assets, the owner(s) will pay the 12.46%, plus the state and local taxes, as a capital gain tax on any profit from such sales.   This ensures that any funds going into the company, no matter what form they eventually took, got properly taxed. Thus throughout the life of one business it will pay the exact taxes as any one individual. These taxes are the tribute to the society which allowed that business to profit initially.

v. Subsidiaries

Subsidiary defined:

1. A subsidiary is a company controlled by another corporation. When that control or ownership is not shared, it is termed a wholly-owned subsidiary.   Subsidiaries are distinct legal entities for purposes of taxation and other forms of regulation. – Wikipedia

2. A subsidiary is a company which is owned or controlled by another firm or company. Subsidiaries include firms in which a company owns more than 50 percent of the outstanding voting stock, as well as firms in which a company has the power to direct or cause the direction of the management and policies.
– U.S. Census Bureau Glossary of Terms for the Economic Census

Subsidiaries no longer exist, being that companies are no longer considered individual entities, they cannot own things. Ownership of any company asset is divided proportionately among its members. Too often subsidiaries are used as deceptions to conceal the breath of the control and interests of a corporation. Additionally, they act as protection for an already too large animal. A company can create a subsidiary and attempt a risky venture under a different name, and if they fail or cause great ill to the society, the majority of the society will never know who was responsible. Thus, a company must have only one pre-fixed name for all of its interactions clearly identifying its presence. This will slow the growth of corporations because the consequences of their actions will directly affect the individuals of the company and may result in criminal punishment, instead of a mere payment of restitution, or dissolving of the subsidiary, neither of which serves justice to the minds who initiated the act. Furthermore, this inability to conceal their actions slows expansion into questionable areas to which their customers would not agree, regardless of the profits which management may see therein.

The setting up of an entity within an entity or outside of an entity controlled by that entity partially or wholly, allots for many types of corruption. This subdividing of one entity countless times creates a myriad of loopholes granting the ability to conceal actions, profits, involvement etc. Thus, a subsidiary is naught but a corporate strategy to avoid and bend law. Allowing for men to do great injustices to the world and to have a non existent "entity" be punished in their place by mere monetary payments whose origin was from none other than the pockets of the exploited mass population. Thus the people simply get some of their money back when a corporation does wrong. But in nearly all cases, no one in the company gets truly punished, thus no deterrent exists, therefore no justice is present. By prohibiting subsidiaries, every activity of a corporation is much more carefully considered and undertaken.

vi. Subsidies

Subsidies defined:

1. A grant paid by a government to an enterprise that benefits the public.
– Cognitive science laboratory at Princeton university

2. In economics, a subsidy is generally a monetary grant given by government to lower the price faced by producers or consumers of a good, generally because they are considered to be in the public interest.
– Wikipedia

3. A payment that a government makes to a producer to supplement the market price of a commodity. Subsidies can keep consumer prices low while maintaining a higher income for domestic producers.
- University of Maryland Research Library Glossary

First of all, the *government's* money *is* the people's money, therefore the above definitions should read; the people pay money to a private entity to get a lower cost at that private entity's elevated profit. To simplify it further; the people pay money to get a lower cost . . .. this nonsense is worth repeating: the people pay money to get a lower cost. To put it simple, the people have just bought something twice, they paid the producer to make it for them, then they paid to buy it from a store. If one pays the producer to make a good or service, it is then paid for, there is no second procedure. Furthermore if a good or service is of such importance to the society, the Populus will have already voted for the construction of such a facility. The Individualist pays for things only once, and does not use public money to the benefit of private entities.

Nearly every subsidy if rife with corruption, agriculture, coal, oil, auto, power, construction, private sports and an endless stream of other private industries thriving off of public dollars. For example, farm subsidies. Subsidy payments awarded to farms are based on their production levels. Therefore, the massive corporate farms get the largest subsidy payments. They use this public money to grow even larger until small farmers, too small to be eligible for significant subsidy payments, are eventually driven out of business and forced to sell their land to these same corporations made tyrants by the people's money. Even Wal-Mart is an empire built almost entirely on taxpayer money yet it returns none of its titanic profits to the people.

Subsidies are eliminated entirely without delay in the Individualistic society. Corporate welfare in any form is an unfair advantage and the use of the tax payers money for the profit of private individuals. If needed, tax money will be used to erect such companies publicly owned, and their end product or service offered at practically cost to the people, to whom any profit made will be redistributed. There is simply no welfare for any individual or collection of individuals in the Individualistic society. All subsidies and grants or any other labels given to the act of lending the people's money to private interests are disbanded without delay.

vii. The 2110 law

Any paid member of a company which has over 2110 employees, whose salary is at least 1% of the company's worth, is considered a "Vital Mechanism". In other words, the individual is more part of the company than an individual, and thus pays the current company tax for his income rate as opposed to the flat rate of 12.46% paid by the Populus. This keeps the profits of companies benefiting the Populus and stops the hiding of profits by distributing them to the elite executives, while still allowing for substantial profits of said elite executives. (Detail page 84)

g. Churches and Temples

The Individualists believe in and uphold the American Constitution when it states that congress shall make no law respecting an establishment of religion or prohibiting the free exercise thereof. Therefore, the following is mentioned as a suggestion regarding religious establishments from an Individualistic point of view.

No holy place of worship should take donations without giving proportional property rights in return. Too often supposed holy men are corrupted and find it too easy to receive and give nothing but empty promises of illumination in return. This action suggested is an attempt to make these individuals more truly representatives of their faith and to have them make better attempts at actually illuminating their students and make their establishment more focused on their religious instruction as opposed to money. Those donating are now part owners and will consequently feel much more responsibility for the establishment and its members. This suggestion does not affect religion, it affects currency which is the Populus' property and thus the property of all people of all faiths in the Union. But again, this is merely a suggested method of conduct and not a law.

h. Decriminalized Activities

i. Illicit Drugs

This subject raises the eyes and the hatred of most just by viewing the words. Therefore, the Individualists request special care of the reader in considering the Individualistic reasoning before making a judgement, while remembering that it is the underworld itself that wishes this activity to remain illegal for its sole benefit. The illicit drug market in the U.S. alone is over 65 Billion dollars per year, and 300 Billion dollars globally. Whether legal or illegal people will still engage in this activity, therefore the aim is to find the most constructive way to handle the subject. To deem something illegal only opens the door for crime which brings with it violence, and all of the other related corruption. The Individualist believes that all drugs should be legalized for a six-fold purpose:

1. All sales can be monitored and the money put into the Populus government and not into the pockets of foreign governments or criminals.
2. If individuals are so senseless as to abuse drugs leading to their death, they were not of strong enough caliber to be among the Individualistic society in the first place, and their death removes their weakness from it.
3. The very act of making a substance illegal creates a taboo and black-market around it. Prohibition of alcohol is the common example. Therefore, making something illegal actually increases interest in the substance.
4. No *government* or any other individual should have any control over the personal decisions of any individual, so long as those decisions affect no other individual outside of the decision maker. For example, suicide and murder, are both the decision to kill, however one involves an exterior individual. Thus the first should be legal, the latter illegal. The Individualists place this much more responsibility in the hands of the individual, where it has always belonged, as a natural result of the increased freedom and independence of the Individualistic society.
5. Legalization removes a huge influx of "criminals" out of the taxpayers' system and makes them tax payers themselves. Thus, there is a threefold gain in Populus profit:
   a. Less justice system influx means less spending, hence more money
   b. A once underworld business becomes a Populus tax generating system
   c. Drug industry related criminals themselves become taxpayers, instead of costing tax by sitting in prison.
6. Legalization lessens violence associated with the industry, and causes a drop in crime, and crime organizations, as well as increases social safety and user safety.

Many believe that the common illicit substances are no more dangerous to the human mind and body than are alcohol and nicotine. The regulations of these substances if legalized would be no different than alcohol, sold in state stores to people 21 or older. Since making illegal a large portion of these substances in 1914 by the Harrison narcotics act, the underworld has marketed an image of terror around these substances to keep them illegal for their own control and profit.

This madness of making illegal some things as hazardous to an individual "for that individuals own good" is a cover up for the control of a market for profiteering purposes. For instance if gasoline is lethal to drink, why is it not illegal to drink it? But safrole, a flavoring of original root beer, was supposedly found to cause liver cancer in rats only after feeding them massive doses, thus it was made illegal to consume. However, not much was said about how it is used to create MDMA, the designer drug called 'ecstasy'. The Individualists believe that a warning on a product is all that is necessary, if one wishes to ingest a potentially lethal substance, it is their freedom of choice to do so, and the repercussions of one's own free choices is how one learns. Else, the society as a whole must hasten to make fire illegal to touch.

ii. Prostitution

No different than the previous subject, it is another subject often kept out of sight and out of mind. It is for this very reason, ignoring reality, that a global market of horror has risen up, with human beings actually being sold into slavery and shipped about world wide. The Individualist does not ignore such topics and subjects them to analysis for the truth, no matter how difficult it is to ponder.

Prostitution has existed since history has been recorded. It obviously is not going anywhere and must be recognized as a fact of human existence and dealt with accordingly. Therefore, the most constructive methods must be drawn up to coexist with the phenomena. Research in countries such as Sweden show that repressive measures do not result in the reduction of prostitution. They merely shift the practice from one area to another.

There are arguments for and against any subject, either side chosen always has pros and cons. However, the repression of this practice has been attempted since history began and has yet to succeed, thus it has proven futile, and now the alternate argument must be considered. The Individualist sees this practice as simply a matter of free choice. If any individual wants to sell sex and another wants to buy it, as long as none is harmed, and it is done in a discreet fashion, then there is no social harm, thus there is no social injustice, therefore there is no crime.

The question of morals is strictly between one's own self and one's god. If one desires to perform this act, it is their body and their freedom of choice to do so. Hence, the Individualists find difficulty in calling this a crime but find ease in calling it amoral. However, personal morality is no grounds for incrimination or laws, simply grounds for self shame.

If legal and regulated, prostitutes and their clients will be safer and sexually transmitted diseases will be lessened. As above, the business will be a $12 Billion per year tax generating system, and an influx of individuals would be removed from the penal system. If written law is allowed to govern morality, one could be forced to dress a certain way, behave a certain way, and live life in a certain way. One's actions, however immoral, simply display to the rest of the population the level of learning and understanding of that individual. Thus, law cannot punish ignorance, for rarely is the ignorant one responsible for being ignorant. If law is to punish ignorance, than the entire current schooling system must be immediately incarcerated.

i. Individualistic Legal Simplicity

The state of having all of the laws and punishments simplified to such an extent, without sacrificing any order, wherein every individual has the entire code memorized is called "Individualistic Legal Simplicity". This statute will be simple enough to fit on a reasonable sized plaque, or set of plates, and will be placed in all Populus facilities and most homes. Complexity of law only assists, supports and encourages corruption.

Once any restriction is set upon man by law, it immediately creates a black-market and all the evils connected thereto. Law's only right is to establish reasonable guidelines for the individuals of a society to use to get along. It is not to be used as a controlling force or a concealing force. Knowledge alone allows the people to live in harmony, with laws only being required as a background framework. Knowledge alone is sufficient to guarantee all liberties, and it is awareness and knowledge, freely shared, that will lead to a free and just society, not an endless doctrine of laws.

3. INDIVIDUALISTIC TAXES

Tax defined:

Enforced charge exacted of persons, corporations and organizations by the government to be used to support government services and programs.
– Sanderco Glossary

A contribution for the support of a government required of persons groups or businesses within the domain of that government.
– American Heritage Dictionary

As one can see, the ambiguous word "government" is used in these definitions. Again, it matters greatly whether it is describing a direct democracy truly representing the people, or if it is describing an entity separate from the people. If it is an entity separate from the people, the people would be paying their tax money to another entity with its own interests and profits independent of the people, which is exactly what is happening in most of the present world. The amount of money being paid by the people compared to the amount of benefits which they proportionately receive in return from their investment is negligible. There have been revolutions over much less a blatant disrespect, abuse and exploitation. But, unfortunately the lack of education and awareness maintained by this separate entity has successfully kept the masses in a state of sensory depravation bordering on a coma, unable to act in favor of themselves.

The word "Tax" is often a biting and contemptuous word to many people, as it should be do to their experiences described above. However Individualistic taxes are utilized strictly for the benefit of the Populus as a whole with numerous public checks on the way they are spent. No dime is spent without a vote by the people, and all profits of those projects initiated are returned to the people. The Individualists therefore define Individualistic tax as such:

A reasonable contribution of all the individuals and businesses of the union for the proportionate support of the individual desires of that union.

a. Income Tax

In 2006 over $2.2 trillion in federal taxes and over $1.25 trillion in state and local taxes were collected. Additionally, over $0.9 trillion in health care was collected from the 7.65% of each individual's wage allocated to health care (as Medicare and social security). Later in this document (pg 90) it will be shown that national health care can be achieved by allocating an additional 2.54% in taxes to health. It will also be shown that the 2.2 trillion (15% wage tax) spent each year to run the federal government is 71% to much (pg 143). Thus, of the strictly federal tax (average of 15%), which is meant only to run the government, 2.54% of it is instead allocated to health care, leaving plenty to run the inflated federal government.

In the present world the average specialized laborers are getting away with only 63%, at best, of the money they earn. Of their paycheck they are taxed roughly 15% Fed income, 6.2% SS, 1.45% Medicare,

82

5.5% state, 2% local, totaling around 30.15%. This net profit is then taxed for all things bought and paid for with it, such as utility taxes, sales taxes, etc, averaging another 7% of the remaining income.

The US federal income tax law is over 60,000 pages long, and just as with anything, complexity is equal to corruption. The Individualists achieve simplicity by implementing a federal flat tax of 12.46% based on income, simple enough for all citizens to file themselves. SSI and Medicare are removed as well as the additional 2.54% of the federal tax which was allocated to health. State taxes will be capped at 5% and local at 2%, and neither may use this money for health related manners. Thus the Individualist pays approximately 10.7% less of his gross income than the average American.

This 12.46% is the bare minimum amount needed to run the government in its present wasteful, oversized and thoroughly corrupt, corpse-like state. However, with the disbanding of the many unnecessary government departments along with the federal reserve, fractional reserve, usury, and the countless other depraved actions of the US "representatives", operating costs will plummet, and this 12.46% will be more than enough funding for an efficient government leading to a bountiful society.

Not only will the taxes lower, but also a great amount of revenue will be generated simply by simplifying taxes:

1. Simplified taxes eliminate the deceptive areas of tax law created and exploited by the corrupt. Amounting to over 300 Billion dollars in the first year from stopped evasion techniques and reduced administration costs.

2. The Department of the Treasury estimates that the cost of conforming to the endless guidelines of the US tax law is around $125 billion a year. Simplifying the code will be able to completely abolish the IRS (with over 10 Billion in operating costs), as well as a myriad of filing institutions. Saving the taxpayer time, frustration and money by completing a simple form themselves.

b. Real Property Tax

Individualistic Property tax is a federal flat tax per acre annually. There is no "premium" land and the alterations to it such as, excavation, buildings, utilities, make no difference in the tax. Each individual's initial acre of land is not taxed, however, every other acre up to ten acres is taxed at a flat rate. Land amounts greater than ten acres fall under the excess land tax (page 82).

The suggested amount of this initial tax is $100 per acre, and adjusted accordingly per year to find the optimum comfortable compromise between the Union and its individuals. This number was generated from various property taxes, from as little as 0.11 cents per acre on plains land, to thousands of dollars per acre for premium lands.

Hypothetically, if every acre in United States paid $100 the (approximately) 2 billion acres of land would bring in 200 Billion dollars in tax revenue. However, the realistic number is less than a third of that figure being that a third of US land is protected and about a third of it is uninhabited or presently uninhabitable, leaving the remaining third able to draw roughly 66 Billion dollars annually.

c. People's Health Care Tax

Being that the Individualistic society encourages self sufficiency, which may lead to a drop in available workers, this tax's form is a voluntary non income based flat fee divided equally per capita of $4090 for each individual. Adults are responsible to pay this fee for their children. Legislation shall be passed forbidding tax spending on Health Care except with strictly this flat tax for the care of only paying members of the system.

The tax credit received from the lower income tax of the Individualist society (+10.7%) will make more capital available to these working individuals to pay this fee. This burden on average will be $2,522 less than the privately insured previously paid, and $1,800 more than what the publicly insured previously paid, yet $4090 more than the10% unable to work paid in the old system, (who must either opt out of the care or have some other pay for them). This makes the total US national average fee approximately $521 less per individual per year than the old system yet all are covered equally well in the new Individualistic system. (For the detailed discussion of the determination of this figure see pg 86).

d. Inheritance Tax

The Individualists disband the estate tax, inheritance tax, or death tax, by other names, being that 1. All property accumulated was bought on previously taxed money and 2. A government, local, state or federal, has no place whatsoever in family matters regardless of the size of those matters. It is simply an attempt to exploit yet another facet of life for profit.

e. Sin Taxes

The "Sin" taxes of the Individualistic society are in place to prevent acts of oppression, deception, inefficiency and damage to the environment and to life, especially human. Do not be discouraged by seeing the many new taxes, for only those who are not in harmony with higher thought will pay these taxes, ideally, no one in the absolute Individualistic society will pay these taxes.

Many sin taxes are split taxes, that is, they are taxed to the manufacturer to place that product on shelf and to the consumer or end buyer for purchasing it, before any applicable sales tax. This discourages manufacturers from making a product effected by theses taxes, as well as discouraging the use the same. It encourages both to take steps towards more intelligent solutions, and keeps the ideals of Individualistic harmony in the forefront of the minds of the Populus.

i. Controlled Substance Tax

Just as Alcohol and Tobacco are monitored and taxed, the Individualist propose all newly legalized controlled substances be treated just as alcohol, taxed accordingly and sold only at secure Populus outlets to adults. Due to the nature of these products these new stores will be designed similar to light duty banks, with the safety of the workers ensured. Fully equipped with separation of the employees and the wares from the customer, silent alarms, and doors which lock any perpetrator within. The workings of these outlets will be posted on the inside and outside so that deviants shall know that robbery is futile.

Experimental and new pharmaceuticals are also taxed. These are those never ending streams of wonder drugs curing any ailment while causing ten others in side effects. These irresponsible toxins making up most of the pharmaceutical industry's product line are more dangerous that any illegal drug to date yet are openly marketed through every medium, displaying the industry's brazen attitude as an immune diplomat. This tax shall assist to slow if not altogether stop their careless actions.

The suggested tax 12.5% to the retailer upon purchase from manufacturer, and additional 12.5% to the end buyer calculated after retail markup and before sales tax. The amount of revenue generated is predicted to be approximately 49.69 Billion dollars annually from taxing 200 Billion in US annual prescription pharmaceutical sales and 65 Billion US annual illicit drug sales.

ii. Excess Land Tax

The Individualist realizes that one acre is sufficient for one individual to successfully sustain oneself, thus by right one must be entitled to one acre. This initial acre is therefore not taxed, as it is a natural right to have enough land to sustain oneself. However, it is not necessary to possess more than this amount of land as it then infringes on the rights of others to possess one acre also. Also recognized is the human desire for spacious land and the desire of ownership over that land thus the low flat tax of $100 per acre is established up to 9 acres over the initial one tax free acre. However to own more than these ten acres of land is an excess and therefore the excess land tax becomes invoked. This is a tax upon any amount of land over that necessary for one individual's sustenance and one's fair desire of spacious land ownership.

For every power of ten (acres) the tax on the new lands shall double, thus 1 acre over the free acre is a $100 per acre flat tax, 10 acres over (11 total) equals the tax X 2 ($200 per new acre), 101 acres is the tax X4 ($400 per new acre), 1001 acres is the tax X8 ($800 per new acre) etc. This makes one not hoard land in vain, forcing the ownership to be advantageous and profitable.

The owner may select any one acre for his capital (the tax-free acre), all remaining tax on land shall be as it was chronologically purchased by total acres owned. Defaults in tax are subject to tax auctions. Partial payments shall cover owned properties in chronological order. Auctions may only be held after the owner fails to report to court summons after six months, and the property duly posted for the same length of time. (To often banks do not pay the taxes of a property when accepting a mortgage from and individual, without that individual's knowledge. The property is often sold out from under them for pennies at tax auction, while they are left with mortgages of tens of thousands of dollars for property practically stolen from them.)

iii. Foreign Soil Business Tax

All goods made in foreign lands either by U.S. citizens or foreigners will be taxed an additional 10% wholesale vale upon entering the U.S. This will encourage all business to remain in the U.S., and reduce exploitation of oversea labor.

iv. Fossil Resource Tax

All fossil fuels and fossil fuel byproducts shall be taxed 12.5% to the retailer, and additional 12.5% to the end buyer calculated after retail markup and before sales tax. This is applied atop the US average combined tax of $0.42 per gallon (using gasoline for an example), adding approximately an additional 49 cents per gallon.

These taxes shall create more responsibility in these companies and slow the consumption of these soon to be banned resources and their entourage of dangerous products. This will funnel inventive thought towards renewable energy sources and the innovative use of natural materials.

This tax shall cover not only all known fossil resources but also their byproducts including but not limited to: Plastics, artificial flavors, scents, and colors, as well as any (fossil) petrochemical derived drug, coating, additive or product.

This covers many products in the market, and thus shows the over use of fossil oil, and how little or no steps are being made to create products from other mediums. Depending on the drop in consumption, the prime directive, the additional revenue generated from just fuel tax using the 2004 figures of 140 billion gallons of gasoline and 40 billion gallons of diesel consumed, would be approximately 88.2 Billion dollars annually. The revenue from the various other products effected by this tax shall also be a substantial figure. However, the actual aim is to stop the use of these fossil resources altogether, not to attempt to generate additional revenue.

v. Hazardous Material Tax

Any man-made material that is found to be harmful to any form of life to any degree is taxed 12.5% to the retailer, and additional 12.5% to the end buyer calculated after retail markup and before sales tax. This will reduce the use and production of many pesticides, industrial chemicals, cleaners, volatile chemicals etc and cause the focus upon more natural and friendly solutions to increase.

vi. Junk Mail Tax

Ad mail is a direct result of a materialistic society, the only purpose of this wasted material is to make a sale. U.S. companies alone distributed 100 billion pieces of ad mail in 2005. At 2 cents per copy, this amounts to 2 Billion dollars per year. The amount of energy spent to generate this, in paper, ink, shipping, distributing is shameful when it could have been used for the free education of the public instead. This amounts to 300 pieces of mail for every US citizen, think of how much knowledge could have been placed on each of those pages. 44% of this mail is never even opened, even less of it is actually responded to. Less than 36% of this mail is recycled costing taxpayers an estimated $275 million dollars per year to dispose of it. Amounting to 5.8 million tons of junk mail ending up in the solid waste system each year, which is tens of millions of trees wasted every year. The amount of such mail increases the size of the postal system, whose increased operating costs come back to the citizen. This is a blatant waste of money and energy from every angle.

Therefore, the Individualists invoke the junk mail tax. For each single page of ad mail to be mailed, the mailer must purchase a three cent stamp in addition to the base mailing fee. Thus the tax is 3 cents per page, resulting in an approximate 150% tax. This is to abolish this practice for good and make those who continue use it, to have a very important message, thereby causing more people to actually read it. This generates a rough estimate of 2 billion dollars additional revenue in the first year.

vii. Large Entity Tax

All companies over 100 people must pay additional large entity tax which is 0.1% of their profit per every ten people over the 100 person limit. Thus a company with 998 employees will pay 8.9% in additional taxes. This controls the speed of growth of companies leveling off the playing field. This makes it difficult for any company to become a controlling force separate from the people as well as making a company plan with more care an efficient method of expansion to warrant the increased taxes.

Limiting the size of businesses leads to a maximum efficiency between competing companies just as limitations on NASCAR engines specs do the same between engines. The larger a business becomes in this system, the more it returns to the populace, the more the populace then cares for it, the more the business then cares for the populace, inspiring efficient innovative solutions, thus expanding and continuing a cycle of firm, healthy growth. As opposed to the malignant and hastened, weed-like growth of the present world companies, where cheap solutions are encouraged, and their pointless products use the people instead of assist them.

This helps younger companies start with just their ideas, keeping most of the profit for themselves and enabling them to reinvest more into their company. As one may notice, companies of over 5000 people begin to pay more to the Populus than to themselves. With over ten thousand people the company works strictly for the benefit of the Populus but is still operated by private forces who dictate their own salaries. This is the origin of the 2110 law.

When a business reaches 2109 employees, the business and personal tax rates become the same. After 2109 employees, the business tax rate grows larger than the personal. Thus, the founders may make their salaries substantially large to absorb the profit and pay less of these higher taxes. This is protected by the 2110 law, listed here again:

Any paid member of a company which has over 2110 employees, whose salary is at least 1% of the company's worth, is considered a "Vital Mechanism". In other words, more part of the company than an individual, and thus pays the current Company tax for his income rate as opposed to the flat rate 12.46% for individuals. This keeps the profits of companies benefiting the Populus and stops the hiding of profits by distributing them to the elite, while still allowing for substantial profits of said elite.

viii. Packaging Tax

The current amount of plastic, synthetically coated papers and paperboard, used as packaging, is unacceptable. Most of these materials are not able to be efficiently recycled, if at all. Even those that are recyclable, are to often discarded into the solid waste system, and not properly marked as to what type of plastic they are. All environmentally unsound products in packages such as these are therefore taxed 12.5% to the retailer from the manufacturer and an additional 12.5% to the end buyer calculated after retail markup and before sales tax. This includes any plastic package or wrapping in any form, be it sheet, bottle, box or petrochemical derived wax papers and paperboard.

This forces wrappings to be of untreated paper and paperboard, glass, foils, cellulose derived cellophane, plant or animal waxed papers, (excludes petroleum derived paraffin) etc. This type of packaging is more easily handled by the environment in a reasonable time frame. Glass and foil are recyclable, and can occur naturally as opposed to plastic, although some plastics may be recyclable, many humans do not participate thus these substance end up in natures hands. This tax helps reduce this problem as well as encourage companies to use safer packaging, and make efforts to develop innovative packaging materials.

ix. Primitive Vehicle Tax:

To encourage the development of advanced electric motors and battery technology, along with the phasing out of fossil fuels, all vehicles will be taxed if they utilize any form of internal combustion engine. The degree of the severity of this tax, with gasoline being the most heavily taxed, is as follows: 1. Gasoline 6%, 2. Fossil diesel 5%, 3. Gas or diesel hybrids 4%, 4. Ethanol 3%, 5. Propane and methane 2%, 6. Hydrogen and biodiesel 1%.

Any fully electric vehicle with no on board internal combustion engine is not taxed. This tax will be paid upon purchase of the vehicle, 12.5% by the dealer from the manufacturer and an additional 12.5% to the end buyer calculated after retail markup and before sales tax. This will encourage the phasing out of the fossil fuel based engines which maintain a society of consumption. It will additionally encourage research into electric vehicle technologies on a much larger scale.

x. Unnatural Foods Tax

All foods which utilize any enhancement, synthetic, or additive which does not naturally occur without the presence of man is deemed unnaturally enhanced and taxed 12.5% to the retailer from the manufacturer and an additional 12.5% to the end buyer calculated after retail markup and before sales tax. This includes but is not limited to:

Any plant or animal with genetic alterations not acquired by selective breeding.
Any plant or animal enhanced with hormones either man-made or extracted by man from some other source.
Any plant or animal fed any man-made chemicals.
Any plant or animal sprayed or powdered with any man-made chemical.
Any plant or animal raised and/or kept in an inhumane and/or unsanitary environment, thus an unnatural environment.
Any food with man-made additives or preservatives of any kind.
Any food with partially or fully hydrogenated oils.

* "Man-made" is defined as a substance that cannot naturally occur without the presence of man, and/or any man-made imitation of a naturally occurring substance.
* Food is defined as anything ingested to be used by the body.

One can see that this discourages the damaging use of the chemical industry's fertilizers, pesticides, mold inhibitors, artificial additives and preservatives, as well as the synthetic drugs from their partner, the pharmaceutical industry. Sadly, it covers nearly all of the available foods, which shows how tainted the food supply has become. This will greatly assist the health and longevity of the society as a whole, while encouraging people to create more of their own food. Making food safer for the Populus and making them more conscious of what they are eating.

The revenue generated from this could be calculated roughly from the U.S. food industry's sales of approximately 600 Billion dollars annually minus the mere 14 Billion dollars in totally organic foods, yielding an estimate of 109.9 Billion in additional tax revenue.

xi. Waste Tax:

The Individualists believe that the "disposable" mentality of the world must stop. For example, millions of plastic freezer bags, all going to the land fill, when one glass container, could be used and used again. Or millions of plastic grocery bags, when each individual should be responsible and bring their own baskets, useable again and again.

The Individualistic society makes its citizens very waste conscious early on in schooling and applies taxes for all non-recyclable wastes. All natural waste is to be dealt with on one's own land. Any other waste it to go to a Populus Waste Handling Facility, where one has to pay a waste tax for any non-recyclable substances. This is an attempt to achieve a zero waste society or as close as possible to it. This tax is paid by individuals or companies dropping off waste. It will be calculated per pound and material type, recyclable materials will not be taxed. Thus, if an individual avoids products containing non-recyclable materials such as Styrofoam, this individual may never pay a waste tax. (See pg. 148 for the waste table and how the Individualist achieves virtually no waste.) This tax rate is to be voted on by the local Populus and is meant to be slightly high so as to encourage efficient thinking and avoidance of products which generate these wastes.

The ignorant and slothful may try to burn, bury or stockpile their waste instead of thinking of solutions to initially avoid waste or pay the small tax. This is the origin of the environmental waste law (pg.73), reprimanding those found burning, burying, or stockpiling unnatural or non-recyclable materials.

All of the above taxes are cumulative, for instance if a company is selling meat that has been unnaturally enhanced, and is wrapped in plastic that has been made from fossil oil, there will be three sin taxes applied to this item. The attempt of these taxes is not to generate revenue, it is to slow and eventually abolish these activities. Those who disagree with any of these taxes show that they obviously support waste, hazard, exploitation, and pollution.

4. HEALTH CARE

Before beginning this subject it must be noted that the figures available to the public are generated by groups either directly or indirectly affiliated with the organizations involved in health care, most of which have billions of dollars in profit at stake. Thus it is highly likely, but not factual, that these figures are either, fully or partially falsified to bias all arguments into their favor. Nevertheless, the Individualists shall use their figures, and still prove the system faulty. The Individualists accuse the entire health care industry of being so full with corruption, waste, fraud etc, that if the true figures were known, as to the total revenue vs. the total truthful and reasonable expenditures, the percentage of squandered funds would be staggering.

a. Breakdown

The Total U.S. Health Care Cost was 1.988 Trillion Dollars
2005 figures

$0.903 Trillion, of total income tax collected in 2005 went to health care. The US population is approximately 300 Million people, a third of which are children. 59% of the population has private health insurance (assuming 39.33% are adults), 26% of the population (17.33% adults) has taxpayer paid care (some wrongly call it *government* insurance) and only15% (9.99% adults) have no insure. Of the total population approximately 5% are unemployed and 5% cannot work, (disabled, early retired etc) and 7% are retired.

Therefore, 75% of the entire adult population contributes (by taxes) to the taxpayer paid health care, amounting to 45.4% of total US health care costs which is 903 Billion dollars. Thus, the majority of the entire adult population already pays for practically *half* of the total US health care costs with their taxes. Therefore the US is, basically, half way to national health care. The remaining 54.6%, or $1.085 Trillion, of the total US health care is all private money. This will be examined in two parts.

1. Private Health Care $694.4 Billion or 35% of the Problem

It is assumed that a negligible few pay private health care costs and are also unemployed, such as a wealthy individual or the retired. Therefore, only the work force is considered to bare these costs for simplicity's sake. About 63% of the entire US workforce of 150 million people has health insurance. (This is 94.5 Million people or 31.5% total Population) However, being that half of the population cannot work: 33% children, 5% unemployed, 5% disabled, 7% retired,(yet only 15% are uninsured); the labor force could be generally viewed as supporting themselves and the other half of the population. Thus, the total tax burden of $1.988 Trillion falls on the 150 million people of the work force equaling to $13,253 per labor force worker.

A. 63% of the workforce pays private *AND* government funding (with their taxes) which is 94.5M people. Averaging $7,348 private health insurance burden per paying worker *in addition to* the $7,333 health tax and out of pocket burden, (2005 average private policy premiums were $10,880 for families and $4,024 for an individuals) for a total burden of $14,681 per worker.

B. 37% of the workforce pays only government funding, which is 55.5M people, amounting to a $7,333 burden of health tax and out of pocket expenses per worker.

Therefore, of the total US citizens available to work, only 37% do not contribute to this part of the problem. Thus only 63% of this portion of the problem is solved or 22.05% added to the 50% from above. Thus, relatively 72.05% of the US is already leaning in the direction of a national health care scenario.

To clarify, in a national health care system all pay the same annual fee and are cared for equally. Hence, what was proven above is that 63% of the workforce is already paying this total fee, and 37% are paying half of it, therefore 72.05% of the US is already paying the fees needed to establish national health, to private industries who profit and lobby for the system to remain in the wasteful limbo between national health care and private health care at the expense of the work force.

2. Private out of Pocket and Misc. Expenses of $390.6 Billion or 20% of the Problem

A. Out of pocket expenses of $250 Billion -$12.5 Billion* = $237.5 Billion (11.9% of the problem)

Considering the out of pocket costs are roughly estimated to originate from each two workman types listed above (A and B) and are distributed evenly between the two groups, yet removing the 7% of the population that is retired, and the10% that are on other programs such as disability, both of whom are also paying some of these costs. Therefore, only 83% of the workforce contributes to this potion of the problem (paying $197 billion), adding 9.88% to the relative figure making it now 81.93%.

89

B. Other misc. expenses of $142 billion or 7.14% of the problem

This figure incorporates many questionable items, including $67.7 billion (almost half the total) for the construction of private hospitals and equipment, and unspecified amounts in spending in cafeterias, parking lots, and gift shops etc. within health facilities. Other funds are from philanthropy support. A satisfactory breakdown of the remaining $74.3 billion was not found. Thus, none of this can be added to the figure.

*. The amount of co pay from the unemployed or disabled is considered double counted because an unemployed individual is receiving benefits paid by taxpayers and thus his out of pocket expense came from the tax payers. Thus it was estimated that half of the unemployed made some type of out of pocket payment so 5% of the 250 Billion or 12.5 billion was a double count.

To briefly summarize, The US is already relatively 81.93% national health care. 100% of the workforce already pays out enough taxes to support a $903 Billion health care program, and pays enough out of pocket expenses to support a second plan of $197 Billion, both together total $1.1 Trillion. Furthermore, 63% of the workforce supports a third plan of $694.4 billion.   This remaining uneven burden could be evenly distributed for a national plan of $1.79 Trillion. Equaling a decreased health care burden of $11,933 per labor force worker. This is $193.6 Billion short of the present $1.988 Trillion health care system.

b. Important Figures

Know That:

Of the $1.988 trillion paid by the people's money:
$100 Billion is Profit of the pharmaceutical industry
$11 Billion is Profit of the health insurance industry
$12 Billion is HMO profits
$29 Billion is Private hospital profits
$68 Billion is Private sector construction and equipment
$150 Billion is administration costs

Totaling = $370 Billion Dollars

$152 Billion in private profit would be practically eliminated in a non profit national health system. An estimated $150 Billion would additionally be saved on administration costs alone by the superior efficiency of central organization. While at least 68 billion would be added to *public* health assets annually.

The following are not considered priority:

$ 87 Billion on dentistry
$170 Billion on nursing home and home healthcare
$100 Billion on pharmaceuticals
$ 57 Billion on misc. professional care (private-duty nurses, chiropractors, podiatrists, optometrists and physical, occupational and speech therapists, among others.)
$ 52 Billion on non-traditional sites (community centers, senior citizens centers, schools, and military field stations) (*Reorganized)
$ 5 Billion on Industrial services (health care or supplies provided by employer for employees at the employer's establishment)
$ 40 Billion on research
$ 57 Billion on government health agencies (*Reorganized)

Totaling = $568 Billion Dollars

- This $568 Billion dollars must be left to the Private choice of people. These are non-vital cares, such as dentistry, a cosmetic care at the expense of the populace, having no rational place in national care. Taking the insurance industry out of these categories will bring these costs down for those who truly need them. Too often one with insurance is told that they need something when they do not, and are exploited for their ignorance, and the insurance company is sent an inflated bill. Such as the millions of children running around with eyeglasses or taking pharmaceuticals, a heinous practice developed only over the last 100 years of mankind. Children's' entire bodies are "weak" compared to that of an adult, they develop and grow strong over time and need not be interfered with. The Individualists observe exploitations like this with horror, how many children's eyes and body chemistry have been forever altered because of money? Without insurance support, people will not go to these places unless necessary being that they must pay the entire cost. Thus, these places will then be forced to lower their cost to maintain business, bringing the costs of all these barely necessary services back down to the rational earth.

- Nursing home and home health care services are not to be paid for by the collective strong. They are places for the weak and the abandoned and shall not burden society. The burden shall fall exactly where it should, on the immediate family. This shall assist all to make better preparations for the future, and maintain better health deep into their later ages, while encouraging the youth to assist the assurance thereof. This system is constantly exploited with preposterous overpricing such as $75,000 per year as the average price for one individual's nursing home care. At this cost one could outright buy one's own home and equip it with a live-in nurse for less.

- The Individualists know that 80% of pharmaceutical sales come from "blockbuster" drugs pushed harder on the public than any street dealer of illicit drugs, for only the survival of hypochondriacs. The nation will not assist the support of needless dependence. No Pharmaceuticals are supplied by the Populus funds, else this leaching industry would exploit the program, skyrocketing the costs and cause the system to fail. As such, fewer drugs will be purchased being that the individuals will have to bare the full cost themselves. This will assist the practice of Individualistic health, causing the people to become more aware of the resilience of the body without synthetic chemicals, causing the pharmaceutical industry to lower prices and turn to more natural solutions to maintain business.

- Various miscellaneous care is considered non-vital and of private interest. Of all of these and similar categories, chiropractic care is the only one recognized by the Individualist as a vital practice and encouraged for its near endless curative and preventative techniques. However, it is too often exploited for dubious insurance claims and must therefore remain private.

- Non traditional spending is mostly misused, mismanaged and misdirected tax money to be dismantled and integrated into the one orderly system of Individualistic care.

- Industrial services must remain private choice.

- There will be no lending of public funds to private researchers. Government lending to private research is thoroughly compromised. It is also a violation of Individualistic precepts to allow any form of government assistance. Thus, all necessary public research will be conducted at the Populus' direction with the amount that they alone specify.

- All government agencies involved in health care are dismantled and organized into one efficient body of the Populus Health System.

1. $309 Billion of this $568 is publicly funded (tax)
2. The selling of any type of insurance is forbidden in Individualistic society, thus all the above labeled 'private' will be paid for totally out of the pocket of the purchaser.

Reasonable expenses:

$421 Billion in physician and clinical services, salaries etc.
$ 58 Billion in medical equipment
$430 Billion in hospital care (less administration and profit)
--- The above three prices are most likely inflated to hide additional private profits ---
$ 20 Billion Public structures

Totaling = $929 Billion
$151 billion of this is publicly funded (tax)

Summary:

$761 Billion in expenditures are immediately removed by implementing the Populus Health System.
$ 88 Billion is now towards Public Health Structures and equipment, as permanent assets of the public. (This amount is expected to drop substantially after the first year, for construction has always been an excellent outlet to hide profits and inflate expenses.)
$109 Billion is reorganized*, inefficient, departments of the old world, into a new centralized management.
$909 Billion remains virtually in the same use but under more efficient monitoring and management of the Populus Health System.

Know that this does not include the spending of these private entities on extraneous costs such as marketing, which for the Health industry alone is over $1.6 Billion.

The Populus Health System would therefore be, at most, a $1.227 trillion plan ($1.988 - $761). With the workforce already presently paying $903 Billion in the form of their taxes allocated to *government* health programs, and $197 Billion in out of pocket expenses, a mere additional $127 Billion needs to be spread upon the 150 Million adult workers of the workforce, amounting to a flat tax fee of no more than $847 dollars per year which could be temporarily implemented while transitioning to a fully Individualistic system. By removing 2.54% from federal taxes and allocating them to health instead, this $127 plus the $197 in out of pocket expenses are both covered. Therefore the system will not even require out of pocket expenses. ($197 + $127 = $324 Billion, which is 2.54% of the 2005 Gross Domestic Product of $12.8 trillion, such is the origin of the percentage used).

Being that the Individualistic society encourages self-sufficiency, and may lead to a drop in available workers, the work force alone cannot be considered. The Individualists remove all health-related taxes and consolidate them into one fee. The tax's final form is a non income based flat fee divided equally per capita of $4,090 for each individual or $8,180 divided over just the workforce as it is presently. Creating an average $5,073 health burden **relief** per labor force worker (13,253 – 8,180).

Legislation shall be passed forbidding tax spending on Health Care except with strictly this flat tax for paying members of the system. The tax credit received from the lower flat income tax of the Individualistic society will make more capital available to these working individuals making the relative burdens on average (14681 – 8,180) $6,501 less than the privately insured workers previously paid (63% of the work force), and (8180-7333) $847 more than what the publicly insured paid (37% of the workforce). These payments by this working half of the population support themselves and the other half of the society, the children, the elderly and the disabled, just as they do today.

A 143 Billion deviation is found in data regarding the amount spent in premiums on private insurance and the amount of revenue taken in by the private insurance industry) Due to rounding in this document the error only seems to be 121Billion)

No one is forced to pay the flat fee for health care, even though at its low cost it would be foolish to do so. In the event that an uninsured individual is harmed, and care administered by a Populus facility, it will be viewed as though a loan was taken from the Populus funds, and therefore, needs repaid within five years, as any other loan, else one is sentenced to a Laborforce assignment.

This fee will most likely drop each year as Individualistic philosophy takes root and corruption subsides under the pressure. The Individualistic system will be evaluated each year for cost, and its price adjusted accordingly to the people's desire. With Individualistic philosophy, the population will become increasingly healthier, as they realize the strength and resilience of nature, for millions of years not needing any drugs, therapies, supplements, assistance, etc. Following the simple health methods of the Individualists (pg 150) the people will most likely only use health care for shear accidents.

The sole reason why the health care costs are high and rising is because of the lack of preventative care, and basic health practices, such as hygiene, exercise, and diet, as well as the countless exploitations of ignorant hypochondriacs created by the mass marketing of health problems and products. The majority of the US now exists as a nation of ignorant, lazy, and out of shape weaklings, who are thoroughly unhappy, all contributing to increased health problems. Over 65% of the population of the US is over weight. The

NCHC suggests that retiring elderly couples will need $200,000 in savings just to pay for the most basic medical coverage. This is simply because of the weakness created and encouraged by the current system and dependence upon it and synthetics as opposed to self-heath practices. The Individualistic elders will be strong up to the moment of death, and will need very little, if any, assistance when aged.

c. Quality of Individualistic Care

As one may notice the amount of physicians and their salaries was not altered in the conversion to Individualism, thus, there is no threat to doctors or the quality of care they proved. However as Individualistic thought grows, the profit driven doctors, with more feeling for the size of the bottom line than for love of the occupation they chose, will fade away with the increasing popularity of the Individualistic doctors, displaying true love of healing and compassion for their fellow man.

The salaries of individual doctors, as all Populus employees, will be based upon their performance. Too often, guaranteed high salaries cause people to become doctors (or any other occupation) for money instead of for Love of what they do. The Individualist does not disagree with the right to earn a high salary, but it must be granted to a worthy recipient of a public funded system by popular vote. Thus each patient must fill out a form after receiving care and mail it to the GEP evaluating their care, on a point-based system. Each year the points are totaled and a subsequent raise or demotion is given to each Populus Health Facility and to each individual employee from doctors to janitors, according to the points which they earned. Thus these Health workers will always remember that they are employees of the people they are serving. Therefore, a truly excellent healer, known nationwide in the Individualistic society, could possibly command a salary much higher than the present average doctor salaries of $156,010 to $321,686.

A Fee per visit system encourages haste within doctors, as more patients seen per day equals more money, leading to poor care. If the fee was 50 dollars and one patient was seen every fifteen minutes for ten hours a day, five days a week, this doctor's salary would be 520,000 per year, over twice the present mean average doctor salary, it is no wonder why some doctors support this option.

d. Quality of Present Care

The Individualists believe that many modern hospitals are money making machines, and nothing else, far removed from places of healing. Facilities where Death is suspended for profit. Such as when an individual arrives brain dead from a massive heart attack, many doctors see nothing but dollars. They perform "emergency surgery" and sustain the body on a myriad of machines each charging by the hour. They fill the corpse with expensive "medicines" while conducting expensive tests with more sophisticated machines, each costing ridiculous amounts. This is dragged on for days, weeks, as long as possible giving a family false hopes, while feverishly writing the bills to the insurance companies accounting for every second and penny.

Individuals entering these doors are potential experiments, guinea pigs for a host of their practices and products. A person in good health can be lead to believe they are ill, and allow themselves to be subjected to endless horror. Hypochondria is nursed and encouraged, the more fear instilled into a soul the more that soul will place all trust in the doctor instead of God and self healing. This is used to the advantage of their pockets by placing these people on countless drugs, tests, and surgeries, killing, poisoning, maiming and mutilating their fellow brethren for income in the blasphemous guise of healing.

Many surgeons have become masters of mutilation, filling men with pins and plates, replacing and removing body parts as if it were a fad. Ignorant to the infinite complexity of the self healing divine machine, the human body, while asserting in arrogance that they comprehend in detail this work of God. Thus they proceed in blindness with great conviction, and their conviction becomes contagion when spoken of with certainty to "lesser" men, which only succeeds in compounding the ignorance of man. Thus, they continue treating the effects of disease rather than their source, disregarding wholly the factor of spirit in their equations.

Thus, much of health care is naught but an unprovable racket, for an individual with no degree in medicine cannot hold an argument against any doctor and be believed, even if in the right, thus a doctor will win every argument regardless of his ignorance. Society hands them a pedestal with their degree and often looks to them as "all knowing". Instead of looking into one's own heart or to God for answers, they consult a doctor, which is just another soul. These doctors exploit this ignorance and trust of these "patients" in the guise of benevolence and use them for their advantage. Even if they know a simple, natural and safe cure, they prescribe "procedures" and endless pills to elevate their profit and that of their contributing industries, the pharmaceutical industry, medical manufactures etc. Such are the countless numbers placed on "Chemo therapy", naught but a poison, and most likely responsible for more deaths than cancer.

Of the $590 Billion in hospital care how many emergencies have been feigned for insurance money, how much money goes into each child birth when the Indians had them in fields. How much "special care" is feigned for newborns? How many are taking drugs or are scheduled for a procedure, that could merely be prescribed a regime of exercise and diet? The Individualists believe it to be substantial, and will remedy great amounts of people and expenses with simple self health care methods. (Pg 150)

For example, the Individualist examines the nonsensical, and purposely unintelligible itemized hospital bills with ridiculous charges such as $5,000 a day for a room, $50 per pill, tens of thousands for one titanium screw, or $75,000 dollars per year as the average nursing home bill for a single individual, and sees the unrealistic markup and blatant theft of these institutions. Corruption is rampant and has many heads and faces. Such as the following five health insurance companies which have profited billions per year on the people's money.

1	United Health Group	71.542B	4.159B
2	Wellpoint	56.953B	3.095B
3	Aetna	25.569B	1.702B
4	Humana	21.417B	487M
5	Cigna	16.547B	155 M

(Italics are total revenues bold are annual profits)

Many often pitch that the hospitals and insurance companies act as separate entities, robbing each other, this is most likely a secondary illusion, with the reality being that the hospitals are owned wholly or partially by other health care industries, such as insurance, pharmaceutical, medical equipment manufacturers etc. Thus the loss shown by most hospitals is simply a front for the great profits of such industries composing and profiting off of all hospitals.

These and similar institutions frequently give "campaign donations" to politicians to bias support, laws, etc in their favor. The people are already paying for every thing, thus, there is no need for private middlemen making $11 billion in profits. These middle men, as all the others, are not of the people or in favor of the people, they are private and for their own interests, a siphon in the middle of a simple stream. As one can see, private establishments such as these stand in the way of a simple, reasonable system of affordable and logical Health Care, without any of the drama and hype. These and similar institutions have billions of dollars in reasons to stop such simplicity.

5. FOOD

In our present insane society, industrial farmers are more worried about the sale of their product than its nutritional value and safety for their fellow man. They drench the crops with pesticides and fertilizers, many which do not fully wash off and are highly toxic. After harvest they then further poison the foods with preservatives as well as chemicals to make them look good, prohibit mold etc, and then send it to the market place.

These industrial farmers are supported by the "government" who pays them, with the people's tax money, to grow crops. Thus, the people paid for the crops to be grown yet they buy them a second time at the market place for a $120 Billion profit to the Industrial farms. The *government* then pays them to burn the crops so that the market isn't flooded with product and diluting the price, (to maintain control of the cycle of waste and consumption). This then taxes the soil from over use, which the farmers then have to pay to have fertilized (more profit for the chemical industry). $25 Billion of taxpayer money, in the form of farm subsidies to mostly massive corporate farms, is squandered in this way annually. This nonsense and lack of reason is the Individualists archenemy, so far removed from logic it is mind numbing.

Approximately $500 billion is spent processing, and distributing these foods. The Individualists, being self sufficient, rear their own small farms. Apart from having safe food, it eliminates the need for a $500 Billion processing and distribution cycle, $120 billion in profit to unnecessary industrial farms and $25 billion in subsidies which will be redistributed to the people to assist them in their personal micro farms. (The US creates 10,000 new processed-food products every year, and nearly 90% of its food spending is on these processed foods.)

This present world madness has extended to unprecedented levels. Within it man feeds his fellow with harmful laboratory creations and calls them "generally recognized as safe for consumption" food (an actual FDA term). All significant efforts to clearly inform the people are impeded or not made at all. Within the average household practically all foods will contain one or more of the ingredients listed below. Many of the "trusted" household names are not to be trusted when one researches their ingredients and deceptive labeling of these poisons in one's food.

All of these ingredients are shown in different tests to be harmful to some degree to the human body but are allowed to be present in food because the US democratic decision making has been compromised by many industries and the safety of the people is no longer a priority. Government departments such as the HHS and FDA, along with back pocket politicians, all benefit by allowing poison to remain in the food for the profiting industries.

These chemical additives were not designed with the consumer in mind, they were designed strictly for profit, making food:

1. Look Better

No sale can be made on even the healthiest food if it appearance is bland. The focus is simply on the sale, not the nutritional value for the buyer.

2. Last Longer

This is so the merchants can maximize their profits, the longer something can sit on a shelf the more chance it has to be sold. The concern is not health, it is profit.

3. Taste and Smell Better

Nearly all of modern food has been so overly processed that chemicals need to be added to give it a flavor and a smell. Most big name fast foods, and high dollar name brands get their smells and tastes from artificial flavor manufactures, and certainly not from their food quality or preparation method. Without these chemical giants you would never buy the substance which tastes no better than dust. The aim is profit, not well being.

4. Lower Calories

The marketing madness of caloric intake pushed upon the world has caused people to rather eat zero calorie cyanide than one calorie of naturally occurring fat, which is essential for the intake of many vitamins and imperative for proper brain function. It has created a slew of feverish mindsets bent on buying anything that is labeled "reduced fat", "low calories" etc. The "generally safe" toxins which achieve this in various ways are created for the sole purpose of capturing this part of the market, thus are simply profit minded.

<u>5. Cost Effective</u>

Substituting artificial chemicals for their expensive natural counterparts is often cost effective for the manufacturer.

<u>The motive in all cases is Profit five fold, with not one concern for YOU.</u>

The below list is by far exhaustive. These are just some of the most common of these chemicals to be aware of. Of all of the chemicals listed below, if one cares not to watch for all of them, at least avoid these four. Just in these four one will begin finding shopping a challenge.

1. BHA and BHT, 2. Anything Hydrogenated, 3. Aspartame (Equal, NutraSweet), **4. Artificial colors:** Blue 1, Blue 2, Red 3, Yellow 6.

a. Artificial colors

BLUE 1: Derived from Coal Tar
BLUE 2: Derived from Coal Tar
CARMINE OR COCHINEAL EXTRACT: comes from drying and pulverizing over 4000 cochineal insects to
    produce an ounce of this red dye, can be at times labeled as "added coloring".
GREEN 3: Derived from triphenyl methane which is made by reacting benzene and chloroform with
    aluminum chloride catalyst. Prohibited in European Union
RED 3: Derived from Coal Tar
RED 40: Derived from Coal Tar, has produced two unidentifiable metabolites in urine. Prohibited in Austria
    Belgium, Denmark, France, Germany, Sweden and Switzerland.
YELLOW 5: Derived from Coal Tar
YELLOW 6: Derived from Coal Tar
All of these chemicals have shown adverse effects on humans to varying degrees, yet still remain in the food supply. All products containing coal tar and coal tar derivatives are prohibited in Norway.

b. Artificial flavor

On food labels will be seen either "Artificial flavor" or "Natural Flavor" but preferably neither. The presence of either signifies a bland food lifeless without this magic component or a food that needs a taste hidden. To distinguish, "natural" flavor may denote a chemical extracted from a real plant, however, it is still added thereby acknowledging that the product one is consuming lacks that property naturally. Also "natural flavors" does not delineate the extraction process used or the chemicals which may have also been employed in that extraction process.

Conversely, Artificial flavors are created with no link to the original substance, they are entirely engineered in a laboratory. Flavor has become merely an ingredient, not a product of the ingredients. Many of the famous flavors of the fast food chains and name brand foods of today are actually purchased from chemical companies composing the flavor industry such as; International Flavors & Fragrances (IFF), the world's largest flavor manufacturer, Givaudan, second largest, Firmenich, third largest, Frutarom, Haarmann & Reimer, Takasago, Quest International etc. This flavor industry has annual global revenues of approximately 10 Billion dollars. There is no law requiring that the chemicals which make up these synthetic flavors be labeled for public awareness as long as each individual component of the flavor is tested as "GRAS" which means "generally recognized as safe". As seen in just a few of the above Colors, GRAS has no meaning when deemed as such by a corrupt entity such as the FDA. A number of these chemicals, such as vanillin, are derived from coal tar just as the above colors, which are known to be harmful.

96

c. Manufactured Fats

These synthetic fats are inexpensive and have long shelf lives thus bring greater profit all around.

i. HYDROGENATED OILS (trans fat)

Derived by passing hydrogen gas through oil. The health effects are numerous including; coronary heart disease, stroke, liver dysfunction, cancer, and obesity.

ii. OLESTRA (Olean)

A synthetic fat developed by Procter & Gamble. Impedes the absorption of vitamins D, E, K, and A, and causes numerous adverse bowel effects.

iii. SALATRIM

A modified fat developed by Nabisco who declared it safe for human consumption and marketed it without FDA approval. There is much debate as to the proper testing of this substance as tests appear suspect. Evidence suggests adverse gastrointestinal side effects.

d. Flavor Enhancers

i. MSG (Monosodium Glutamate)

Or "free glutamic acid." Allows the reduction of real foods by multiplying the taste of smaller potions. An arguably addicting substance, it is often disguised in many ingredients that contain or create it during manufacture such as; autolyzed yeast, carrageenan, "Enzymes", hydrolyzed vegetable protein, sodium caseinate, yeast extract and many others. Disodium inosinate and disodium guanylate often signify the presence of MSG in one or more of the ingredients being that they enhance MSG action but are impotent alone. Similarly, the phrase "seasoning" or "spices" may also indicate added flavor enhancers. The FDA, HHS, and USDA do nothing to ban the use of this deceptive, ambiguous and misleading labeling of foods knowing that it would capsize the entire food industry due to the fact that most foods contain harmful chemicals as these for strictly profiteering purposes.
Some claim MSG triples insulin release causing obesity with excessive use. Some claim possible links to ADHD, ALS, Alzheimer's disease, Autism, Diabetes, Huntington's disease, Migraines, Parkinson's disease, and a myriad of other adverse nervous and endocrine system effects do to excitotoxicity of free glutamic acid.

e. Preservatives

i. BHA (butylated hydroxyanisole) and BHT (butylated hydroxytoluene)

Derived from petrochemical hydrocarbons and outlawed in Japan, Romania, Sweden, and Australia for possible liver and kidney damage and carcinogenic health hazards. These chemicals are added to food to slow spoiling in fats and oils. Some suggest that neither compound is needed and can easily be replaced with Vitamin E as a natural preservative.

ii. SODIUM NITRITE

Used primarily in Meat and fish to fix a lively color and add longevity. It is also an anti bacterial agent against botulism, however, it forms known carcinogens in high heat cooking and has been linked by some to colon and pancreatic cancers.

iii. PROPYL GALLATE

Slows spoiling in fats and oils. A suspected carcinogen.

f. Sweeteners

i. ASPARTAME (AKA NutraSweet and Equal)

Derived from aspartic acid (a known excitotoxin) methanol (Known toxic alcohol) and phenylalanine. Upon ingestion it breaks down into its harmful component parts. What is more dangerous is that out side of the body it rapidly breaks down at room temperature into 1. DKP (diketopiperazine) which converts to a suspected potent brain carcinogen upon ingestion 2. Formic Acid, a component of insect stings 3. Formaldehyde, an embalming fluid 4. Methanol, a toxic alcohol known to cause blindness.

Aspartame has been linked to brain tumors and lesions, blindness, convulsions and many other adverse nervous and endocrine system affects, common to excitotoxins. Most commonly found in 'low calorie', 'diet', or 'sugar free' products.

Aspartame was discovered by accident in 1965 by scientist James Schlatter while working on a drug for peptic ulcers for G. D. Searle and Company, a US pharmaceutical corporation. It was approved by the FDA in July 1974, but withdrawn in December of that year because of brain tumors found in rats tested with aspartame. In 1977 the already 20 year political veteran, Donald Rumsfeld, became the CEO and president of G.D. Searle. In April 1981 shortly after Regan took office, newly appointed FDA Commissioner, Arthur Hull Hayes, appointed by the Secretary of HHS Richard Schweiker, overruled a Public Board of Inquiry and approved aspartame for use in dry foods before any further tests were conducted. Then In 1983 it was approved for use in beverages.

Upon leaving the FDA September of 1983 Dr. Hayes became dean and provost of New York Medical College. Then in 1986 he became a paid consultant for G. D. Searle's firm Burson-Marsteller, one of the largest public relations firms in the world, a mere one year after Donald Rumfeld assisted the sale of G.D. Searle & Company to Monsanto chemical corporation for a suspected profit of $12 million dollars in 1985. While G.D. Searle's Lawyer, Robert B. Shapiro, became Mosanoto's president.

There is Great debate over the authenticity of the safety tests performed regarding this chemical as noted in 1987 by toxicologist Dr Jacqueline Verrett, before a US Senate hearing describing the tests as, "serious departures from acceptable toxicological protocols". Obviously, as shown above, the *government* departments are compromised by corporate interest thus all tests conducted by them including NCI (national cancer institute) will all be likewise compromised.

ii. CYCLAMATE

This synthetic sweetener was discovered in 1937 on accident by Michael Sveda while working on the synthesis of an anti-fever medication. It was banned in October 1969 as a Suspected Carcinogen about four years before the legalization of aspartame, but has been making a comeback and the ban has been being lifted.

iii. SACCHARINE: (sweet N low)

Derived from coal tar and discovered by accident in 1879. Has caused cancer of the bladder, reproductive organs, skin, and other organs in laboratory tests. Therefore, 1977, the FDA attempted to ban saccharin but Congress allowed its used in foods so long as they had warning labels. In May 2000, the HHS removed saccharin from its list of cancer-causing chemicals and that same year, Congress revoked the need for a warning label while this chemical remains banned in Canada.

iv. SUCRALOSE: (splenda)

This product of Johnson and Johnson is derived from sugar (sucrose) and chlorine. There is debate over whether it has been significantly tested, and concern that approximately a third of it is absorbed by the body. Claims have been made that it causes thymus gland shrinkage and enlargement of liver and kidneys as well as general concern that prolonged use may result in adverse nervous and endocrine system effects.

g. Irradiated foods

A newer practice arising in food production is irradiation. This process allows for more filthy foods to be irradiated and become "safe" for consumption. This allows the corporate slaughterhouses and other producers to speed up their production with less concern for cleanliness.

This irradiation can leave trace levels of radioactivity and animals eating such foods have been shown to exhibit an increase in tumors. The radiation breaks up molecules not only in harmful bacteria but also in vitamins and other nutrients as well as any preservatives or pesticides etc. This myriad of broken chemicals then combine with each other forming new chemicals called unique radiolytic products (URPs) which can be any chemical, some possibly unknown. Known URPS include benzene and formaldehyde, two known toxins. The irradiation causes nutritional value loss of 5-80% depending on food type and application method. Irradiated foods must be labeled with the following logo:

h. Diets

The dieting population is suckered with countless poisons to cater to their fear of weight gain, each worse for them than if they'd eat pure fat doused with sugar. It is arguably better to just eat sugar than to ingest laboratory produced synthetics. To believe that man, in his few thousand years upon earth, knows what is best for the human body, a product of 300 billion years of natural earthly evolution, is outright foolish.

There are those who then decide to simply eat organic, where another slew of deceptive merchandise lies in wait as well. "Natural" flavors are additives produced by laboratory processes, as are "modified" starches, flours and proteins. Each of them laboratory products, which may have degrees of safety, however, the point is that they are many times included in supposedly "organic" or "all natural" foods over twice the price and half expensive to make. Many times companies succeed in using all organic and truly natural products and then add unnatural preservatives and inhibitors to the mix and claim that they "protect taste" or "freshness" or "flavor enhancer" when it is strictly profit oriented as above, and remains marketed as "organic" or "all natural".

i. WEIGHT GAIN

The population's concern with weight is based mostly on misunderstanding. Fat is light compared to muscle and water. So to measure health by weight is completely irrational. If one works out one most likely will build muscle and drink more water, thus becoming heavier. Fat itself, regardless of weight, should be watched as a degree of tone. And effort should be made to keep such tone as all animals in nature are active and thus hold a healthy fat to muscle tone ratio. But the lazy are concerned with the magic pill, and become host for an endless supply of poisons, from diet pills to steroids. All wanting something with out putting forth any effort. Excess fat is simply the result of laziness coupled with overeating and nothing else.

ii. VITAMINS

Strict amateur vegetarians are exploited because of their usually incomplete diet is in need of countless supplements eagerly supplied to them by the chemical industry. It would be no surprise if the chemical industry were actually a major proponent for vegetarianism. All vitamins and minerals supplied by the chemical manufacturers can all be had by simply eating a certain food. Unlike the synthetics, real foods have an additional overlooked quality, that of life itself.

All synthetics are devoid of life. The vitamins, minerals, proteins etc. are only a part of the body's needs, the material part. The subtle energy of life feeds the spiritual body, a more subtle body. This is actually the true philosophy behind vegetarianism which most fad vegetarians are unaware of. The energy is very high in freshly harvested plants yet the energy begins to fade the moment a plant is harvested or a beast slaughtered, and that rate is much faster in animals. Thus bottled juice and canned fruits and vegetables, have much less life, if any, than fresh picked food. The Individualists are aware of the importance of this ingredient and have no shortage of it with the practice of self-sustenance.

iii. WATER

With the proper amount of water nearly every common aliment can be alleviated. One should drink one fluid ounce of water per pound of body weight per day, and have 1 gram of salt per 150 lbs. while drinking such quantities. Water is used by the body to carry all things from foods to wastes, thus a shortage of it slows the entire procedure. Dehydration, or simply inadequate hydration, thus causes a lack of waste elimination resulting in countless toxins in the body reeking endless havoc. Couple this with the resulting lack of efficient transportation of food to rebuild and combat such damages, and the signals of these various internal, "wars" are many: From, aching joints, muscular cramps and inflexibility, head ache, dry skin, eyes, nose, lack of mucus causing asthma like symptoms, heart palpitations, restlessness, etc. Thus, this inefficiency of food/energy delivery and waste elimination, set a stage for pathogens to thrive causing the situation to greatly worsen. This drinking water should preferably be pure water, as in distilled, free from chlorine, fluorine and other added toxins. (Chlorine is a suspect in kidney and bladder cancer, and fluorine is suspected to accumulate in bones with adverse effects)

i. Animal alteration

i. GMO (genetically modified organism) and Synthetics

Genetic engineering and alteration of animals and plants, making them produce more or different things than in nature is seen as an abomination to the Individualists when it is done with a profit oriented mind. Many of the chemicals fed to the animals or their side effects end up in the final product consumed by man. Such as the adding of milk production boosting hormones to cows which have side effects on the product, causing excessive white blood cell count (pus) to be contained within it. The Individualists set up the Unnatural Foods tax to counter these horrific acts. As well as initiate proper education to inform the people and to raise future chemists with a more compassionate demeanor. All people in Individualistic society will thereby be aware of the detail of their foods' origins.

j. Food Bill

A bill called the "Personal Responsibility in Food Consumption Act" or the "Cheeseburger Bill", bans anyone from suing food manufacturers, sellers and distributors regardless of the harm caused by food one has eaten. The only way this bill if fair is by passing a companion bill forcing the full disclosure of all industry ingredients and methods of production and distribution, in a clear unambiguous manner. Only then can one be responsible for what one is eating. This is further proof of the profiteering mindset of another industry who has the entire *government* bought and paid for.

6. PRIVATIZED BANKS

Of all of the need suppliers the banks are the pinnacle of their vile hierarchy. The need they supply is a medium required by all to do any and all things, a restriction which masterfully channels all activities through them and their selfishly biased system successfully controlling all involved. A bank once was simply a heavily walled structure designed to only protect money. Banks have since evolved from such secure facilities into powerful entities which exercise many controlling abilities over the very individuals who deal with them and whose investments fund them.

Before one places one's hard earned funds in these establishments where they charge one to do so while they then invest those monies and make a profit which in no way is shared with the depositor, one should ask oneself: In how many ways do banks thieve money off of the workers? How many lives have banks destroyed by foreclosure and crippling usury? (It is much more often than not, yet one will never see it reported in one's faithful news broadcasts.) How many families exist in which both parents work just to make ends meet? (This is not merely ridiculously accepted today but it is a distraction from an even greater terror, because of this, who then is raising the children?) How many people are in their sixties and still slaving for the impassive and unappreciative machine? Because of the banks there is no question in anyone's mind as to the right to enjoy their life, which means every second, not just the last four hours of the day because of toiling on the machine which has no goal, point or purpose, successfully expending their most vibrant hours of life each day for nothing.

How, one may ask, are the banks responsible for all of this? Because of the long reaching effect of usury. Today most every major possession is financed, and the financing is commonly orchestrated to have the borrower pay three to five times more than what the item is worth. Therefore, every individual works three to five times longer than what is fairly required. The grand picture of this is an entire world working three to five times longer for the face value of all they possess. Funneling all of that excess profit to only the banks as the spirit of the people and their over all demeanor collapses as a direct result of this meaningless and overly taxing drudgery. One may say it is right to pay the banks for borrowing their money, but as will be shown, it is not their money and most of it doesn't even exist. (see also pg 46)

For just one example of their countless debased practices let one examine foreclosure. A man only owes $1,077 on a home which appraises for $81,000, the same amount borrowed from the bank some 29 years ago. He falls late on his last two payments and the bank forecloses taking the property and selling it for $81,000, meanwhile up to this point the bank most likely had already collected $192,768 *before* this sale (81,000 at 7% for 30 years minus two months). Hence in this scenario the bank grosses roughly $273,768 and profits $265,668 (the bank only paid $8,100 for the house because of fractional reserve) while the man has nothing after 29 years of his life, hard labor and $192,768 of timely payments. This is an unacceptable outrage, yet evils of this nature go unquestioned in the old dying world because no one has the incentive to stand up to it. The Individualist clearly sees these heinous acts for what they are and hastens to eliminate them and all those who perform them upon their fellow brethren.

The Banks have ensured their existence by passing laws which makes their existence and their use a necessary step within the society, practically forcing all to have at least a checking account just as one is forced to have insurance. What better a business to be in where the people are forced to do business with you? A case in point, for a business to open and be able to do business, it must first possess a "business checking account" at a local bank. What other businesses can do this? This is absurd yet it goes unquestioned. In the guise of "keeping track of lawful business" the banks entrench themselves, embed themselves into the system no different than a burrowing tick. In numerous other guises, laws and methods they have done the same. Nothing of any significant amount can be purchased with cash, it must be had by check, again forcing one to use the banks. All private institutions controlling the actions of the public and profiting off of their forced use.

As money is time and power, the collection of money is synonymous with the collection of time and power. Any entity who collects pools of money is collecting pools of time and power which can then be utilized however that private entity desires regardless of if that use is in the interest of the individuals it was collected from or the society it is contained in. Too often this money is used in ways not clearly disclosed to the contributors. Such as when a bank invests in a corporation (such as a loan) with the people's savings, whom if informed of the nature of said corporation, may not agree to their funds being applied to it, furthermore these people will see none of the profits gained by utilizing their money. If these customers would have placed their money into a business of their own choice, a profit would have been returned to them and only that business would have become powerful, not a business one did not choose who is fed by the unaware funds of thousands. The ability of large corporations to set up subsidiary banks, allows for them to acquire such a block of unregistered, powerless, non-voting, unaware investors so that they may proceed with plans unimpeded by concerned investors.

To funnel more of these unaware investors (the common bank account holders) into the system, all systems that assist independence are eliminated. To be independent in this world only two things will allow for it 1. Sufficient funds (to supply all one needs) or 2. The knowledge of self-sufficiency. The first is greatly removed by usury and market regulation (prices and wages), the second has been purposefully kept from schools to force man into the system of money use, and by this action only the ones with the money grow in power. Each low dollar individual is a potential servant, the more taxing the market and lending practices the more low dollar individuals can be created and locked into the system, or taught and encouraged to use the system.

The money of the banks *is* the people's money. The bank only exists by having people feed it money. Without account holders installing money, there is no bank capital, as a result there is then no bank lending or investing capabilities, then there is simply no bank. Yet banks continually take more from their account holders, their lifeblood, and award them less and less while profiting from their funds. May this be a reminder of the nature of a bank, a servant and product of the people, and not vice-versa. A private bank is simply a pool of the people's money which an independent private entity controls by its own rules and profits therefrom returning nothing to the people who compose it. If it is the people's pool of money then only the people should control and profit from it. Otherwise the money should be returned to them.

What follows is the mechanics of fractional reserve which deserves full attention. It is practiced by every bank everywhere every day and is allowed by law, (for only banks that is). A person deposits $1000 into his local bank account; this bank can then loan 90% of this amount to a second individual and only be obligated to maintain 10% physically in the bank. (Thus a fractional reserve) Therefore, the initial person still has $1000 in their account, but now a second individual also has $900 from thin air, and the cycle indefinitely continues. From bank to bank the money is transferred and grows, thus from this $1000 the chain of lending would be:

1000, 900, 810, 729, 656, 590, 531, 478, 430, 387, 348, 313, 282, 254, 229, 206, 185, 166, 149, 134, 121, 109, 98, 88, 79, 71, 64, 58, 52, 47, 42, 38, 34, 31, 28, 25, 22, 20, 18, 16, 14, 13, 12, 11, 10, 9, 8, 7, 6, 5, 4, 3.5, 3, 2.7, 2.43, 2.19, 1.98, 1.78, 1.6, 1.49, 1.3, 1.17, 1.05, 0.94 etc. Totaling $8962.08, and these figures have been rounded off for sake of simplicity, the actual value would be $9000.

Thus is shown the bank's unwarranted license to print money by private individuals and none of it is backed by anything meaningful. None of the profits go back to the consumer whose backbreaking labor in the form of currency was used to build this exponentially increasing phantom wealth. There is no material backup for the worthless paper and digital credits that are deemed your net worth. It is a blatant exploitation of the working class and must now come to an overdue end.

From a snap shot of a single bank the practice does not seem dangerous. It is when the entire industry is analyzed that this creation of phantom wealth becomes apparent. For the entire industry acts as one entity exchanging money with itself in this manner producing 90% non-existent funds. This very practice can be used by corporations and banks behind closed doors to erect lending circles between themselves generating potentially endless funds.

Thus, as shown, the banks create 90% of the currency thereby controlling a nation's money supply. It is the Government of the People who are to control the money, not privatized individuals who are separate from the government and who have interests which may not have anything to do with that government which should be of the People. Therefore, by this clear description it is a direct threat to the people which is fueled *by* the very people it threatens.

The only reason today's hollow currency has any power whatsoever is because everyone believes that when they take the currency to another person, that person will give an expected amount in return. Hence, the banks can be destroyed by making their money useless simply by refusing to use it. By this very same method one becomes immune to their enthralling powers. The instant doubt becomes injected into the system the bank's dollar and welfare is threatened. This is done by simply creating a new currency and first getting many individuals and companies to begin utilizing it because of their belief in what it represents, trusting only in it and refusing the other currency. As it grows all will have the right to get paid in either currency. Some businesses in the highest technologies run by Individualists will refuse to do business with the old currency or banks. Doubt will then grow in all the populace as to the power of the bank dollar, as it now cannot be used for anything and everything as in the past. As a result, to do business with the most evolved companies of the new world one must use the new currency because undoubtedly these companies will be Individualist owned and by their very nature will posses overwhelming technologies. Soon the bank dollar will only buy primitive technologies, and useless material items. May no law be made to stop the people, as a whole, from printing their own money or having their own recording institutions, beware of such acts of tyranny and suppression.

An argument that states that the Populus Common Wealth system is no different than the One World Bank system. Here are the clear differences: 1. The One World Bank promotes utter dependence so that no one may buy sell or trade without having their currency. Individualist currency can be had by simply trading in surplus food, power etc. generated directly on the homestead by the hand of the Individualist, if said Individualist chooses to be utterly self sufficient as opposed to having an occupation within the community. The Individualist society actively encourages this self sufficient, independent behavior by way of incentives, where as the world bank would discourage this by erecting veiled stumbling blocks to discourage its practice and encourage dependence in its stead, not assisting self sufficiency because its very nature threatens the bank's existence. 2. And greatest of all, the Individualistic society forbids usury in all forms and the pooling of money by any private individual or group for any purpose, which is contrary to the one World Bank system.

Banks have the world convinced that it cannot function without them. The truth is, it is the banks that cannot function without the people. A bank cannot exist without the account holders who blindly use them yet it taxes and charges their every action, profits on their money and returns little or nothing to them. They have accumulated trillions of dollars from exploiting their enslaved (deceived) brethren in this way. Why are they enslaved? Because the law supports the banks' usury and debt collection, thus the law favors the bank and not the people who compose the bank. The people are powerless to change the law when they are deceived into believing that it is a just and fair system.

Yet there once existed small clauses which had lenience toward these slaves, who were sadly working three to five times over the value of the amount they borrowed from their captors. These clauses have since vanished leaving no hope for the escape of any slave. One was bankruptcy but it has since been restructured by the banks in favor of the banks to force their slaves to pay back every cent of the obnoxiously inflated debt, which without interest they most likely have already paid back numerous times. The slave cannot even refuse to pay this unconditional judgement because the banks and the compromised justice system will simply garnish one's wages forcing this repayment of three to five times the amount borrowed. Say the frustrated slave wishes to run away, being that all records go directly to the credit bureaus this makes it very difficult for a "run away slave" to escape for long. The moment a job is acquired or personal information is listed on any official paperwork, the slave masters know their slave's location and will come for him. Bankruptcy only forgives the case of the extreme poor. After taking all that the individual owns, the bank is still entitled to its "lost" money through federal government insurance, which is naught but tax money. Thus the taxpayers, even those who are not voluntarily enslaved, are, in fact, also enslaved. They involuntarily pay for the bank's losses through their hard work in the form of taxes. Thus the bank has excluded no one from its tyranny.

Now the true face of the bank is becoming apparent, yet it will only reveal the totality of its hideous features once its collapse begins to fully manifest and its life blood, the people, flow away from it. Its claws will then be set deeper into those that still remain and blatantly it will begin ardent campaigns for laws hindering the noble Individualist movement. Therefore, act quickly, the least that needs done is to make illegal usury and fractional reserve. However, even then it will be seen that privatized pools of money still only breed corruption, then it is understood that the thorough dismantlement of all banks must come to pass to realize a complete solution. As this manifests, be advised of banking lobbyists who will assure the people that the doctrine of Individualism has exaggerated the facts about their establishments to an unacceptable degree, as they then continue to charge the people while using their money to the profit of only the bank.

Concluding with this description of the true nature of the banking system as a degenerative disease afflicting mankind and its healthy evolution, the suggested remedy will now be disclosed. Many people will say that the dismantlement of the entire global banking system is unfair to the banks or an impossibility. They may insist that the money is the banks' because they have 'earned' it, or that the creature is too large to be dispatched. The banks have raped their fellow men since the day they opened for centuries, it is only just that they are eliminated and the funds redistributed. Here is now shown the Individualist solution to slaying the great beast.

Suggested Method of Dismantlement

The following activities will be handled by the local HVR and any disputes may formally appeal to the next higher HVR within 10 days.

a. Privatized banking is made illegal. All banks are closed and their activities are frozen.

b. A detailed audit of the bank and its owner(s) and shareholder(s) is conducted reaching back thirty years. Most importantly it will contain:

   i. All loans.
   ii. Land and Buildings which the bank operates from.
   iii. Balance and history of all accounts (Hereon defined as THE COMMUNITY *Yet Excluding The Owner(s) and the Shareholder(s) or any individual who is found to be an owner or shareholder in any other bank, as none of them may be considered part of THE COMMUNITY. Neither may accounts or individuals with less than $100,000 spread over more than two banks less than one year old, any account less than six months old with an average daily balance less than 2,000 dollars or any account less than two months old be considered part of THE COMMUNITY.*)
   iv. All other Holdings and assets in any form.

c. The owner(s) and/or shareholder may at this point liquidate 10% of their holdings and account balance, if one exists, which is all they are entitled to, do to the nature of fractional reserve creating 90% phantom wealth. If however, in the audit there is any suspicious activity of boosting holdings with foresight of this dismantlement, all of these funds will be liquidated and returned to THE COMMUNITY leaving these cheating individuals without anything. In either case they must remain within the locality for the remainder of the dismantlement for reasons outlined in the following section **d.**

d. All accounts are closed and each account holder is to be given the full amount within his account in cash. * If the owner(s) and shareholders cannot produce this, it will come out of their liquidated personal belongings, if after that that there is still money owed, the owner(s) and shareholders shall become indentured servants to those owed as special Laborforce workers in the field chosen by the creditor (the individual(s) owed). Any owed accounts will be in this way repaid from the smallest to the largest. Upon opening of the local HVR facility, the account holders may deposit or exchange their cash.

*If the owners/shareholders cannot meet the required account cash out, the shortage will be converted into a percentage of the amount owed in full and each member of THE COMMUNITY will be shorted that percentage of their account cash out. They will then be repaid as outlined in this section.

e. The total amount of monthly payments successfully applied to the amount which the account holder initially borrowed is calculated for all loans. If this amount is more than the amount initially borrowed the borrower is reimbursed this amount. However, if the amount is less, the borrower must continue the monthly payments until paying off EXACTLY what was borrowed, as usury has been removed. 10% of these funds are to be divided evenly among the past owner(s) and shareholder(s), the remainder of these funds, if any, are then distributed evenly amongst THE COMMUNITY.

104

f. All remaining holdings the bank possesses, if any, are liquidated and the wealth evenly distributed to THE COMMUNITY. (Some buildings may be initially purchased for fair market value by the Populus, see section **h.**)

g. All monies returned to the people must be exchanged for Populus Energy Certificates, the Populus printed currency backed by the Populus Resource Reserves, at an exchange rate calculated at that time. Old Currency of the deceptive Federal Reserve is deemed valueless and not accepted for exchange after one year.

h. Suitable bank buildings will be converted into Populus owned HVR facilities. Each being a "Hall of Vital Records" capable of exchanging money, shredding Federal Reserve notes, lending, and all other normal banking activities without the practice of usury or fractional reserve in any form.

This method will take great time to realize, and it is known that there exists those fervent Individualists who would rather deliver a blow immediately. For them there is simply the boycotting of all banking: no accounts*, no loans, no credits, and the convincing of all others to do the same. Money orders can be utilized until the "Populus Energy Certificates" become more recognized. Above all, stick together with your fellow Individualists and combat laws which restrict or encumber these activities.
* Keep an account with a tiny balance so as to be considered part of a COMMUNITY to benefit from the dismantling process.

Let it be clearly seen that all that has been done to the banking system is 1. The elimination of Usury 2. The elimination of fractional reserves 3. The returning of the money stolen from the people by the two aforementioned evils 4. The establishment of the Just bank of the Individualist which is owned and controlled by all the people of the nation, making illegal the privatized bank and similar establishments such as the Federal Reserve. 5. The establishment of safes and vaults as now being local treasuries, military protected compounds of real concrete wealth of the people backed by the Populus energy reserves, as it was in the past with the gold standard.

"If the American people ever allow the banks to control the issuance of their currency, first by inflation, and then by deflation, the banks and corporations that will grow up around them will deprive the people of all property, until their children wake up homeless on the continent their fathers conquered. The issuing power of money should be taken from banks and restored to Congress and the people to whom it belongs. I sincerely believe the banking institutions having the issuing power of money, are more dangerous to liberty than standing armies." -- Thomas Jefferson

7. INSURANCE COMPANIES

The Individualists erect the Populus Accident Fund eliminating the need for a private insurance industry. A play on fear, these establishments exist only because of the irresponsibility of one's own risks. By these means they gain large pools of wealth, exactly as a bank, which endow them with the very same powers and corruption. Such as lawmaking capabilities with which they practice making laws in favor of only themselves. Masters of deceit, their contracts are so wordy that few have the time to read every portion or understand their purposely cryptic language. The details are such that there is an escape clause for almost every claim one may present to them. Fast to demand their money, and faster to evade one's claims of need, these fraudulent and cheating beasts lay in bed with the darkest sides of governments, banks, hospitals, unions and a endless list of other writhing worms. Privatized insurance leaves too much room for corruption as the people have no say about its actions and fees nor can its claims versus premiums, and type thereof, be accurately verified by external sources.

Exempt from federal laws, (such as anti trust laws, opening the door to the ability of price fixing, and market and consumer control, the very same laws which Alan Greenspan condemns), and automatically chosen by banks as defaults, they tirelessly practice and exercise their legalized extortion upon their fellow man. Their rackets are further solicited by brokerage firms just as insidious, claiming no alleged allegiance to their masters who reward them for every soul lured into their contracts of illusions, and twisted words, wrought full of holes visible only to their wicked eyes.

Within the Individualist's society all "insurance" premiums will be paid to the Populus Accident Fund. (See page 51) The monies collected will pay for any and all accidents which occur that year for the entire nation. If there is any surplus it is divided and returned to the population evenly with their tax returns. If there is a deficit the money from the surplus of the following year will make up for it. If there is a continual deficit, then either the people are too accident prone (which is absurd, if this were the case then all insurance companies would have went out of business long ago) or the annual fee per individual is not high enough. Being that insurance companies make huge profits each year and expand at alarming rates, one's common sense will allow one to foresee the substantial return each year if all paid their present premiums to the Populus as opposed to their private companies.

1. There will be no life insurance which is simply a gambling form of usury, usury with an escape clause - death, so one won't be around to ensure the follow through or to argue a case. Most likely the returns received at the time of one's death are less than the total amount paid into the fund over the many years.
   And the amount of profit gained, if any, is insignificant to the amount of profit these institutions made on   that money in the guise of benevolence. It is illegal for any purpose to sell money in the Individualistic   society.
2. Health insurance is no longer needed as all health care is now Populus provided by the PHS. A private company is obviously in business to make money thus its goal is tainted, this initial taint causes a focus on   money not on healing, which should be the prime focus. Thus from the onset the concept is flawed.
   Having people pay out of pocket for non covered items, as dentistry, keeps prices realistic (because the "health care" professionals know there is no longer access to an endless pool of insurance money to be raped with inflated charges and dubious itemization) and the people taking better care of themselves initially to avoid such fees.
3. Workman's compensation is now a sub division of the PAF, all job accidents must be filed as an accident to
   the PAF. At the end of the year the remainder of this fund will be redistributed evenly among all contributing employers.

All insurance companies shall be dismantled with the same basic procedure as outlined with the banks.

An argument may arise of how the Populus can seize the funds "earned" by a private corporation. The Populus will respond that unjust earning in any form found will be returned evenly to the nation. The proof of this unjust earning are the laws which force one to have insurance, and a society which practically ignores the uninsured. This is an industry in collusion with health care providers, unions, banks (as homeowners insurance etc) the automobile industry, and corrupt lawmakers, in violation of anti trust laws from which they are mysteriously exempt. Therefore for years they have been profiting and erecting bias laws, exaggerating the probability of accidents and their costs, all the while injecting doubt and fear into society to their own benefit. The property will be seized just as a bank seizes the property which individuals paid for more than twice.

8. WELFARE

The U.S. has over 70 welfare programs distributed by six departments: 1. Department of Agriculture (DoA), 2. Department of Energy (DoE), 3. Department of Labor (DoL), 4. Department of Treasury, 5. Department of Health and Human Services (HHS), and 6. Department of Housing and Urban Development (HUD). In 2006 the Federal welfare spending alone was $359.5 billion, with an additional $138 billion in state and local welfare spending. Approximately 51 percent of these figures went to Medical assistance of low-income persons and 38 percent of it went to Cash and food handouts and housing aid.

Welfare began as a good measure but has since been molded into an efficient tool for dependence which is naught but enslavement. The welfare offices are strategically placed near poverty-stricken areas making it easy for the poor to get to them, rapidly addicting them to dependence. The poor (created by the increasing class contrast caused by perverted capitalism) then learn the details of the system and its different "hand out" or "free money" programs and how to qualify. As a result they purposely will not seek employment so as to qualify for poverty income level checks. Furthermore, they will feign madness or suicidal tendencies to gain disability and actually brag over the amount of checks they receive. They will either sell food stamps or else buy food for other people with the stamps, in exchange for the money, causing little of the food money to actually go to food. Very little of this money goes to any good.

With all of this free time on their hands, it would be nice to think that they would apply it to lofty aims as the noble Individualist, but unfortunately the chores they prefer are prostitution, drug using and selling. The pharmaceutical companies have happily set up a market as large or larger than the illicit drug market in this environment because under the *government* hand out programs the people get their drugs for free, addicting these poor creatures no differently than illegal drugs do. These new addicts then get the drug for free every month paid for by tax dollars which go right into the pockets of the pharmaceutical industry. The free drugs received are often then sold on the street to gain money to use for alcohol, tobacco or illicit drugs. This in turn becomes a large block of votes, because a politician knows that if he supports welfare he will have the support of all these slothful souls submerged in debauchery and decay as well as the contributions from big Pharma.

Wherever these offices of dependence spring up the surrounding neighbor hood falls into ruin, businesses shut down and the economy collapses and is then in need of even more support. Therefore the formula is clearly apparent that when a facility intended to assist is implemented it only causes dependence. Just as a narcotic the addiction becomes worse and worse, and needs more and more assistance (in the form of tax dollars), until it reaches a point that if assistance is withdrawn, death ensues. Thus, resulting in the total collapse of the neighborhood. This system is nothing but a cesspool where tax dollars are lost and changed into drugs, alcohol and tobacco profits.

The Individualist sees this and therefore does not implement any assistance in the first place. It may seem cruel but it makes for powerful individuals and a collection of powerful individuals creates a powerful state. Each individual has weaknesses that must be overcome. The universe places trials and tribulations before every soul so that it may hone its skills to be worthy before the perfection of God. If another takes those trials away, even with good intent, then the necessary development never occurs and stagnation results.

This is not to say that this is the only way dependence is initiated. If an individual is kept from learning the foundation skills of self sustenance which every native American and primitive peoples knew, a birth right which has been muddled over, and at times blatantly hidden, without this knowledge they indeed also become dependant. These two modes of dependence are a ploy of the need suppliers since antiquity, no different than a mother lion that does not teach its cub to hunt, but instead supplies it with food until old age. It is a ridiculous and unnatural scenario but it is exactly what is happening. The knowledge of self-sustenance *is* the knowledge of True Independence.

As can be clearly seen, the ignorant and lazy are the ideal subjects for the need suppliers. In their corrupted societies will be seen many systems and programs fortifying existing weaknesses and others which are creating and cultivating new ones. For these reasons there are NO crutches whatsoever in the Individualist society. A crutch is a system that nurses weakness, when you nurse a weakness it only grows to larger weakness. Any type of social welfare is a system that encourages proliferation of the ignorant, inept and socially impotent sheep, which were created by, and only exist to feed and serve the need suppliers' parasitic requirements. The supplying of one with all they need creates no incentive, ambition or skill in any occupation because they have never experienced work. If experience is had, it is usually in an underground, black market of some type of social and morally degenerative activity. By eliminating this crutch you will not only have stronger individuals, but the socially degenerative activities will slow if not stop, including the degenerative influence of the drug, alcohol and tobacco industries, preying upon and assisting the implementation of these types of environments.

Many Economic overviews fail to take into consideration the full impact of the poor, disabled and retired, neglecting a shadow side of the market. There exists a massive black-market here greatly effecting the working taxpayer. These monies dumped into these people are not used for the intended purpose but are transformed by many heinous methods into cash for prescription and illicit drugs, alcohol and tobacco. Thus in the act of kindness the taxpayers are fooled into sending their money to these three dark industries, when the intent of taxes is to benefit the strength and integrity of the Union.   Furthermore, the massive Health Care attention to these exploited people (sick from laziness and drug abuse) and the complimentary Pharmaceutical interest, both in the guise of benevolence, are corrupt industries, fully aware of how greatly they benefit from this system of dependence on the tax payers bill. Thus welfare causes the taxpayer to lose all the way around and actually causes harm to the Union because it weakens and corrupts the people who it was intended to assist as well as the taxpayers. In the end it supports only corrupt industries, all of which have no concern whatsoever for the taxpayer or the union.

a. Unemployment Compensation

No assistance is offered in the Individualistic society to any for any reason besides the free information housed at LAFKI. The instant a group is defined as needing assistance, one has caused separation within the Union. The new "group" is defined different and it is thus separate. Separation causes a cascade of evils even if with good intent. "United we stand, Divided we fall!" is very true, any degree of separation is division in the union which is a crack in a diamond. If an individual is inept for whatever reason to make his own living, he can volunteer in a "Laborhood". In time the individual will learn all trades necessary to forge their own independent path to social and spiritual success. Nursing weakness only strengthens it, and creates a medium for its spread.

b. Foreign Aid

The current US foreign aid budget is about $26 billion. Approximately 30% of the US foreign aid budget has been going to Israel since 1949 totaling over $85 Billion, with $50 Billion in interest being paid by the American people (since the money so generously given away is "borrowed", reflecting a deceived nation), totaling over $135 billion and growing. $15.2 billion has gone to Japan from 1946 –52 and from 2003 – 2006, $28.9 Billion was given to Iraq. The logic here seems to be: pay money to destroy, pay money to rebuild, all on the taxpayer's dollar, to the benefit of private corporations with no profit returning to the taxpayers. The taxpayers pay all the way around, and the corporations and war manufactures profit all the way around. Thus, war and foreign assistance is simply a racket.

Most of these "loans" are never paid back, and 70% of them go toward "economic recovery". Which is simply corporate interest, building their new factories, machines and successfully implanting a new system of waste and consumption, fully paid for by the taxpayers to the profit of private industries.

The Individualist taxpayers will not pay to help strangers in other nations for no return. When is there ever a public vote as to whether the people would like their tax dollars to go to a foreign nation? When is there ever an itemized receipt for the use of those funds? When has a public board ever investigated the accuracy and verified the legitimacy of such expenditures? This is the result of corporate interests and has nothing to do with the integrity of the Union which tax money is meant for. If corporations have interests in other countries they are welcome to pay for them with their own private funds.

9. CREDIT BUREAUS

All credit bureaus (Equifax, Experion, Trans Union and Innovis Data Solutions) will be dismantled in exactly the same way the banks were. All records will now be kept by the HVR, whose practices shall be much more humane than the credit bureaus. The HVR will practice a more detailed judging system, taking into account reasons for late payments, years of on time payments, as well as adding bonus points for early and overpayments.

With the present method of operation, an individual who has had excellent credit for 20 years and then goes through a six month streak of bad luck, now has a terrible credit score, no better than bankruptcy or an individual who has never paid anything on time or at all, for the next seven years. The current bureaus are merely a treacherous agent of the banking system possessing no human compassion or regard for the advancement of society. They hide facts about the data they keep on the public and with whom it is shared, yet they claim that they are independent of the banking industry, while selling this information on people which should be free public knowledge. The HVR will keep free public records of each individual's past public deeds, financial and otherwise.

With the dismantlement of the banks, the demise of the credit bureaus naturally follows, as well as all debt management and credit counseling services (dismantled as the banks). Establishments as these use the ignorance of their fellow man against him and make him settle with the banks in various ways for a fee. Some even make the individual's situation worse by preying on his desperateness, and placing payments in a trust, not paying the creditors, causing endless added fees and lawsuits, compounding the nightmare of debt.

III. LIBRARY OF ACCREDITED FREE KNOWLEDGE AND INSTRUCTION (LAFKI)

The Library of Accredited Free Knowledge and Instruction is the collective mind of the Populus, containing all of their knowledge. As the GEP is the active knowledge of their awareness, and the HVR is their static knowledge or wisdom, the LAFKI oscillates between these two as the sum total of all of this knowledge and clearly communicates it to man. With its massive collection of unrestricted free knowledge it aids the understanding of man in all subjects and applications thereby enlightening his existence, purpose and goals. This creates a populace wherein every individual is fully competent to wisely vote on all decisions of the GEP consensuses, resulting in a society whose greater harmony, meaningful social projects and facilities, consequently arisen out of the PHMC, are the direct reflection of the desires of the entire people as a whole. This then allows man to create and discover even higher ideas for the future, continuing this synergistic cycle of healthy growth and evolution.

~ See color diagram on back cover ~

A. STRUCTURE OF LAFKI

Unlike the bogus and impotent "freedom of information act", LAFKI practices truly unrestricted freedom of information. It shall be made law that no entity, government, public or private may withhold information from LAFKI, who represents all of the people, each of whom having unrestricted access to LAFKI data (save in war, see '6M' pg 73). It is the right of each citizen to know all information within their society being that a society is one unit which must work together, the only reason to withhold information is to keep others at a disadvantage. It is illegal in the Individualistic society for any aspect of the *government* to withhold, or make unclear, any information being that that information was had by using the people's money, therefore that information, by definition, is the property of the people. Furthermore, any just government is to be strictly of the people, again making all "government" information the property of the people. Any *government* that separates itself from the people in anyway should be dismantled without delay for the sake of freedom. It shall be stressed that deceit, suppression and dependence begin by withholding knowledge from one's fellow man. Thus, those who hoard and privatize knowledge and insights which The One has given them, directly impede the evolution of mankind.

The Individualists begin empowering each individual by first overhauling the impotence of the present education system, from the elementary to the colleges. These shall be made more demanding and informative focusing more on practical knowledge and detailed awareness, including but not limited to, the mechanics of government, law, economics etc., to make competent souls instead of corporate tools. Furthermore all knowledge shall be readily available as a free digital database accessible to all at any time. LAFKI will thus dwarf the library of congress and their "THOMAS" (an acronym for "The House's Open Multimedia Access System"), and world digital library of congress (www.worlddigitallibrary.org), by being unrestricted and actively reaching out and communicating, constantly, with the people.

The LAFKI section of the Populus Informer will actively included valuable methods of self-sustenance, self-creation, self-defense and practical lessons on the newest breakthroughs in science and technologies etc. It will then refer the reader to databases where the details of the knowledge down to the equations and harvesting of the natural materials will be found. It will be written in an easily understandable method outlining the how and the why of the technology in question with links to the history of its evolution prioritizing the full comprehension of the average reader. This will create a thinking and involved society of Scientific artists who by their very nature will be immune to control by others, and who will make wise decisions for their society in harmony with each other and God's creation. Furthermore, the public shall be made more aware of, and encouraged to use, public facilities, such as libraries. These shall be broadened in scope in the spirit of Individualistic free knowledge, active information distribution and teaching, becoming additional outposts for LAFKI Instruction which shall further assist the ease of access to this tremendous wealth of knowledge.

Note: Patents shall still be given, but the knowledge will be publicly useable, (too often patents restrict the proper uses of knowledge) however credits must be given to the patent holder and homage be paid in the amount of 2% wholesale royalties to the individual for his work in attaining the idea. However the patent holder may grant the use for anything less than 2% if so desired.

1. THE POPULUS MEDIA

The Populus Media acts as a completely free and independent balance to the GEP's researchers and to privatized media giants. It has a large portion of rotating volunteers in addition to its Populus paid staff, and is constantly monitored and directed by the consensus of the entire population, making it very difficult to corrupt. Its media includes a paper, radio station (satellite and local where necessary), television channel, and cellular service. All of which (save for the cellular service) is accessible on the Internet. The cellular service of the Populus Media not only gives inexpensive phone service to much of the population, but will serve as the foundation for a completely free, global, wireless internet system. Allowing all of the worlds knowledge to be accessible to anyone, at any time, any where on Earth. With the advancement of laptop computers each individual will be able to carry all of mans knowledge with them wherever they go. (More detailed information of the Populus Media continues on pg 115)

2. POPULUS FREE EDUCATION

a. Populus Colleges

Besides the active distribution of free teachings via the many outlets of the Populus Media and the full data base of LAFKI online, LAFKI also erects public colleges from existing community colleges and other buildings, such as dismantled prisons. Unlike other media instruction, physical colleges can teach knowledge in 'hands on' applications. These colleges will only be erected at the request of the locality because, unlike online instruction, these facilities will have substantial operating costs in comparison. In the event of a locality without such a building, classes as these can still be taught at hosting facilities, such as a Populus Fabrication shop, which would be able to hold fabrication oriented classes, or a Populus mine which could host geology, prospecting, metallurgy etc. All of these services would be free as the result of the amount of taxes previously allocated to the program, agreed upon by the people as a whole. If there is a demand for more 'hands on' classes as these, possibly exceeding the tax budget, it will be voted upon in the Populus Informer whether to increase taxes to hold more of such classes, or to have a certain percentage be paid for, at cost, by each student.

The placing of a price on knowledge is another method to restrict the knowledge of mankind and thereby impede their evolution. The Populus, therefore, maintains knowledge as free as possible, exacting the minimum fees allowable to make up the cost of the mediums used to transmit that knowledge. However, any individual who gets below average grades at these facilities, must pay (at cost) for the next semester of learning, because individuals as this are wasting the time and energy of this generous system and possibly taking the place of another who will excel. This minor penalty shall act as incentive for every truly appreciative student to excel.

b. Populus Militia Colleges

There are two other LAFKI instructional institutions which both operate out of the PHMC. One is the chain of Populus Militia Colleges, and the other is the various Laborhoods. The Militia Colleges are the facilities which train every member of the society in defense of their person, locality and nation, as well as survival and paramilitary occupations, such as citizen police. After the initial two year training is concluded, any citizen may return to the college for additional schooling but must reenlist in the Militia for another two years and thus hold a paramilitary occupation, in exchange for the additional free training. All of this information is indeed freely available from LAFKI, however, what one gains by trading in their personal time, is expert hands on training and experience.

c. Laborhoods

The Laborhoods are a place of learning for the mind, body and spirit. The students are placed on a site in temporary, mobile housing and rise each day for class. Class is the teaching of the building of a homestead from the ground up. The entire project is preplanned by the Populus, from the number and types of houses in the proposed community, to the project's location. It is carried out by the students at the direction of skilled instructors, (tradesmen, engineers, architects etc). The students are not only taught how to build an entire home, but to farm and to hand build renewable energy devices. The materials needed are paid for by the Populus as a loan to the students. When the project is complete the student may move into the new homes that they built, or leave them for the Populus to sell, at cost, to a buyer. The only expense for the student is to repay the cost of the materials for the home and the accessories (only if moved into), as well as the room and board rendered during the time which they were learning. When this project is over each student not only has a home, but the skills and knowledge of many trades to assist in the community from that day forward.

The Laborhood will not only be used by curious students, but by those in need of a home. This remedies the act of *government* projects handing out housing to individuals who then have no understanding of the amount of effort and skill gone into the structure, and thereby possess no appreciation of the privilege handed to them. With this out dated method, the taxpayer pays for the home and gets nothing in return. Conversely, with the Individualistic Laborhood, the Populus *lends* the amount and is repaid in full within five years. Furthermore, those receiving the Populus home through the Laborhood program, at its completion, are consequently endowed with great understanding of the entire construction process and possess many new skills. They are therefore competent contributors to their society either by employment within that society, excess production upon their own homestead, or teaching others the valuable skills which they have learned. They are not left incompetent and inept as in the dying world's system of housing handouts. For the elderly and the disabled, one of their able-bodied family members may sign on to a Laborhood on their behalf. However, any one going through a Laborhood program cannot go through again to gain an additional home*.

Similar to the Laborhoods are the Populus Conversion classes. Held at Populus Conversion facilities, they lend the student the money to, hands on, convert one's internal combustion engine driven vehicle into a fully electric vehicle. They will also give a student a vehicle if the student has no vehicle for going through the class. The student can then repay the Populus by whatever method chosen, especially volunteering for a Laborforce assignment and requesting to work at a conversion facility to hone the new knowledge acquired.

As mentioned earlier housing and transportation amount to 80% of all household debt and supply massive interest profits to the banks. (Remember that interest is wasted energy see pg 47) Therefore, the Laborhood eliminates one of the largest sources of energy waste in present society while simultaneously enlightening the people and strengthening the integrity of the Union.

*Laborhood built homes may not be rented under any circumstances. Else one would make profit on the generosity of one's society. Anyone caught engaged in this activity will have the home confiscated and be sentenced as grand theft.

3. THE LAFKI INFORMATION DISTRIBUTION CENTER (LIDC)

As the GEP is responsible to collect and compile the people's will, the LIDC is the aspect of LAFKI which ensures the delivery of all information to the people so that they may wisely respond to the Populus Informer. The LIDC is responsible for the printing and delivery of the final version of the monthly Populus Informers, via the Internet, post office and the various outlets of the Populus Media. The LIDC also allocates the people's end commands (final consensus responses to the Populus Informer) to the proper departments in a clear and organized manner for that department's efficient access and use, so as to execute the people's will immediately.

B. EXECUTIVE DEPARTMENTS ASSIMILATED

1. DEPARTMENT OF EDUCATION (ED)

a. Federal Student Aid
DISBANDED Education is free in the Individualistic society. If one chooses to go to a private school one must fund it oneself.

b. Institute of Education Sciences
DISBANDED Their motto is "promoting educational excellence for all Americans" Obviously they are failing, for most Americans are insignificantly educated. The little research they conduct will be covered by the GEP.

c. Office for Civil Rights
DISBANDED Being that there are no funds given for education, because it is free, there is then no need to enforce compliance over such funds. Civil rights apply to all citizens in the nation no matter where they are or what they are doing, and shall be handled by the HVR. The 650 attorneys in this office, whether for good or ill, see much of reality as a quota to be filled which can be used as a leveraging tool for various purposes. Any private institution may do whatever it desires on its property, allowing or not allowing service to anyone for any reason, such is freedom. Populus facilities, on the other hand, shall assist all equally.

d. Office of English Language Acquisition
DISBANDED This is segregation, to teach and assist one group and not all equally is not equality. All languages are taught for free to all tax paying citizens of the Individualistic society.

e. Office of Innovation and Improvement

DISBANDED This office is obviously failing in its innovations and improvements to the education system. The innovations and improvements LAFKI shall implement through all media, in a short period of time, will show the full extent of the incompetence of this department of the old world.

f. Office of Intergovernmental and Interagency Affairs

DISBANDED "Encourages public understanding and support for improving American education." Obviously it is failing at its claims. LAFKI's free education system will solve all of these "problems", mostly implemented to keep the majority at a disadvantage.

g. Office of Management

DISBANDED "Performance and results" is the objective of the Department of Education's Office of Management (OM). The result is that the Performance of the children is as sheep, perfectly ignorant to the fact that the government is to obey them. "OM is aggressively moving in new directions in support of the President's Management Agenda, . . ." That agenda is nothing but the stupefaction of the America people and is rapidly succeeding.

h. Office of Safe and Drug-Free Schools

DISBANDED There is no need for a federal office to conduct duties that should be performed at a local level by local authorities.

i. Postsecondary Education

DISBANDED There is no need to give grants when education is free. There is especially no need to send tax payer money out of the country, or to give grants that favor one an not another, all practices of this department. All of these monies shall be relocated to free education.

j. Special Education and Rehabilitative Services

DISBANDED Unfortunately, as cruel as some may see it, inequality begins when assistance is given to one and not another. Special aid is the concern of the family, not the society. Disabled individuals are looked to as wholly equal and welcome to take part in all Populus services, and are expected to achieve the same high standards as all others.

k. Vocational and Adult Education

DISBANDED Most of what this office does is redundancy of the other offices coupled with much wheel spinning on tax dollars with no remarkable results. LAFKI immediately implements programs to assist all freely and efficiently, not just adults, and not just in certain conditions.

l. Office of Elementary and Secondary Education

ASSIMILATED into LAFKI

m. Office of the Chief Financial Officer

ASSIMILATED There are no grants given for education as it is all free in the Individualistic society, unless one chooses private education, which one must fund oneself. This allows this department to be downsized to focus only on the projects of LAFKI ordered by the people.

n. Office of the Chief Information Officer

ASSIMILATED This office will be very important to ensuring the free education of all, if not in a college, within their homes. It will strive to have better teaching techniques then the best schools, allowing the rapid assimilation of the most complex knowledge in the shortest amount of time at the youngest possible age. Such are the high standards of the Individualists.

C. OTHER DEPARTMENTS ASSIMILATED

1. SBA

DISBANDED There will be no monetary assistance offered to anyone for any reason, as such help is a crutch that generates weakness as well as a guise for corruption. Individualism does not only condone handouts to giant corporate conglomerates, but to anyone in any form. In the guise of helping "small" or "minority" businesses, the SBA allots cash to all government personal interests. It has no definition of 'small' and has even considered the American Motor Corporation as a small business. It was intimately involved in the whitewater and wedtech scandals, and major defense contractors like Northrop-Grumman and General Dynamics were given money as "Small Businesses". In fact, rarely does this office help small companies, it is mostly involved with medium sized companies, but has many huge companies it considers as "small" so that it can grant loans, backed by the people's money, to the private corporate interests of the perverted American *government* "representatives".

2. DOL

The following three departments are assimilated from the department of labor, which mostly became absorbed by the HVR.

a. Veterans' Employment and Training Service (VETS)

ASSIMILATED into LAFKI, Unrestricted Education is given freely to all in the Individualistic society, whether a veteran or not.

b. Employment and Training Administration (ETA)

ASSIMILATED into LAFKI, unrestricted Education is given freely to all in the Individualistic society, thus, this type of knowledge would be readily available.

c. Bureau of Labor Statistics (BLS)

ASSIMILATED Reduced to freely accessible information at LAFKI collected by the GEP.

3. POSTAL SERVICE

ASSIMILATED into LAFKI, left unchanged.

4. MISCELLANEOUS

a. Consumer product safety commission

ASSIMILATED Dissolved to information and rules accessible at LAFKI

b. Federal citizen information center

ASSIMILATED Dissolved to information accessible at LAFKI

D. IMMEDIATE LAFKI REFORMS

1. SCHOOLS

Ignorance creates poverty which then creates ignorance and repeats the cycle. Dependence is directly proportionate to this ignorance, and slavery is directly proportionate to the resulting dependence. The simple fact that people do not know self-sustenance causes their dependence upon the machine, which demands them to work, expending all of their time, leaving little or none for the acquisition of knowledge. With less knowledge they therefore earn less money. Thus impoverished, the condition then worsens because the children of such homes, 1. are raised by parents who are working most of the time, thus not passing on their knowledge, leaving the children more ignorant than the parents, and 2. cannot afford to go to college thus continue in ignorance and raise more children, again with deeper ignorance, compounding the situation. Even some who achieve college are often no better off, as many private colleges are producing workers for the machine, as opposed to free thinkers. No matter how "free" they believe that they think, their minds remain confined by parameters taught to them which they accept as fact without proper research.

Let it be known that the Individualist has sympathy for his fellow brother of the old world. It is not his fault he is ignorant, for he was borne into the trap. In his schools he was taught nothing useful but to be a passive slave relying on the system for sustenance. His potential for noble deeds and ambition for evolution and higher purpose was snuffed out in the monotonous repetition of meaningless mundane tasks which only serve to maintain the machine and weaken and corrupt the human spirit. In stark contrast, the school of the Individualists creates powerful enlightened freemen.

As knowledge is the cornerstone stone to Individualistic success, the school is the foundation for that stone. Knowledge is useless unless properly conveyed. The very first, most important, and constant teaching of the Individualists from grades K-13, is the teaching to the students that they are infinite, limitless spirits. Come to this earth to perfect themselves in mind body and spirit, and are not fragile, limited "human beings", which was the weak concept with which the old world used to imprison the children of God. This is not a religious teaching, as any religion can be laid over its foundation, it is a philosophical teaching which adds courage and force to each individual.

This very same concept will change the way parents and teachers look at children, and consequently alter their teaching methods. Presently, parents and teachers look at children as if they are incompetent, when in fact they are ancient spirits. Thus, they present teachings to them in a very slow manner, so that the children can grasp it (and wonder why attention deficit disorder exists). This lack of understanding of a child being a vast soul capable of feats of genius, and therefore taught and spoken to as an inferior being, wrongly convinces that soul that it is a weak and frail mortal thing, (as opposed to an indestructible spirit sparked from the genius of God), thereby crippling its confidence. Therefore the Individualists apply rapid and complex teachings at the earliest of ages, successfully rearing a society of prodigies.

As such, the Individualistic school year is continual, proceeding all summer long, yet the length of each grade is dropped to 173 days. Within this year are four one-week breaks, one beginning each season. Thus in 12 years with the traditional 3 month vacation and 180 day school year, a student receives approximately 5.9 continuous years of training. With the Individualist method, in 12 years a student receives 230 school days per year or 7.6 full years of training*. This amounts to an additional 3.3 (600 days) traditional 180 day school years completed by the same age. This allows for the introduction of a thirteenth grade and 2 years of mandatory militia instruction to be achieved in three months less time than the mere 12 grades of the outdated schooling method. In the final year of the two-year mandatory militia service, the student is a paid member of society in a chosen (temporary and practice) social service. (see pg132) Not only do the students receive more time learning but also the intensity of that learning is twice that of the traditional methods. Amounting to, relatively, 16.4 years of continuous learning creating individuals 2.8 times as adept as the traditionally taught students in less time.

* (Traditional time off = 36, 2 day weekends + 20 holidays + 3, 31 day months. Individualistic time off = 52, 2 day weekends + 31 holidays off. Grades 1,5,9 and13 begin after spring break. Grades 2,6,10 and the first and second years Militia training begin after winter break. Grades 4,8 and 12 begin after summer break. These 173 day school years still allow that grade's teachers their three months vacation as in the past, if desired.)

More sophisticated subjects will be administered at much earlier times than present schools. For example, three languages shall begin to be taught in the first grade when the brain is best suited to learn language, and continue to the 7th grade, as opposed to modern methods which wait to teach languages well after this optimum period has elapsed. All Individualistic learning shall be taught utilizing techniques that stimulate both the right and left brain simultaneously to facilitate rapid information absorption by the students.

At 7th grade the student begins a "Populus" class which continues up to the 13th grade. In addition to traditional classes, it teaches Individualistic philosophy, simplicity, law, voting, active government participation, etc. as well as the four Populus departments, who's duties and functions shall be memorized in detail to ensure continued simplistic operation of the Individualistic society. It does not teach these things in a matter of fact manner, but gives the reason why these things are implemented. It therefore speaks deeply on types of corruption, from usury to tyranny, that can afflict a just nation. The entire constitution, amendments, bill of rights, along with the detailed working of the economic and law system, shall likewise be memorized by every student to make it impossible for corruption, ignorance and dependence, to grow uncaught in the Individualistic society. Thus, ensuring that it will not revert back into the inadequacy and chaos of the old system with its countless departments and inept citizenry.

The 13th grade will be focused primarily upon assuring each student's preparation to be a self sustaining, contributing member of society with a firm understanding of civilization's workings. From the finding of raw materials and the extraction thereof, to fabrication, economics, self-sustenance, renewable energies, to understanding the reason that humans exist in such societies in the first place. There shall be numerous hands-on projects, raising food and shelter from the earth, building wind and water turbines, various solar collectors, electric motors and generators etc., to understand in detail the principles and methods of energy efficiency. This grade thus teaches aspects of real life, unlike modern schools whose students are left dumb to some of the most important areas of life, and are primed to depend on another. From real and practical economics, to basic moral and social conduct, this grade makes all citizens wise, understanding members of the community able to uphold such an advanced system of social living.

The need suppliers have purposely allowed the schools to become shameful jokes of useless information. To combat this degeneration of the schools, starting pay for all of the teachers shall be the same. Teachers annual pay raises shall be based upon their student's scores on administered Populus tests. These tests shall be drawn up by an elected group of accepted and accredited citizens based out of LAFKI. These tests will be updated each year, and copies of the updates will be sent to all parents to approve and comment thereon before the final test is printed and administered. The students of each class are graded on these tests by an independent Populus panel, far removed from the teacher's access, so that the teacher cannot purposely pass his students to gain a pay raise.

Each teacher's merit will thus be clearly exposed with this grading system, and evaluated at the end of each school year based upon this premise, granting a proportionate raise or demotion thereby. This removes the competitive nature from the students and puts the responsibility and stress of learning on to the teaching adult, leaving the child's mind free from negativity. It is therefore the teacher's responsibility to understand the learning methods of each child and to ensure all children are perfectly prepared for the Populus issued test, and thus, pass. Therefore, if a child fails, it is not because of the child's lack of intellect* but the teachers lack of skill and understanding to successfully teach that child. Thus, the greatest teachers will be able to teach any type of child, any level of understanding.

As can be seen, the children are not the ones with learning disabilities, it is the growing number of ignorant adults who have developed teaching disabilities and irresponsibly blame the children. This creates a doubt in a child's mind from an early age that the child is deficient, when, in fact, it was the adult who truly was. This system will create extraordinary teachers and will expose all incompetence.

*Disadvantaged children are welcome to participate in all Populus systems and will be viewed as wholly equal and therefore, expected to achieve the same high standards. Due to the "No child left behind" action, classrooms of advanced children have become compromised with severely disabled children. This causes strain on the teachers with the implementation of the Individualistic "salary by grade" system. Therefore severely disadvantaged children's test will be sent to a separate department for review so that the teacher's salary is not affected by such an anomaly. The panel will ensure that a disadvantaged child may only pass on to the next grade when that grade is duly earned. Furthermore, due to the fact that public education is paid for by tax dollars, no child may stay in school for more than 16 years plus 2 grace years. It is therefore probable that a severely disadvantaged child be held in the second grade for 16 years, being that lowering the standards to accommodate one's disadvantage directly thwarts the doctrine of equality.

Lastly, it must be made clear that the Individualists erect no laws against private schools or what they may teach. It is simply hoped they can match the effectiveness of the noble Individualistic education methods. Furthermore, any education of the masses can be used for control, the Individualistic teachings are thus distinguished by avidly teaching independence and corruption awareness amongst the traditional types of classes to negate the possibility of such control.

Child Psychology

The diabolical practice of child psychology must be briefly mentioned here. A child's psychological makeup is not developed enough to 1. be analyzed 2. develop a psychosis 3. be tampered with. Child psychologists hurt children far more often than not, because they have forgotten what it is like to be a freethinking, imaginative child, filled with boundless creative energy (just as their Creator). Thus in their dull, ignorant and blind view of life, enslaven to their soulless modern teachings, they force a child to grow just as dull as they are. Thus the children grow into adulthood shackling their free minds and spirits to melancholy, whereat a psychosis is sure to develop as they are made fit to be pacified slaves as opposed to vibrant free thinkers. It is the child psychologist who has the psychosis – one that believes children have mental problems, when the children do not fit into their belief of what is the "right" way to think and act. Most likely one of this profession had no vivid and vibrant childhood because of being raised in the empty and restricted world of the need suppliers.

Furthermore, Attention Deficit Disorder is not a disorder, it is a product of today's lame and pointless society which creates no desire or incentive for children to pay attention to its senselessness. A soul finds interest in the pursuit of its creator and in activities mimicking its creator, thus it must create and seek, all else is empty and futile, just as is the entire present world. Instead of these simple facts being seen by the supposed "learned" these children simply become guinea pigs and income to the pharmaceutical industry, as they are drugged at a stage of rapid cell growth, with amphetamines such as Adderall and Ritalin. All the while the brilliant newscasters wonder why such chaos and murder exists in the schools.

2. COMMUNICATION

Privatized media groups have become too large and influential, rarely for the good and advancement of the society. These groups are owned and/or influenced either directly or indirectly by corporations, mostly to advocate their sales. No different than much of modern journalism and marketing which has mutated from an informing mechanism to a belief mechanism. Instead of informing the people, the people are led to believe misinformation, half truths, or opinions, as truth. Over time, practices as these assist the compounding of the ignorance of the masses instead of enlightening them, whether done intentionally or not.

The Individualist highly respects the freedom of speech and does not intend to dismantle or regulate these mostly corrupt organizations who take pleasure in deceiving and misleading there fellow brethren 24 hours a day. On the contrary, The People's Media will be erected as a dynamic communication system paid for by a small percentage of the Union's annual collected tax. Completely free and equally owned and governed by each member of the union.

It shall begin as a fully public paper, first on the Internet, and if votes agree, to paper also (for those without Internet access). Half of the paper will have available open columns, where, on a first come first serve basis, the people's documents will be published and express their unedited social opinions (save vulgarity) in topics chosen by the writer, from law to art, government to science. This conglomeration of multiple perspectives, stances and beliefs will negate any possibility for bias in any subject.

As opposed to written media, broadcast media has also been perverted. In the present world there exists an over abundance of aimless RF communication, a noise. Encouraging the ability to speak of meaningless and non-constructive topics, a waste of time and energy for both parties and the system utilized to allow such mindless activity initially. 60% of all teenagers now have cell phones, 66% of all cell phone communication is mere gossip. Less than 15% of cable and radio stations are educational. (Talk shows are not included as educational due to their frequently bias content, bordering on propaganda).

The Individualist creates a more meaningful and constructive broadcasting system as The Populus Media grows from a newspaper. It will be a Public broadcasting system similar to the existing public broadcasting system in the US, except that it will be funded with a small amount of tax money, therefore it will be owned equally by each individual of the Union whose votes and desires shall control its every action. It aims at the highest quality and method of information transfer to enlighten all of its viewers most efficiently. With superior teaching of unrestricted knowledge, great attention shall be drawn to it, lessening the use of privately funded channels that teach little or nothing, and are constantly interrupted with materialistic ads.

In its early stages the Populus Media will broadcast a weekly program12 hours long twice a day. Each day of the week the entire program moves 1 hour forward. Each week the entire program is changed. Thus any citizen of the populace should be able to find the information they desire at the time they desire it, if not watch all 12 hours of programming. This initial channel shall present detailed practical knowledge taught rapidly and efficiently, as opposed to the supposed learning channels that use up an hour to describe something that could have be expressed in a single paragraph.

A typical program lineup would be similar to this: Hour 1. Science (all types) 2. Art (graphic, literary, theatrical, martial etc.) 3. Languages 4. Practical techniques (Homestead hands on techniques such as foundry work, hand wound and built generators, machining etc.) 5. Philosophy (physical, metaphysical, political to divinity) 6. Self-sustenance 7. Individualistic simplicity (thorough understanding of the importance of maintaining simplicity in Law, society, etc) 8. Mathematics 9. Individualistic philosophy 10. News (local and national) 11. Open (for petitioned broadcasts from any of the Populus, from amateurs to professionals. Initially on a first come, first serve basis until significant growth is achieved, then Populus voting shall determine its content.) 12. Also Open

The Populus Media will eventually extend to having one channel for each of these topics, soon growing to a complete college level course per channel. The Populus Media will be assisted in growth by the Large Entity and Excess Land Taxes which will cause large communication companies to raise their bills or increase the length of commercial breaks to cover the cost of these taxes. This will cause their customers to utilize The Free Populus Media more frequently and abandon paid programming. This loss of customers will cause communication companies to sell off their assets. The Populus Media will then grow by buying all of this discounted, already erected broadcasting equipment. Those companies remaining in private communication, to survive and compete with the practically free (considering it comes from a small tax allocation) Populus Media, will necessarily be of profound skill and innovation thus being a great benefit to their users. The Populus Media radio programs will be organized in much the same way. The amount and type of music, programming, and open public spots etc. will all be decided by the Populus.

When of sufficient size the Populus media will begin a cellular phone service. All phones will be bought at cost by the user. The service issued will be a flat amount of minutes per month, useable at anytime, with calls timed in ten-second increments. There will be a fee for this service initially, but as it grows to the proper size, it will become totally free (save for the initial phone purchases and necessary tax allocations). Each user will be responsible to purchase one's own phone and will be issued a reasonable amount of minutes decided upon by the Union, such as 150 minutes per month. Upon reaching the maximum there is no overage, the connection is simply denied, (one would pay for amounts over this initial equal allocation). This will pressure the existing cellular companies with the same forces which pressured the broadcasters, and in the same way the Populus Cellular system will grow. With a large base of phone and cable systems, the Populus Media will ensure a totally free Internet (and ideally, fully wireless) for the distribution of its free media and for the free use of all of the Union

As can be seen, Individualism focuses great energy to keep all informed of *All*. Those who say that this is unnecessary refuse to see that the smallest amount of ill informed people, and therefore ignorant people, is a seed for the propagation of ignorance which is the adversary of efficient progress, and the base element of subjugation.

---

* The Populus media will endeavor to grow to the point where it may allocate its money to mass produce, "efficiency computers" which are the very basics of a computer able to get on line and communicate, and sell them to the people lacking the ability to get online at cost.

Dominating Corporations of Media

The elite: Time Warner (formerly AOL-Time Warner-Turner -- 2004 U.S. media revenue, $37 billion -- January 2000 merger with AOL recently approved worth $178 billion. Total corporate worth: $350 billion. Also directly connected to Comcast (see below) and Liberty Media Group, which also owns 3% of Vivendi (see NBC below) and has holdings in 7 of the top 100 media companies; as of late 2003 was talking with EMI about combining music divisions -- worldwide Time Warner's revenue was $39.5 billion

Viacom (2004 U.S. media revenue, $21.4 billion -- separated from CBS into two companies beginning in 2006 after years of being combined. CBS was formerly held by Westinghouse.)

Comcast -- linked to AT&T, by a $72 billion merger (2004 U.S. media revenue, $20.1 billion -- owns E! Network, part of QVC and Golf Channel, Comcast Cable Systems, and linked to Liberty Media Corp. (not a media company but investors in media companies such as Time Warner) and owns Philadelphia 76ers and Flyers.

Disney/ABC-Cap Cities (2004 U.S. media revenue, $17.4 billion -- possibly being acquired by Comcast in a $54 billion merger, Disney is also directly connected to AT&T's Liberty Media Group -- it has 10 TV stations)

NBC Universal (GE) (2004 U.S. media revenue, $12.4 billion -- NBC recently acquired Vivendi (French owner owner of Universal, whic owns USA network and is huge into music and theme parks and also holds 26.8 million shares in Time-Warner) -- GE has 44 TV stations. It is also into areas such as aircraft engines, lighting, plastics, medical systems, nuclear fuel services, satellite, electrical distribution). GE's worldwide revenue was $134.1 billion before 2003.

News Corporation (2003 media revenue, $11.4 billion -- Rupert Murdoch controlled corporation holding Fox TV, MySpace.com and into books, cable, books and magazines around the world, is also directly connected to Echostar (owner of DISH satellite network) and Gemstar (owner of TV Guide) -- News Corp. worldwide revenue for 2003 was $19.2 billion -- it has 37 TV stations

DirecTV (2004 U.S. media revenue, $9.7 billion -- owned by General Motors Corp.

Cox Enterprises (2004 U.S. media revenue, $8.5 billion -- into newspapers, TV (owns 16 stations), cable, etc.)

EchoStar Communications Corp. (2004 U.S. media revenue, $6.6 billion

Clear Channel Communications (2004 U.S. media revenue, $6.5 billion -- nation's largest radio owner, also holding TV stations -- including Bellingham's KVOS and other media)

Advance Publications (2004 U.S. media revenue, $6.4 billion -- owner of Parade magazine, Conde Naste's 17 magazines (such as Vogue, Esquire, etc.) and 25 newspapers, and linked to Cox. Enterprises

Gannett (2004 U.S. media revenue, $5.7 billion -- owns USA today and around 90 daily newspapers, along with TV stations (21 of them), cable, billboard, etc.)

Tribune Co. (2004 U.S. media revenue, $5.5 billion) -- owns 30 TV stations, 15 newspapers, including the LA Times and Chicago Tribune, and has holdings in radio and cable and owns the Chicao Cubs

Bertelsmann (German corporation holding books, magazines, music, multimedia and broadcast in Europe -- $15 billion -- as of late 2003 was combining music divisions with Sony)

Six parent firms -- General Electric (NBC Universal), Viacom, Disney, Bertlesmann, Time Warner, News Corp. -- (ordered on annual media revenues) have more of such revenue than the next 20 firms combined -- Ben Bagdikian, The Media Monopoly, 6th ed. In the 7th edition, Bagdikian lists Time Warner, Disney, News Corporation, Viacom and Bertelsmann as the "Big 5."

Above list courtesy of Mr. Tim Pilgrim www.hope.journ.wwu.edu/tpilgrim

3. ENTERTAINMENT

The Individualists do not wish to control people's choices of entertainment, just enlighten them to the propaganda of mass entertainment. Entertainment only exists because the one in need of entertainment has no constructive activities in which to engage one's mind and abilities for the progress of oneself and mankind. However a small degree of entertainment is acceptable, but look at the scale of it today. It has become a focal point, a titanic 1.5 Trillion-dollar industry. As you have seen above, most media, the main outlet of entertainment, is controlled by a handful of multi billion dollar groups. The control lies in what is allowed to be seen and what is not. Rarely any details of practical knowledge are made apparent and the over all nature is usually of low moral and intellectual character and it is getting progressively worse. Such as much of present day music, broadcast programming, and even spectator sports. All the result of art and action produced by the desire of material gain instead of being produced by the inspiration and love of the act itself, thus it is hollow. Be aware that it can easily be used to distract, and subtly guide opinions, understanding, beliefs, and acceptance of the same while drawing one away from sources that can bestow truth.

In the society of the Individualist entertainment will naturally decrease as the Individualist has his time occupied by much more lofty and meaningful practices than that of the present day world. When he would desire entertainment it would be appreciation of true artists expressing their love for their art. The Individualist sees clearly the priceless value of time and very few of them will waste this time for "entertainment" or even for material gain. Most Individualists will find an overwhelming amount to learn, practice, and create that they will not seek to waste time, being that they are entertained to the highest in the pursuit of their own works.

Spectator Sports

The Individualists witness the countless numbers of people watching someone else play a game, as opposed to playing the game themselves, and persons who, ingeniously, have every statistic, player and rule memorized but know nothing of any knowledge that would make one self sufficient. The Individualists are saddened by such a waste of time and powerful intellectual capacity. Ideally they would dismantle and restructured Spectator Sports altogether. However, they refuse to interfere with free enterprise, yet aim to educate its followers as to how beguiled they are.

A great portion of the sports industry is in frequent violation of anti-trust laws, which are laws designed to prevent monopoly and conspiracy. Too often the courts rule in favor of the sports industry allowing the continuance of such violations. Such closed markets cause the consumer to bare an unwarranted burden in the form of spiked ticket prices and other associated inflated expenses.

Ideally the Individualists would bust such trusts and cap all salaries at two times the mean average of the salary of the nation. If anything the pioneering scientists, places of learning and instruction etc. should be paid millions of dollars per year for the advancement of evolution. (In all due respect to the athletes and their talent in their game.) But, think of how much free teaching could be given to those in need, by utilizing the inexpensive Individualistic methods, with all of these millions.

These salaries have gotten out of hand, and encourage school children to do less thinking because of the amount of money that lies in games as an occupation. All of these monies could be utilized for far more lofty goals and necessary projects for the people, and not simply thrown away into deep private pockets. Teams should be owned by the community as well as all of the facilities. All profits beyond operation and maintenance fees are either returned equally to the individuals of that community or put towards a community project. If the players win the championship, they are entitled to 15% of the entire pool (of each locality/state involved) before it is returned to the Populus. Being that all stadiums are paid for by the tax payers money, thus owned by the Populus, all private entities must pay a fee for stadium use which is also returned directly to the people. However, these are merely suggestions, the people are fully entitled to throw away their time and money. It is for this very reason that private commercial gambling is completely legal in the Individualist society, yet subject to large entity and excess land taxes as all other business.

IV. POPULUS HOMESTEAD MANAGEMENT CENTER (PHMC)

This department is the workhorse of the four departments. As the above departments are mostly knowledge based, the PHMC is where that knowledge and will of the people gets crystallized into reality, physically building the body of the society. Composed of various facilities and services, from mines, to farms, utilities to highways, all means of production and distribution will have at least one such PHMC establishment representing, paid for, and directed by the Populus, and employing numerous Populus paid individuals.

A. STRUCTURE OF PHMC

1. POPULUS SERVICES

The types of services performed by the PHMC are too extensive to describe here in detail, however a few are briefly mentioned to convey the general idea. These "services" and "facilities" will often overlap, or be one in the same. Operating costs of services and facilities are had by a specified amount of tax dollars allocated by Populus vote, rendering the products and services generated, able to be given to the people free or at cost.

a. Populus Construction Service

Divided into national, state and local levels, the Populus construction service is the builder of all Populus projects within the nation, from houses, highways, to Populus facilities. The projects they undertake are not planned in haste as many modern projects. They are reviewed countless times until the entire Populus agrees upon the final plan.

In contrast, most present day developers (develop: to grow or evolve) develop nothing but the destruction of the earth in inharmonious ways. Land is changed in ignorance to higher goals and harmony with nature, for money, not for necessity. Had they these thoughts in mind they would then truly be developers as is the Populus Construction Service. Until then they are merely destroyers.

The use of all Populus forces for Populus projects eliminates the common practice of political favoritism to one private construction company (at times even owned by a politician), causing inflation of prices to the people and ambiguous and misleading itemized expense sheets supposedly detailing the incurred costs of public projects.

b. Populus Electronics

This facility and service produces electronic devises at cost to the Populus at their collective demand, including TV's, radios, computers and cellular phones. The projects undertaken are decided upon by the Populus in detail. "Cost" is not to be mistaken with "cheap", for the Populus workers will be well paid which will be reflected in the price. However they will also be highly skilled, increasing efficiency, also reflected in the price. As well as all materials used will be had at cost from Populus mills, also reflected in price, causing an inexpensive end product, made by the people, for the people. Obviously no profit is placed on Populus products and services because the profit would simply be returned equally to the people, creating a pointless step.

c. Populus Militia Industry

It is illegal for any private company to have their products used in war. The reason is because one who would profit by selling one's product in times of war, for example munitions, would therefore be a supporter of war. This not to say that a private company cannot produce war-related items, such as weapons and machines, it simply cannot sell them to the Populus militia. Therefore their products must be sold to private interests, and at risk of treason, those interests may not be foreign. Such individuals wishing foreign war customers are more than welcome to move to their customer's country and establish a prosperous business there.

As such the Populus Militia Industry's factories, plants and mills, are erected to build all tools of war preventing private interests from coercing a nation to war for private profit. Their strategic focus will be upon homeland defense as a neutral nation. Unlike today's active invasion and patrolling of foreign nations being defined as "defense".

d. Populus Utilities

All utilities are owned equally by the local Populus, no privatized utilities are allowed. This system will not be a monopoly because every single citizen is equally a part owner. A localized service upon which people depend upon cannot be privatized because it opens the door for exploitation, captured markets and price gouging. Each utility's actions are directed by the Populus. All remaining poles and lines will be strictly Populus property. Any other way 1. allows for anyone to place poles and run conduit wherever they desire, and 2. disallows anyone to place poles and run conduit because all the property has been monopolized by another private entity.

Nearly all personal electricity is to be generated on site and supplemented with biofuels, if necessary, until efficiency is achieved. A large portion of the electrical transmission grid shall be dismantled. The towers and wires removed from the sky and wisely recycled. All remaining transmission and communication lines must be below ground in an underground conduit system owned by the Populus.

Water shall also be mostly generated on site with wells and rain collection devises and methods, coupled with electric distillers. A substantial amount of sanitary waste shall also be processed onsite by advanced means. The operating cost of any remaining utility is divided equally by the amount of people receiving service, with the people paying proportionately for their consumption amounts.

Natural gas will be slowly phased out. All Populus phone and Internet service shall focus upon achieving completely wireless systems. Private phone and cable companies must use Populus line, or pull their wire through Populus conduit, renting the line and space.

With a central point of generation of any utility, in times of war, one bomb could deprive an entire city of a utility. Self-generation keeps all in supply in times of war. This in itself is an immunity to the ever rising threat of "terrorism" which is most likely simply small groups paid by the need suppliers to justify more spending. (Need to sell security technology? Blow something up. Need more resources to exploit? Deem a nation as a terrorist capital so the people don't mind conquering it. Need the support of allies? A small thousand-dollar car bomb in their country will do the trick.) The Individualist is immune to terrorism by self-generation and through detailed knowledge of military defense of the self and of the homestead, armed and unarmed.

e. Regional Environmental Management Authority (REMA)

REMA is the DEP and EPA both purged and combined. It fulfills all of the same duties yet is strictly directed by the Populus. A mere 200 years ago man could drink his fill from any stream, now he can drink from none. REMA shall begin ardent campaigns of reestablishing mans harmony with nature as well as maintaining it. It works in connection with the Populus Construction Service conducting general maintenance of all lands and Populus properties, federal, state and local.

2. POPULUS FACILITIES

Similar to the previous section, the complete description of facilities to be erected is too extensive to present in this work, however a few are briefly mentioned to convey the general idea. All erected Populus facilities are agreed upon by the Populus direct democracy. They will be constantly monitored the entire time they are operational by the GEP, who shall report clearly to LAFKI, so that the reports may be read by all the people, who may, at any time, demand more detailed information. The itemized breakdown of the cost of each facility's construction, daily operational expenses, and returns to the people, (products, services and or profits) will be placed upon a plaque at the facility in clear view of all. Thus, this shows the exact amounts, and reasons, of tax money expenditures or returns generated by the facility.

a. Populus Conversion Facilities

With the implementation of Individualism, all existing devises utilizing fossil fuels must be converted to a renewable energy source within five years. Therefore, the Populus Conversion Facilities will be one of the most utilized mechanisms in the move towards a fully electric society. These facilities will be located near hydroelectric power plants, thus having the capability to make powerful magnets and batteries with these high voltages. The magnets will be used in Populus electric motors and generators of all sizes, assembled at these facilities. These facilities will also convert all internal combustion engines into fully electric vehicles. Recycling the engines for metal to be used for more electric motors, wound with the copper salvaged from the dismantled electric grid. All products and services of these facilities are given at cost to the Populus (payable by energy certificates, allowing various methods to pay), or by loan or a Laborforce trade.

b. Populus Equipment

Each locality will have a warehouse of Populus purchased equipment, from power tools, tractors and attachments, construction equipment, to cars, trucks and recreational vehicles. Each piece of equipment, and its rental price, was agreed upon by the locality prior to its purchase. Any profits made by this facility will be either returned equally to the locality or used for the purchase of additional equipment, dependant upon that locality's vote.

c. Populus Fabrication Shops

These shops are open on a first come first serve basis, having a sign-up list, with a maximum successive time limit per each individual. Taxes pay for the general construction and upkeep of the facility, and the people pay individually for the length of time using the facility. The price of that time is decided upon by the locality. As with any Populus facility, people who do not use such a facility may file to be exempt from its taxes, but then may not use the facility. (However this would be unwise, for this tax would amount to a very tiny amount of money when divided over all of the people, and after the initial construction, facilities as this will most likely be self sustaining, gaining their upkeep from their use and generating a yearly profit, returned to the people.) Any profit is returned evenly to the contributing people of that locality. The equipment includes, lathes, drill presses, band saws, welders, milling machines, sheet and pipe bending equipment, vacuum forming machines, injection molding machines etc. This gives access to the commoner to use such machines for a project of one's desire, whether professional or hobbyist. LAFKI instructional classes will be available there to instruct the inexperienced on the proper use of such equipment.

d. Populus Farmlands

The Populus farmlands include agricultural farms, fisheries and animal ranges, as well as solar and wind farms, all erected at that locality's desires. The agricultural farms grow food for the resource reserve. If it is not used in a certain amount of time it is converted to fuel (when able) or another form for storage. The wind and solar farms will have a small, on site, Populus Resource Reserve office, where the people can charge any type of battery, from home storage batteries to fully electric vehicles. Any surplus of energy generated there is either converted into hydrogen (by water electrolysis) or stored in large deep cell battery banks for future use.

e. Populus Laboratories

These various laboratories of all of the sciences, are directed by the Populus for their interest, curiosity, and necessity, as opposed for material gain at the expense of ignoring and hiding cures, or creating toxins and titling them as medicines, as do the perverted modern labs. They will be unhindered by corporate directives, and restrictive funding requirements, allowing the scientists to truly pursue their love and the interest of humanity, causing science to evolve at an incredible rate.

f. Populus Seed Bank

This facility supplies the people with every type of seed that they may need. They will not supply the modern, genetically modified seeds which produce seedless plants causing the people to have to buy the seeds every year. On the contrary, they will be perfectly natural seeds, so that if reared correctly, the grower will have an endless supply of seed. Seeds will include fruits, vegetables, trees, tobaccos, teas and coffees, to tropical plants for those with greenhouses. Freeing anyone from having to buy such products.

g. Populus Vehicle Works

The Populus Vehicles will be designed as a national, state and local cooperative project. The Nation will most likely agree on a general design, while the localities will come up with customized versions. Each car will thus reflect the unique desires of that locality. They will be fully electric vehicles, sold at cost to the people, utilizing materials from all Populus facilities, mills, mines, etc. Built for the people, by the people, as it always has been, save that the private profits have been removed, as well as usury, resulting in a very inexpensive end product. Yet the comradery formed in such a cooperative project, by highly educated people, will also cause that vehicle to be of substantial high quality. This is not to say that the Nation will only make a single car, as the system grows they will produce, trucks, motorcycles, and all other vehicles by the same cooperative procedure.

B. EXECUTIVE DEPARTMENTS ASSIMILATED

1. DEPARTMENT OF AGRICULTURE (USDA)

a. Center for Nutrition Policy and Promotion

DISBANDED all of the knowledge that this center contains is far surpassed by that which will be contained within LAFKI. Furthermore LAFKI's overhauls in education will promote dietary awareness far more effectively, with virtually no necessary funding.

b. Cooperative State Research, Education and Extension Service

DISBANDED Grants are not given for any reason by the Populus. All monies go to tasks chosen directly by the people, not by supposed "representatives" with personal motives.

c. Farm Service Agency

DISBANDED no subsidies are given to anyone for any reason in the Individualistic society.

d. Food and Nutrition Service

DISBANDED As discussed on page 104 there is no welfare, such as food stamps, of any form in the Individualistic society. Regardless if those claiming need are wealthy corporations or poor slaves.

e. Marketing and Regulatory Programs

DISBANDED The taxpayers money will not go towards "marketing" of privately produced foods at home or in foreign nations. Such private entities can market themselves on their own dollar. Further more regulations are healthy and promote safety, but can also be used as tools to leverage unfair advantage by the ones wielding the enforcing power if they have interests (or competition) in a business covered by said regulations. They can ease the enforcement upon their self and colleagues while impairing the competition. Thus the GEP (controlled by the people) is responsible for all regulation compliance and informing the people thereof. They cannot enforce regulations directly, but may suspend one's activities if deemed suspect until judged by the people.

f. Natural Resources Conservation Service

DISBANDED Concerned only with water and soil instead of oil, coal, and natural gas, which are dwindling by the second, it is an arm of the chemical industry pushing fertilizers. It is also another "regulatory" tool used to leverage the few and disadvantage others. Possibly started with good intent, the few grams of righteousness left within it shall be salvaged by the PHMC and applied logically and efficiently within the refined REMA.

g. Office of Community Development

DISBANDED Grants are not given for any reason by the Populus. All monies go to tasks chosen directly by the people, for the people, never for private interests, the results thus being owned wholly by the people. Any development is discussed in detail by the entire locality and agreed upon before any development of any kind takes place. Too often "development" is undertaken strictly for profit with all higher ideas unconsidered.

h. Research, Education and Economics

DISBANDED Much of this department is redundancy. Specific applications of science to industry will be decided by the people not by the few. Again the people's tax dollars will not be used for marketing or grants to private entities.

i. Risk Management Agency

DISBANDED There shall be no insurance on crops, a form of subsidy. Furthermore the people's tax dollars will not be spent on marketing solutions for private entities. All "risk management" is to be conducted by the private producer with one's own funds, not the people's funds. All information to assist such private entities will be researched by GEP and posted at LAFKI for the use of all. Lastly, this agency's regulatory and compliance powers can be used to leverage unfair advantage.

j. Rural Development

DISBANDED Grants are not given for any reason by the Populus. All monies go to tasks chosen directly by the people for the people, never for private or select interests, the results being owned wholly by the people. Too often this 16 Billion in programs goes to assist massive corporate farms with ties to government officials. Little of these funds make it to the common farmer, which is just enough to conceal the extent of this racket. This is why the Individualists stress the disbandment of all grants and subsidies bar none.

k. 1. Rural Business-Cooperative Service, 2. Rural Housing Service, 3. Rural Utilities Service

DISBANDED Grants are not given for any reason by the Populus. All monies go to tasks chosen directly by the people for the people never for private or select interests, the results being owned wholly by the people.

l. Economic Research Service

ASSIMILATED into the GEP as a research branch and its information posted at LAFKI. The economy will be monitored by the people, advised by the GEP and LAFKI.

m. Food Safety and Inspection Service

ASSIMILATED Refined and given more responsibility to make sure labels are not ambiguous and food is actually safe.

n. Foreign Agricultural Service

ASSIMILATED There will be no food aid to foreign nations when we spend tax money to give out food stamps in our own nation. Foreign imports and exports of food will be overseen, however it will be encouraged to cease these activities and be fully self-sufficient. If such is realized, at the direction of the Populus, this department will be disbanded.

o. Forest Service

ASSIMILATED into the general duty of the PHMC

p. Grain Inspection, Packers and Stockyards Administration

ASSIMILATED into the GEP as a research branch and its information posted at LAFKI

q. National Agricultural Statistics Service

ASSIMILATED into the GEP as a research branch and its information posted at LAFKI

2. DEPARTMENT OF COMMERCE (DOC)

It is no department's right to allow or restrict the flow of goods, or the way they are packed or shipped (provided the common sense of safety is present). Only the producer is concerned with the most advantageous method. The department of commerce's regulatory powers are often used as leveraging tools by those in the department or in bed with it. The producer of the best goods should be allowed to thrive naturally, not because of payoffs. Their "promotion" of US goods is nothing but the exploitation of every last market of the world with the products of the few, paid for with tax dollars of the people who see no share of that profit.

a. Economic Development Administration

DISBANDED Grants are not given for any reason by the Populus. All monies go to tasks chosen directly by the people for the people never for private or select interests, the results being owned wholly by the people.

b. Minority Business Development Agency

DISBANDED Grants are not given for any reason by the Populus. All monies go to tasks chosen directly by the people for the people never for private or select interests, the results being owned wholly by the people. Any agency, policy, etc, that affects or benefits one group and not another is bias and thus unequal. Therefore to maintain Individualistic true equality, this department is disbanded but its spirit, the desire to educate, lives on in the unrestricted knowledge and teachings of LAFKI.

c. National Telecommunications & Information Administration

DISBANDED Grants are not given for any reason by the Populus. All moneys go to tasks chosen directly by the people for the people never for private or select interests, the results being owned wholly by the people. Contracts are not awarded to private entities, all needed projects will be erected by the PHMC at the direction of the people who will equally own the final product.

d. Bureau of Economic Analysis (BEA)

ASSIMILATED into the GEP as a research branch and its information posted at LAFKI

e. Bureau of Industry and Security (formerly Export Administration)

ASSIMILATED into the general operation of the PHMC until full neutrality and self sufficiency is realized.

f. Bureau of the Census

ASSIMILATED into the GEP as a research branch and its information posted at LAFKI. Its activities shall be directed strictly by the Populus.

g. National Institute of Standards & Technology (NIST)

ASSIMILATED into the GEP as a research branch and its information posted at LAFKI. All funding to private sectors shall be eliminated. All products, physical or intellectual, are now owned equally by the people, who are also the directors of its research activities.

h. Economics & Statistics Administration

ASSIMILATED into the GEP as a research branch and its information posted at LAFKI

i. International Trade Administration (ITA)

ASSIMILATED into the duties of PHMC. It shall be reviewed and refined, its practice of promoting foreign trade reversed to discouraging foreign trade. When true neutrality and self-sufficiency is realized, this department is disbanded.

j. National Marine Fisheries

ASSIMILATED as a function of PHMC

k. National Oceanic & Atmospheric Administration (NOAA)

ASSIMILATED as part of PHMC

l. National Technical Information Service

ASSIMILATED into LAFKI and all of its information made free, as opposed to presently having to buy its information which the taxpayers paid to have them collect.

m. Office of Technology Policy

ASSIMILATED into LAFKI

n. Patent & Trademark Office

ASSIMILATED into LAFKI

o. Technology Administration

ASSIMILATED into LAFKI all technical information and training will be given free to all citizens.

p. National Weather Service

MAINTAINED as part of the PHMC

3. DEPARTMENT OF DEFENSE (DOD)

This entire department will be forced by the people, who compose and fund it, to stay true to its title of DEFENSE. All foreign activities and support are stopped, all forces brought back to the continental US. Strict neutrality is declared and all alliances are severed in a peaceful and respectful manner. No US soldier will be sent to foreign soil for any reason. All combat will be fought on US soil if the enemy can get to it. Navies and air force will be no more than 500 miles from the US coast at all times. The policy is Strictly Defense.

a. Office of the Secretary of Defense (OSD)

ASSIMILATED into the operations of PHMC. The secretary shall execute the commands of the people, none other.

b. Air Force

Academy, Band, Combat Command, Direct Reporting Units, Education and Training Command, Field Operating Agencies, Materiel Command, Mobility Command, National Guard, Pacific Air Forces, Recruiting, Reserve Command, ROTC (Reserve Officer Training Corps), Space Command, Special Ops Command, U.S. Air Forces in Europe
MAINTAINED as part of the PHMC composed of the people

c. Army

Bands, Corps of Engineers, Criminal Investigation Command, Europe Command, Forces Command, Intelligence and Security Command, Materiel Command, Medical Command, Military District of Washington, National Guard, Pacific Command, Recruiting, Space and Missile Defense Command, Special Operations Command, Surface Deployment and Distribution Command, Training and Doctrine Command, U.S. Army South, U.S. Military Academy, West Point
MAINTAINED as part of the PHMC composed of the people

d. Navy

Air Systems Command, Atlantic Fleet Forces Command, Band, Education and Training Command, Facilities Engineering Command, Forces Central Command, **Marines**, Medicine and Surgery, Meteorology and Oceanography Command, Military Sealift Command, Naval Academy, Naval Installations, Naval Network and Space Operations Command, Naval Network Warfare Command, Naval Observatory, Operational Test and Evaluation Forces, Pacific Fleet Forces Command, Personnel Command, Recruiting, Reserve, Safety Center, Space and Naval Warfare Systems Command , Special Warfare Command , Supply Systems Command , U.S. Naval Forces Europe
MAINTAINED as part of the PHMC composed of the people

e. Joint Chiefs of Staff

MAINTAINED as part of PHMC

f. Combatant Commands

Central Command (CENTCOM), European Command, Joint Forces Command, Northern Command, Pacific Command, Southern Command, Special Forces Operations Command, Strategic Command, Transportation Command
ASSIMILATED these divisions will be brought back to the continental US. A small percentage may remain in their respective foreign nation for intelligence purposes as directed by the people. A Policy of strict neutrality and Defense is adopted and strategies erected from those principles. With the power of these concentrated forces and soon larger army (when mandatory two-year service is implemented) the US will be impenetrable.

g. Inspector General

ASSIMILATED into the GEP

h. Defense Agencies

i. Defense Contract Audit Agency (DCAA)
DISBANDED there are no contracts given to private entities. All projects will be built by the PHMC at the people's direction and equally owned by all citizens.

ii. Defense Contract Management Agency
DISBANDED there are no contracts given to private entities. All projects will be built by the PHMC at the people's direction and equally owned by all citizens.

iii. Defense Security Cooperation Agency (DSCA)
DISBANDED The Populus does not give contracts to private entities and does not assist foreign nations in any military applications from weapons systems to training and counsel with the tax payer's money. It is advised that private entities not be allowed to sell weapons systems to foreign nations if it was built or assembled by US resources. Such entities are welcome to erect a plant in said foreign nation on their own funding.

iv. Defense Logistics Agency (DLA)
ASSIMILATED all contracts will be built by PHMC at the people's direction.

v. Defense Security Service (DSS)
ASSIMILATED no division shall have a permanent head, as this one. All Populus offices will cycle all heads to avoid corruption. Information in a nation whose collection was paid for by the people is property of the people. There thus can be no restrictions, save in the time of true defensive war, and then a policy of a six-month delay should be substantial.

vi. National Geospatial-Intelligence Agency
ASSIMILATED into the GEP

vii. Defense Advanced Research Projects Agency (DARPA)

MAINTAINED policy shifted towards neutrality and defense, renewable energy power, and fully electric vehicles.

viii. Defense Commissary Agency

MAINTAINED this division's role will expand ten fold with the mandatory two-year service plan.

ix. National Security Agency (NSA)

MAINTAINED Information in a nation whose collection was paid for by the people is property of the people. There thus can be no restrictions, save in the time of true defensive war, and then a policy of a six-month delay should be substantial.

x +. Pentagon Force Protection Agency - Defense Finance and Accounting Service (DFAS) - Defense Information Systems Agency (DISA) - Defense Intelligence Agency (DIA) - Defense Legal Services Agency- Defense Threat Reduction Agency (DTRA) - Missile Defense Agency (MDA)

MAINTAINED all relatively unaltered

i. Field Activities

i. American Forces Information Service

ASSIMILATED into LAFKI as part of the People's Media

ii. Defense Technical Information Center

ASSIMILATED into LAFKI under the 6M delay when applicable.

iii. Economic Adjustment Office

ASSIMILATED into the general duties of the PHMC.

iv. DoD Education

ASSIMILATED into the basic functions of LAFKI 's free education system, being that all citizens will be military families.

v. Human Resources

ASSIMILATED into the general function of the PHMC

vi. TRICARE Management

ASSIMILATED into the Populus health system. All current beneficiaries are grandfathered into their policy, no new policies shall be excepted. This department is disbanded upon the expiration of the final recipient.

vii. Washington Headquarters Services

ASSIMILATED all 2000 contract employees are disbanded and rehired as employees of the PHMC if necessary.

viii. Prisoner of War/Missing Personnel Office

MAINTAINED

j. Joint Service Schools

1. Defense Acquisition University, 2. Defense resource management, 3. Joint Military Intelligence College,
4. National Defense University, 5. Uniformed Services University of the Health Sciences
ASSIMILATED into the Militia colleges of LAFKI

4. DEPARTMENT OF ENERGY (DOE)

a. Fossil Energy

DISBANDED "Ensuring that we can continue to rely on clean, affordable energy from our traditional fuel resources is the primary mission of DOE's Office of Fossil Energy." Obviously they plainly admit that they have no intention of eliminating fossil fuel use and going to fully renewable energies, regardless of the cost. They are thus immediately disbanded as a threat to mankind and the planet.

b. Federal Energy Regulatory Commission

DISBANDED All large energy facilities will be equally owned by the Populus and their "regulation" a predetermined transmission value based upon operating cost. The amount of large energy facilities in the Individualistic society is reduced due to the amount of self-generation. Only the Populus shall grant permissions to build facilities, not an independent agency, which is funded by charging those it regulates.

c. Civilian Radioactive Waste Management

ASSIMILATED The need for nuclear power is lessened with Individualistic self-generation of energy, thus the production of radioactive wastes is curbed.

d. Energy Efficiency and Renewable Energy

ASSIMILATED This department's name is all that is kept. In stead of producing any real solutions this department spins its wheels and wastes the taxpayer's money. It often hands out millions for audits and "research" to large corporations and universities, whose findings do not become publicly owned even though the public has funded them. This money will be put directly to solutions by the PHMC. One first action being the construction of conversion facilities.

e. Energy Information administration

ASSIMILATED into LAFKI

f. Environmental Management

ASSIMILATED The need for nuclear power is lessened with Individualistic self-generation of energy, thus the production of radioactive wastes is curbed.

g. National Laboratories

ASSIMILATED All laboratories will be strictly monitored by the GEP to avoid instances such as the DOE transporting weapons across country in modified armored 18 wheelers. This has nothing to do with the taxpayer's money spent on energy efficiency. All projects will be directed by the fully aware will of the people.

h. National Nuclear Security Administration

ASSIMILATED However all information placed under the 6M policy when applicable.

i. Nuclear Energy, Science and Technology

ASSIMILATED yet all results are owned equally by the people being that the people funded it, and the people (the tax paying scientists) developed it. At the people's discretion the 6M policy may be applied.

j. Office of Health Safety and Security

ASSIMILATED into the general functions of PHMC

k. Office of Science

ASSIMILATED All projects shall be directed by the people, and all results owned equally by the people being that the people funded it and the people (the tax paying scientists) developed it. The information will thus be immediately published at LAFKI.

l. Office of Scientific and Technical Information (OSTI)

ASSIMILATED into LAFKI. This department makes an attempt at the vision of LAFKI but is disorganized, cumbersome and restrictive. It will be refined and incorporated into the unrestricted LAFKI system.

m. Power Administrations

1. Bonneville Power Administration, 2. Southeastern Power Administration, 3. Southwestern Power Administration, 4. Western Area Power Administration
ASSIMILATED these plants sell electricity to pay operating and infrastructure costs as well as the cost of their initial construction. All of these costs and "debts" will be audited by the GEP. The "debt" (which is owed to the tax payers who funded the project) is divided between each tax paying customer of that locality, generating a dollar figure which is converted into the amount of energy these individuals are given for free, thus repaying the "debt". Then the only costs would be the cost of maintenance divided by collective annual consumption, to give a predicted yearly price per kWh paid by each customer (possibly

amounting to less than half the previous expense). The need for these power administrators will decrease as self-generation becomes prevalent. All sites not hydropower will be dismantled. Any overages of electricity will cause Populus facilities to be built near such plants, to smelt ores, charge batteries and magnets, etc.

n. Office of Administration

MAINTAINED

6. DEPARTMENT OF HOUSING AND URBAN DEVELOPMENT (HUD)

a. Community Planning and Development

DISBANDED No group is favored in the Individualistic society. Community planning and development will be directed by the people's wishes. Those who are not self sufficient and jobless may join a Laborhood to learn such skills.

b. Government National Mortgage Association (Ginnie Mae)

DISBANDED The people's money will not be used to assist private banks (mortgage lenders) to profit while returning no money to the people. Furthermore the people will no longer take the loss for the privatebank should the debtor default.

c. Multifamily Housing

DISBANDED All necessary government housing projects will be built as Laborhood projects.

d. Office of Fair Housing and Equal Opportunity

DISBANDED Discrimination is common sense in the Individualistic society. There is no need for a department funded on public money to hand out public money to ensure common sense. Too often "fair" and "equal" become bias themselves and only one group ends up benefiting from the funds of the entire group. Enforcement powers of these departments are similarly used to leverage unfair advantages in the name of equality. Private entities have the right to refuse any one for any reason. Conversely, Populus facilities must be equal, and will be constantly monitored by the people due to the networking mechanics of the Individualistic society, thus have no need for such a bias department.

e. Office of Federal Housing Enterprise Oversight

DISBANDED This division openly admits its loyalty to two massive private entities: " OFHEO's mission is to promote housing and a strong national housing finance system by ensuring the safety and soundness of Fannie Mae (Federal National Mortgage Association) and Freddie Mac (Federal Home Loan Mortgage Corporation)." This department is disbanded without delay along with those it protects.

f. Federal National Mortgage Association (fannie Mae) (not actually a department of HUD but will be discussed here)

DISBANDED The second largest US financial institution. It is a *government* founded agency turned private after a 30-year monopoly of the secondary mortgage market, but masks as a public entity due to its "public" investors who are all private entities. With a revenue of $58.3 Billion, it is allowed to sell securities with only half the capital to back it up. This creature was founded on the people's money and should have remained as such, instead it was handed to privates entities, which is the stealing of public assets. It will be returned and disbanded, its assets shall be distributed to more logical and just causes.

g. Federal Home Loan Mortgage Corporation (Freddy Mac) (not a department of HUD but will be discussed here)

DISBANDED Like its twin above it was only created to be a competitor against Fannie Mae. With a $44 billion dollar revenue, this creature will be dismantled just as the privatized banks. Usury in any form is forbidden in the Individualistic society.

h. Office of Healthy Homes and Lead Hazard Control

DISBANDED This is the responsibility of the homeowner not the society.

i. Office of Housing

DISBANDED Supports the "Expanding American Homeownership Act" which should rightly be called the expanding American private bank ownership act". This does nothing more than ensure that every one possible is indebted to a bank. Most likely paying minimum payments thus buying the home two or three times, if they do not default, which merely starts the money making all over again for the bank on that one property, who most likely had less than half the capital to back the loan initially. In the guise of kindness and assistance the people are raped by usury and reduced to a lifetime of indentured servitude.

j. Office of Public and Indian Housing

DISBANDED No assistance other than the Laborhood programs are offered. For elderly and disabled, one of their able-bodied family members may sign on to a Laborhood in their behalf. Benefits to Indians are discussed elsewhere in this paper.

k. Policy Development and Research

DISBANDED Due to the fact that the entirety of HUD has been disbanded, there is no need for policies. All public housing will be handled by the Laborhood program, a joint effort between PHMC and LAFKI.

7. DEPARTMENT OF THE INTERIOR (DOI)

a. Bureau of Indian Affairs (BIA)

DISBANDED This 55.7 million acres of land will not be held in trust by the US *government*, it will be given to these people for decimating their culture. 9 acres per surviving Indian shall be given tax free, complete with a free Laborhood home. Education programs will continue, but will encourage the teaching of their heritage as well.

b. Bureau of Reclamation

ASSIMILATED The distribution of water and power will be lessened with the growth of self-generation. Surplus resources will be utilized to assist the Individualistic goals. Surplus water will be used to generate additional electricity in solar steam towers.

c. Fish & Wildlife Service

ASSIMILATED However, one area dismantled will be the giving of grants (taxpayer money) for international purposes. Such as the 5.8 Million currently proposed.

d. Geological Survey (USGS)

ASSIMILATED into the GEP

e. Mineral Management Service

ASSIMILATED No private entity will be given permission to explore Populus land for resources. All expeditions will be directed by the Populus and conducted by the PHMC, and all resources found will be the property of the Populus. Too often are the oil, gas, and other private resource corporations on public land, and paying no royalties to the people because of the compromised members of the *government* with interests in those businesses.

f. Office of Surface Mining, Reclamation & Enforcement

ASSIMILATED The mining of coal shall be significantly reduced with the fossil fuel tax and increased self-generation. Reclamation operations will continue on the bill of the private entities which have caused the damage. This office will regulate all mining public and private.

g. National Interagency Fire Center - National Park Service - Bureau of Land Management (BLM)

MAINTAINED all relatively unaltered

8. DEPARTMENT OF TRANSPORTATION (DOT)

a. Federal Aviation Administration (FAA)

DISBANDED This division is thoroughly compromised by corporate interests, and is suspect in many disasters, amongst other things. The general functions of this department will be performed by the PHMC, monitored by the GEP.

b. Bureau of Transportation Statistics

ASSIMILATED into the GEP

c. Federal Highway Administration

ASSIMILATED No contracts will be given to private entities, all works will be constructed at the direction of the people by the PHMC.

d. Federal Motor Carrier Safety Administration

ASSIMILATED This policy is altered too often causing the drivers to take the brunt of the punishments for driving faulty company vehicles. The punishments will, henceforth be delivered to the owner of the vehicles.

e. Federal Railroad Administration

ASSIMILATED All activities such as research and "assistance to rail industry" will be strictly for Populus owned rails. No tax payer assistance will be given to private rails.

f. Maritime Administration

ASSIMILATED All ships owned by the Populus will not carry foreign commerce, or domestic commerce to foreign lands. Populus carriers will have usage fees to cover operational costs, all surplus funds are returned equally to the Populus.

g. National Highway Traffic Safety Administration

ASSIMILATED This division's regulatory powers will be revised. Too often they are used to leverage unfair advantage in favor of the massive US auto industry and impede all others, such as very small manufacturers with innovative designs.

h. Pipeline and Hazardous Materials Safety Administration

ASSIMILATED Regulations of this agency will be refined and made more strict, and monitored closely by the GEP.

i. Research and Innovative Technology Administration

ASSIMILATED into the GEP

j. Saint Lawrence Seaway Development Corporation

ASSIMILATED

k. Surface Transportation Board

ASSIMILATED Its regulatory powers will be revised, and its jurisdiction over the rails maintained as the rails are switched to Populus control.

l. Federal Transit Administration

MAINTAINED

C. OTHER DEPARTMENTS ASSIMILATED

a. FCC

DISBANDED Any entity with this much regulatory power can be easily be used as a tool to disadvantage some and assist others. Regulation of any sort will be discussed and voted upon by the Populus alone. As for freedom of speech, violence and indecency, these things cannot be hindered. As terrible as it may sound, once one limits personal freedom in the slightest way, one is no longer in a free state. * (Such limitation can be increased until one cannot speak out about one's government, etc). It is the parents and viewers who are responsible for what they and their children listen to and watch, not the society. The nature of an artist or broadcasting station will be thus clearly seen for its level of evolution, and will be consequently avoided by those seeking less debased activities. Debased artists and stations will therefore only attract the debased, who will be few in number, due to the spread of Individualistic philosophy, thwarting the artists and programming of such natures by common sense, not by the restriction of freedom.

* The argument here is that individualism limits business size. It does not limit business size until 100 people, and then minimally. Collections of people controlled by a private owner are units of power allotted to that one owner. In no way, upon ones own, can one become that powerful without the assistance of many people. Thus the power is unnatural and must be regulated. Personal, or singular power, that is, individual freedom, cannot be limited.

b. EPA

DISBANDED The EPA is out to protect the chemical companies and silence and impede any investigating and/or concerned citizen. Independent investigators and researchers using their own private capital stand no chance against the enormous resources of the chemical giants, or the law firms and *government* agencies protecting them. Often because of being invested in them and/or receiving "contributions" from them.

D. PHMC IMMEDIATE REFORMS

1. MILITARY

The only way a peaceful nation can exist on a planet without a military is if there are no other foreign nations. If a nation, no matter its power, disbands its military in a world with separate nations, even if they are all at peace, it leaves the door wide open for a malignant power to rapidly rise up and lash out at these defenseless nations. It is unwise to assume that man lives in a perfect heaven, and that peace can exist unthreatened. The earth and man are imperfect by nature and thus the peace they achieve will be likewise. Perfection exists only in archetypes such as "heaven". Therefore the Individualist strives for the highest ideal yet maintains realism, understanding the necessity of a military for defense against the unpredictable malice of man.

Even within a peaceful nation with a strictly defensive military, a war can be started simply by the greed of man. The need suppliers love war. Within it, or in preparation for it, armaments and munitions of all types call for an increase in the mining of metals and explosive minerals, skyrocketing the manufacturing of all things, from tanks, radios, to clothing and all other war merchandise. For such profitable reasons they purposely start wars without the care of the loss of lives while their profits are soaring. In war these material things are twice as expensive, yet rapidly destroyed and thus, they need rapidly replaced therefore, for them, war is a perpetual gold mine of consumption and waste. Waste of lives, energy, and resources, for the high profit of the few, who are always eager for another war. Each new territory gained is exploited for its resources, with its men recruited to do battle in the next moneymaking scheme. All the while, the most extreme profit is funneled to the international bankers who are financing all sides.

It is for this reason that only Populus owned facilities may create war machines or supplies, solely at the vote of the entire Populus. No private party will start a war to initiate this cycle of waste for private profit at the expense of the tax dollars and lives of the people. For the same reasoning, all Populus meetings, especially in times of war, are broadcast live and immediately made available at LAFKI.

The Individualistic Union is strictly neutral and claims no allies, for allies have exterior interests. Its military force is constantly a passive defense. Too often the word "defense" is used for an active attacking force far from the US boarders. The Individualistic Union only defends when a force threatens its boarders and it never fights off of its own land, or sends its people from theirs. Its Forces will never be more than 500 miles off of their coast.

The Individualistic armed forces remain the same in organization. However its forces are now made up of all able citizens, with one percent of the population being full time, professional soldiers. Upon high school graduation all individuals serve a mandatory two years in the Populus Militia, with a three-month boot camp, modeled and operated by the US Marine Corps. They are taught how to defend themselves as well as their friends, loved ones, home, and locality, thus the nation. They are taught hand to hand combat, firearms, war strategy, and given a general understanding of the divisions of the armed forces.

The 2nd three-month period shall be instruction in the detailed defense of the homestead and locality as well as familiarization with the war machines of each armed force. In this military protection of the homestead they are shown the value of civilization and social cooperation as opposed to the savagery of dealing with nature on one's own. Each student is made face the wilderness, with the bare essentials, to prove an understanding of the survivalist techniques which they were taught, consequently granting the students clear sight to the appreciation of a society and the ease with which cooperation of mankind (a society) makes life. With this understood they will know why it is their duty to protect such a society, so long as that nation maintains a doctrine of Liberty. Finally the infamous "crucible" finishes their six moths basic training. Upon successful completion of the crucible, they are given an M1 Carbine rifle, engraved with their name and *"omnes homines aut liberi sunt aut servi"* for graduation, theirs to keep for the defense of their homestead.

They are then allowed to pick a military specialization at which they will work on for the remaining 18 months under their chosen branch of service. The next six months will then be instruction on the selected specialization, as well as instruction as to the proceedings around a locality, such as passive policing, Laborforces, and methods of regular training upon return to civilian life. They are then paid for their last 12 months (approximately 500/week) as they practice their duty within the union. The knowledge and teaching in the first 12 month period shall be their pay for the first half of their military training, and the M1 being the reminder of such. Concluding their 24 months of service, they may chose to return home as a reservist, or become a professional soldier.

All such citizens returning home are considered members of the Populus Defenders until the age of 50. Each entire local block rehearses once every two months with their fellow neighborhood, and is visited, twice per year, by an overseeing general to keep all drills, skills, knowledge and awareness at the highest possible level of mastery. This very challenging visit includes a standardized test which each division must pass, or face being sent back, for one week, to basic training for their deficiency.

All Populus Defenders are required to train at local facilities one weekend every three weeks, totaling 17 weekends per year until the age of 30. Thereafter, one weekend every 6 weeks up to the age of 35, and then one weekend every two months up to the age of 45. (Thus those from 35-45 need only train at the neighborhood drills) After age 45 there is no required training until age 50 when one becomes officially retired from the Militia. Wardens reserve the right to detain unfit reservists for a health regime at any time during these training sessions. Furthermore, there is no restriction to train at these sessions more often than required.

Each locality is divided by homesteads and rank of the citizens composing that locality. If the highest ranks are numerous, one individual is chosen to be the block captain. The training drills shall focus mostly on the defense of their particular locality, but are not limited to such. The organization and efficiency of the alert of their locality and preparation for its defense, will be flawless, down to the execution of all strategic maneuvers. Besides the reasons already mentioned and those that are obvious, the Individualist turns practically its entire adult population into this active reserve, or retired soldiers for the following reasons.

"Government" militaries can become the power of an entity separate from the people and thus suppress the people. Else they can become a power in and of themselves, and overthrow the orderly rule to initiate a tyranny. Today's militaries are the tools of corporations, causing war for material wealth, ownership and control. In the past they were the tools of the church, causing wars for spiritual ownership and control, and before that they were the tools of single rulers, kings, emperors, and pharaohs, for their own ambitions in all of the above.

The Individualistic Military shall be a tool of the people for their security in all of the above. It must be composed wholly of the people, bar none. The instant exclusions are made, a division takes root and will grow into exactly what exists today, two groups, "civilian" and "soldier", ignorant of each other, who could be turned against one another. Separation in all of its forms is observed with a watchful eye by the Individualists. Unity, harmony, cannot have separation, else it is not One. Separation immediately causes contending forces. With a common experience a comradery is formed, strengthening the union. The wealthy and the poor, man and woman, all in the same trench under the same stress. All illusions of separation are shattered as each see each other as fellow humans upon Earth to cooperate together to survive. With all people experienced as soldiers each one knows the inner workings of the military and the reason for its necessity to protect the society they love, in the event of malice.

The present day US military is 1,427,000 soldiers or 0.47% of the population. About 13% of the US is elderly (about 39 Million people (+65)), 18% is of age 50-65, 34% are Children, and 2% are mentally retarded and or criminals (some believe it is the entire nation). Leaving 33% of the population to contribute to reserve military duty. Whether male or female, mother with child, disabled, or obese, there is a small contribution from every one, as it is their duty to be an active part of the society and assist its protection and welfare. (Only a few will be excused from local reserve training; pregnant females and the disabled. Yet they must still report and be given suitable light duties and practical knowledge tests)

Approximately 2% of the total Populus, or 6,020,000, are 17-18 years old and will be active in their military induction. Possibly an additional 1% will voluntarily remain in active service becoming professional soldiers. Thus 30% of the Individualist population is a standing reserve army with 3% being active soldiers. Additionally, Approximately one third of the reserves will be dwelling in fortified, strategic homestead structures, a common Individualistic, energy efficient home building method. (see pg 145) This is an active military increase of over 600%. However, unlike the military of the old world, the might is composed of the people thus controlled by the people, not by separate interests.

This possession of all the citizens with military knowledge and weaponry, negates any possibility of authoritarian attempts of control whether by corporations, political corruption, or military coup. It causes neighbors to have elevated respect for one another and a common foundation, thus closer bonds. Additionally it makes for a much safer home, locality, and nation from foreign invasion as well as criminals, being that all potential criminals will be made into cooperative citizens by the bonds of comradery formed with their mandatory two-year training, and that all potential victims are now well armed and well trained.

With this trained populace there is thus, no need for a police force. The active militia members of that locality will be assigned for patrol of their locality. These citizen police stop law being used as a control force, as all will be familiar with the law, from its creation to its execution, including documentation and prosecution. Policing duty is never more than a two-year period, unless volunteered for longer service in the position, and accepted by local Populus vote; this method deters the corruption of police. Police with over four years experience may request to become local wardens. Over eight years experience is required to become a senior warden. The word warden was chosen to remind them of passive policing; to "Ward" off malice, not to Police the citizens.

2. LAND

Sovereignty over land is God's alone, not man's. When one is born, one randomly appears on some piece of God's land. Often a "ruler" declares this one born under his rule, because this newborn is on "his land". This assumption of the possibility of land ownership, not to mention the governing of others, is the initial fault of the entire psychosis. The rules which all mankind are to follow, are the rules of God's land, not the rules that any man decides to place over those lands. The clear thinking Native American Indians had a difficult time understanding this flawed logic of land ownership. Unfortunately, the psychosis is contagious.

Without the consent of the newborn, this "ruling" group immediately places its limitations (laws) upon the infant. This is not hurtful if the society is enlightened and truly free, but today, nearly all of man's actions are far from such virtue. Thus, more often than not, the individual grows to adulthood under such limitations, and is often exploited by those claiming ownership of the land, in defiance to the Creator of All. Being raised in such a manner, one often never questions the lack of freedom to a section of land for one's own independence and survival.

The Individualist, however, has an alternate view of land ownership. The Individualist instead looks to oneself as the custodian of one's land. Fully responsible for its well being, and aware that it is a natural right of every human being to have one tax-free acre to freely sustain oneself. The lack of which is forced servitude. (Maintaining Individualistic simplicity, mineral rights are no longer separate from the land, the land is one unit. Furthermore, cremation is preferred, but home burials on one's own property are allowed and encouraged, both practices save land and allow it to be used for those living who need to sustain themselves.)

a. CITIES:

Concentrations of people create a myriad of unnatural filth, disease and pollution. Few places in nature is the waste of any species concentrated in one spot, in a way nature cannot properly absorb, (sanitation systems) along with the species itself clustered together in an unchanging location. The Native Americans never had diseases because they never had concentrated cities, they were spread out. It is this concentration that generates a great deal of unnatural microbial life, creating an environment fit for their growth and increasing the probability of new strains. The Individualists will be even more spread out by having at least one acre per citizen. Sprawl will be of no concern to a self-sufficient society, which consequently works at home, and uses fully electric vehicles as transportation.

The Individualists shall apply their minds to eco-cities if they retain the belief that cities are necessary. Cites will be designed for air flow, limited population per unit of space, use of sun, plenty of vegetation (even upon the structures, exterior walls and roofs) etc. Building new cities and renovating old ones into healthier, harmonious, energy efficient, communities.

b. RESOURCE EXTRACTION

Some Populus facilities (mines and quarries, etc) will focus upon extracting all needed materials for the Populus' interests. As all Populus facilities, they will be run on tax money and their size regulated by the annual vote of the people. A flat fee tax shall pay for the initial construction of the facility, its employees, as well as its operation and maintenance expenses. The price of the plant's product will be set by these annual expenses, according to the amount of product created, divided equally among the amount of tax payers. This unit amount is simultaneously the price of the product and the amount of the flat fee tax.

For example, the 100 people of a locality are each required to contribute 25 cents to a copper plant to cover its costs. The copper plant produces 50 pounds of copper annually, thus every half pound is 25 cents. Each individual is thus eligible for this half pound of copper for free. If it is not wanted, they may sells it back to the plant who then sends it to the resource reserve and issues that individual an energy certificate for the 25 cents. Thus this individual gets his tax money back if he does not use copper. However another individual might need two pounds, his first half pound is free, yet he pays 75 cents for the other 1.5 pounds. Thus this man using the facility pays taxes on it.

If no one uses the facility an abundance takes place and the plant is shut down until needed. Abundance and shortage is monitored by the Resource Reserve of the HVR. Any single individual who purchases more than 40% of the plant's product must pay a 15% gratuity on every unit thereafter. Therefore the plant profits if only one or two individuals are buying most of the copper. Accordingly, the people profit as this amount is divided amongst them, and the one or two buyers of most of the copper undoubtedly profit also. Thus this system helps private businesses (and individuals) by creating low material costs, which creates yet another small profit for the people, due to the low prices on the products manufactured by those Individual's who bought most of the copper.

This does not imply any laws against private resource extraction. However, large plots of land are subject to excess land tax and other applicable taxes, while the Populus facilities are not. Private facilities will obviously have to be more innovative to compete with the low prices of the Populus facilities. This is simply to ensure that a publicly controlled aspect of each market is open to all individuals' input. Ideally this makes for the most efficient company in the business, while keeping the public actively involved with their society, from its foundation to its pinnacle, as opposed to encouraging the least possible involvement of the people, such as in the present world.

i. OIL

The total US petroleum consumption in 2006 was about 318 billion gallons. Any feasible alternative to this oil addiction is rapidly thwarted by the oil and automotive industry and their many allies. Much like the recall and destruction of all fully Electric Vehicles after the California Air Resources Board withdrew its quota for Zero Emission Vehicles. (One of these destroyed vehicles was GM's EV1 which had a range of 160 miles and top speed of 80 mph with a sticker price of $40,000. Very reasonable, but hardly any of the public knows about it to this day)

The Individualists strongly advise that all Fossil Oil be phased out in ten years. All of the people must be actively educated as to its waste, its wise alternatives, and demand that the alternatives be developed, so as to be able to abandoned this product. The people must demand cooperation from their corrupted government to make much more efficient strides towards phase out and implementation of fully electric vehicles. (If the entire US workforce of 150 Million people all contributed $10 to an Electric Vehicle fund, this would amount to 1.5 Billion dollars, more than enough for the construction of a fully electric vehicle plant. The people would then simply pay up front, at cost, for a vehicle and wait until it was built. Thus, is the first Populus factory.)

If as much time, money and research went into batteries, electric motors, solar cells and magnets, that has gone into the oil, coal, plastic, pharmaceutical and automobile industries, this phase out would have already been achieved. Biodiesel, hybrids, and hydrogen vehicles are merely brief stepping stones to the end solution of fully electric. They should quickly become secondary backup systems to the fully electric system. With the implementation of recharging stations, and increased battery, motor and magnet technology, distance problems will be eliminated.

President Bush himself admits the possibility of reducing gasoline consumption (which is only 50% of the oil market) by 20% in ten years with his "20 in10" plan. If an oil baron admits this, the average energy aware soul will agree with the Individualists 50% in five, phase out in ten plan. At first, only twice as demanding as the president's plan, but possible. However, the difference is when the president achieves his goal he stops, he applies no further effort to the hundreds of years to come, obviously because he and his children benefit therefrom (so they ignorantly suppose). The Individualist does not stop mid-stream in a task, nor build half a building. Thus they shall achieve their goal of phase out, because they continue to apply the same energy that achieved the initial reduction. With the president's admittance of 20% reduction in ten years, he indirectly admits phase out is possible in fifty. The Individualists put forth all of their effort to beat this deadline by landslides, mostly with *fully* electric solutions.

Once this is realized the use of fossil oil can be made illegal. All oils needed must then be derived from plants. All civilians will receive credit for their gasoline engines when they install an electric motor in a local Populus conversion facility. All chemical companies dependent on oil (plastic manufactures) will be forced to apply their research skills to plant oils. (The earth is not the only place to get oil, this "easy way" with little thought of the consequences, is long overused and abused). All other companies dependant upon oil and its byproducts must also utilize plant oils, further encouraging scientific research, and expanded cultivation into this area because of plant oil's current expense and limited volume. (With the expanded cultivation of plants comes the need for acreage to grow these plants, this will undoubtedly encourage exploration into vertical greenhouses, recalling the myth of the hanging gardens.) With time plant oil will be inexpensive and abundant, just as Edison vowed to make the light bulb so cheap that only the rich would have candles. So too, will the brilliant Individualists solve the problems of the future, and conquer the blind materialists stripping the earth for nothing but money and power over others.

There will be no assistance programs here, the wisest will succeed and blaze a trail, and the others will follow or be forced into new fields or into the crop fields. The only assistance offered is the knowledge of self-sufficiency for those long relying upon raping the earth for sustenance, unable to support themselves without depending upon another's backbreaking labor, frightened to lose the security of their empire begotten by taxing the earth and returning nothing to it.

Some suggest that if fossil oil is removed the economy will collapse. This is sad, as it shows how dependant upon one substance a deceived people can be, unwilling and uneducated to utilize other means.

It is simply the lack of thought that leads to that conclusion, for if there is a will there is always a way. The implementation of a new system grows as the old system is phased out, it is not an abrupt overnight change. The low expense of a product, the speed of the production of a product, or the power a product gives one in offensive war, does not mean it is a wise solution. These factors only indicate "wisdom" in the haste of a wasteful, and/or war seeking society capitalizing on a product regardless of its consequences to humanity and their globe. This mindset will become a painful memory in the dark past of mankind. Taking a little more time, and money (in the beginning) to utilize renewable means, will benefit the society by the many new areas of research and heightened awareness and responsibility for their species and planet.

(Fossil fuel lobbyists support hydrogen cars only because hydrogen can be made from fossil resources. Any technology that does not support their fossil fuels will always be demonized to the public, who they prey upon. *Government* research and development is too often skewed to the interests of these giants as opposed to the interests of the people who are supposed to be in total control of the actions of that government. Hydrogen should only be used as a storage method for any surplus electricity generated. This can then be used in a hydrogen powered generator to convert that energy back into electricity for use in a fully electric society.)

ii. COAL

Coal also must phase out in ten years, for any burning purposes, directly or indirectly, as well as any attempted oil creation. All electrical power plants based off of Coal must find the solution to their own survival by utilizing only elemental means such as wind, water, biodiesels (a temporary solution), solar, etc., else they will be shut down and dismantled. All establishments and residences dependent upon the plant are expected to assist its solution or find their own solution of elemental means. It is possible that assistance will be provided depending on the Populus' vote of that locality.

All companies who create products based on coal tar or similar coal products must find new solutions in the plant kingdom. This may included the industries of dyes, pharmaceuticals, artificial flavors, scents and colors, and a plethora of other synthetics. All others dependent on coal have ten years to realize a solution to how they are effected. Some may be forced into Individualistic self-sustenance until they realize an alternate path. This will further encourage this practice assisting the people to realize a richer form of life, dependent on none other but oneself. As for cities, they will find it difficult to make a solution, however not impossible. This will encourage the thinning of some cities, the vanishing of others, and the propagation of some wise and industrious cities of the future.

To give one an idea as to why the Individualists strongly encourage the phase out of coal, the following data is presented. To generate one kWh of electricity (which would light a 100 watt bulb for 10 hrs) at the most efficient modern power plant, requires, on average, 8,000 BTU (about one pound of coal) of heat energy. To convert that electricity back into heat when it reaches its destination, it is only possible to get 3,412 BTU of heat in return. That is an instant loss of 58% of the energy within the coal. Every plant uses millions of tons of coal. Thus, for every million tons in, over half a million tons is wasted. This is absurdly primitive yet goes on unquestioned. Furthermore, This figure does not take into consideration all of the BTUs (energy) required by the colossal mining and transporting of the coal or transmission line losses, all of which would make this figure so low as to be shameful.

A quarter of the US's total energy and over half its total electricity is generated by coal. Coal burning power plants are the largest source of air pollution. They are immune to clean air regulation (which target new plants) due to "grandfather" loopholes, and there have only been a few new plants erected since. They are active in the corrupt practice of emissions trading, (including the compromised "carbon market") which is a money making scheme on pollution itself. Wherein polluters buy "credits" which are, basically, the right to pollute, from a less polluting company (at times at the expense of the taxpayer). In this way the buyer is thus fined for polluting and the seller rewarded for not polluting. However, while this is a nice way for brokers, and a select few to make money off of the trillion dollar market, (money which could be used for, Populus owned, non polluting, wind, water, and solar farms) little has been done to the amount of pollution being emitted.

Money is not a part of the equation, one cannot buy the emissions out of the sky, incentives only lead to collusion and delay. It must simply be made law to not pollute and the people must be willing to generate their own power or create Populus facilities so that prices of the new systems remain affordable with the removal of private profit and usury (such as inexpensive wind turbines and solar cells). The people (who *are* the government) should not support or utilize coal and initiate its overdue dismantlement. The Individualists aim at the eventual dismantlement and recycling of the entire grid. All of the telephone poles used as paper and wood products, and the miles of wire to be used in the industry for new efficient generators.

iii. METHANE

The harvesting of methane (natural gas) from crustal gas fields must phase out in ten years. All methane must be produced by controlled anaerobic means (biogas). Nearly all home heating must be electric within ten years (biodiesel may also be sparingly used as a direct heat source, or to power a generator which in turn powers electrical heat). The use of natural gas will be used only in special cases, such as certain chemical reactions which must utilize it, and will be strictly monitored.

iv. CHEMICALS

The modern chemical industry is almost entirely an extension of the oil industry. The largest portion of this entity has no concern for orchestrating its activities in harmony with nature or for the benefit of human evolution. As long as it makes the largest possible profit in the shortest amount of time, no matter how many men or how many parts of the Earth are diseased and destroyed, it has accomplished its desire. These thoroughly ignorant souls would dissolve the entire Earth and all of mankind in their crucibles for an ounce of gold, even to their own blind destruction. Their minds are focused strictly on personal gain, not even the well being of their own children, who will inherit the Earth they poison, enters into their confined minds. Their concern for emissions, dumping of wastes and the testing of any chemicals they create thoroughly for human safety, goes only as far as their bribed regulations agents insist, which is not even a half step in the right direction. As long as their new, unnatural, and unnecessary product sells, and sells big, giving raises to their executives and bonuses to their scientists, none of them care of the effects of their deeds regardless of what they tell the public.

They have become so huge that a one million dollar fine is nothing to them. For a sole proprietor, fines as this would destroy such a small business for life. Thus, justice accidentally ensures the chemical giants' clear territory. This instills fearlessness within these monsters from the tiny stings which justice can inflict. Further more, being that a large portion of all of their products come from oil, most modern day politicians, knee deep in it, protect their alchemical brethren by slyly delaying what little justice can do. Diverting the eyes of the innocent public, answering their cries with impotent circular speeches and actions. Their pockets overflowing with payoffs, mocking all that the title of their position "representative of the people" stands for, as they are caressed by their blind masters like a rabid dog beside the throne. Completely numb to morals and love for their fellow man, these beasts see the people just as what they call them "consumers", and in the title that they give their fellow man they openly admit their disrespect. Their household cleaners leave chemical residue behind more dangerous the dirt they were intended to remove, when all that was needed was water, or plant oils. Their Pesticides "deet" and "anvil", pushed with an industry induced global scare, such as the infamous west Nile virus, frightening the people into buying their product as a magic bullet. (Aids may be no different, of the 3 million that die of aids each year, how many of them were taking supposed "medicine"?)

Large chemical companies such as: Du-Pont, Eastman-Kodak, Syngenta, Monsanto, Dow, BASF, and Bayer etc. should be forbidden to use any chemical for any reaction if that chemical or its product is in any way, to the smallest degree, hazardous or not found in significant quantities in nature. These companies constantly spill and secretively cover up their grossly unnatural substances, endangering all forms of life in many unforeseen and unpredictable fashions above and beyond the few know or admitted ailments which they cause. The only few spills the common man hears about are the ones in which some eye witness happened to see, or in an area to populated to conceal. By setting these strict standards it would force corporations to use their scientists to make all discoveries in harmony with nature, opening a great door to the future of chemistry.

One of their biggest products is plastic. Plastics exist simply for haste and merchandizing reasons. Hastily created from oil to ensure the quickest profit, it is then turned around to a merchandiser just as hasty to implement it.   The merchandisers are likewise concerned more with their profit than with the buyer's health or that of the environment.   Seeking only easier, cheaper, and faster packaging, and production. At all costs their product must "stay fresh" and "look good", regardless of if it is either. This haste of creation and implementation generates a haste of usage, which is the seed and foundation of the "disposable" attitude of much of the modern world. A disease given to them by the need suppliers, who would have the entire Earth covered over with heaps of garbage and smile, because for every discarded object there is a penny in their abysmal pockets.

With proper thought plastics could be replaced by "bioplastics" or specifically bred plants to make new durable woods and pulps eliminating plastic altogether. These solutions may be more time consuming, yet are definitely an advanced and more intelligent solution of the higher Individualist mind. The wisdom of the Individualist creates products and fuels which are endlessly reusable and biodegrade in a reasonable time frame without profit being the primary focus. Woods will last as long as they are cared for, this is all the longer that any object needs to last, else one simply builds with stone as the nearly immortal pyramids profess.

The plastics are a danger outside of the human body, but much territory still remains to be destroyed. These feverish scientists advance their shambling kingdom to the very bodies of men with their unnatural patented potions and have him ingest them, and cover his body with them. All the while lying about how helpful and wonderful their new substance is and the depth of the safety research they have performed. Hiding the chemical's origins and effects, that is, if they have even endeavored to exhaustively ascertain all of its effects.

Great portions of flavors, fragrances, and colors are made from petroleum chemicals (such as the popular synthetic vanillin, synthesized from the petrochemical precursors guaiacol and glyoxylic acid). If it is not to falsify the food's look, smell and taste, it will be made unnaturally imperishable. Harmful preservatives are placed in foods, clearly known to be capable of harm, yet are not listed in the food's ingredients because of FDA loopholes, which these butchers have created and paid for.   They jeopardize the life of every individual, who supports their empire by eating the product, just to make their product last forever.   This allows laziness and irresponsibility on their part because they need not worry about efficient transit and logistics, or an excellent product to make a quick sale for their perishable item. Instead their practically imperishable poison can wait on shelves for eternity for an unsuspecting victim, while their profits from minimized product urgency measures soar. Sadly even the words "green" "herbal" or "Organic" merely prey upon ignorance when many of these products have numerous petroleum byproducts and lab manufactured chemicals in them, or if not, are packaged in plastic.

But behold, pharmaceutical companies are at the bottom of this pit of treachery, creating concoctions for human consumption in the blasphemous guise of Healing, with side effects greater than the disease they claim to treat and understand. The side effects are full proof of their complete misunderstanding of the human physical body which they arrogantly believe that they understand. With prescription and retail sales at $200 billion *each*, and distribution reaching $140 billion, this den of scorpions desires no cures, for that would place them immediately out of business. They are the creators of propaganda inventing numerous phantom ailments, nearly all of which would be self cured by a simple natural diet, plenty of water and exercise, combined with deep breathing and conscious relaxation. They care not about the dangers of the side effects of their products, for they will make a product to "cure" that also, it too with its own side effects, and on and on through a murderous money making cycle.

Their scribes and professors are the dukes and barons of Lie, licking their masters' hands clean with forked tongues and shining their guilded masks with their sweet venom. Worse than the lowliest street drug pusher, they convince all men that any feeling is a disease for which they have a magic pill. Through this method much of mankind has been led to believe that they are merely weak and fragile animals, and have lost sight of their powerful immortal spirits.

Man has gone thousands of years without drugs and supplements now suddenly in the last 100 years they have become essential. The Pharmaceutical industry practices only madness, for they claim the ineffectiveness of natural remedies, yet market vitamins and minerals and attempt to alter them, and natural extracts, so that they can patent them for their own exclusive sales.

The Populus Laboratories will be erected and directed by the people for logical and sane applications with regard for only the advancement of humanity, not personal profit and exploitation of the ignorant. They will be unhindered by illusions and stumbling blocks of altered facts, figures, and distorted reason, all of which are only erected to lead man away from truth, and into the lairs of pirates. Thus, Populus scientists will not be limited by corporate agendas and similar selective funding, accelerating the growth of rational science.

3. TRANSPORTATION

The invention of the car made placement of "developments" haphazard and impractical. People drive from miles to go to one store, and often get their produce, shipped to local stores, from the other side of the nation. This overage of travel, individual and commercial, is a waste of energy, time (average commute is 104 hrs/year) and a source of pollution. This is greatly reduced by self-sufficiency in three ways. 1. The individual is employed by oneself not having to travel to work being that one's homestead is one's work. 2. One needs not to travel as often to procure products, as one produces them oneself. 3. This reduced demand and market for products causes companies to focus only on their localities, thus travel less, as profit in distant markets has lessened.

Furthermore, if individuals chose to work for another, where able, employers should encourage employees to work from home. Many US homes are empty in the day while the "places of business" are filled, and at night, the situation reverses. Obviously there is a large amount of structures using up land and energy (mostly climate control) that don't need to be, empty half of their existence, and people moving back and forth between them. Not only would this save travel energy, but also places of business would save money by not having the expense of a secondary building.

In this same way many service companies, who travel all day long, would be down sized by individuals servicing all of their own needs, such as, trees, landscape, minor construction etc. Lastly, if all vehicles were fully electric, and the people generating most of their own power, there would be zero emissions from the remaining commercial and personal travel. Such as businesses which cannot be performed from home (mass ore smelting, Populus assembly lines etc), people who choose to live far from their occupation, or an occupation erecting a place of business in a remote area.

But beware, by prematurely making it law to have zero emissions or fully electric vehicles, one only assists the profit of the private car makers, granting them an excuse to sell electric vehicles two to three times their worth, creating a haven for the bankers. There must first be an erected facility, owned and controlled equally by all of the people of the union, *without* "representatives". It will be erected by a small contribution from every working citizen (e.g. $10) and create, at cost, fully electric vehicles. Only then can strict laws on zero emissions be made. Strict emissions themselves will discourage the production of the Internal combustion engine, for it will become more expensive than the fully electric car in its attempts to achieve zero emissions, or ultra low emissions.

a. RAIL ROADS

Out of sight and out of mind, few see these massive payloads, multiple times per day, being constantly consumed behind the scenes. With the increased focus on localized shipping caused by self-sufficiency, businesses will rely more on the railroad for shipping long distances. This will give the railroads free reign to spike transportation costs. Therefore, railroads cannot be privatized. Just as a highway cannot be privately owned, or rights granted to any citizen to build their own private highway wherever they may choose. Similarly, any free citizen cannot build rails wherever they wish, thus, the limited places allotted to rails are already "owned", creating a monopoly, as it excludes any other from the freedom of the same practice. This allows control over the prices of goods distributed to the people. Furthermore, if rails were to remain private, the implementation of the Individualists' excess land tax would cripple them, causing them to again raise the prices to the people, who would not accept them, freezing transport. Thus, the Populus rails will be an at-cost service, and their thoroughly itemized bottom line will be annually reported to the people.

4. UNIONS

Unions force pension and health care upon their members, extracting this substantial portion of their pay whether they agree or not. This is not only a pool of money which gains the same powers as a bank (as any other pool of money) but it is also a guaranteed block of insurance customers, and political votes. They take the workers money just as fast as the Bosses before unions, and give no guaranty that the pensions promised will be returned when needed. As numerous workers before have lost their pensions, weeks away from retiring, forced to start over with decades of their lives stolen with a signature of a politician. Unions in the past were needed and well founded as the people were exploited by "bosses". Today the union members are exploited by the bosses *and* the unions.

Unions also have no competition. For instance there is not a Carpenters union A and a Carpenters union B to compete against each other for the best plans and service, thus it is a monopoly controlling the work force and were the people may work. It therefore plunders liberty, the freedom to work where one chooses, to affiliate with whomever one chooses, and is forced upon the industry like unwritten law. Contractors awarded contracts must utilize a monopolized work force giving unions sovereign control. The most significant projects or processes are often fully unionized.

It would be no surprise if the unions were founded by the corporations who hire employees of that union. In such a scenario, the corporation paying out the wages keeps a large portion of that payment (pensions and health care) as an interest gaining pool, granting the corporation kickbacks from the various Health insurers for these guaranteed clients and payments. These health insurers also use this money (the health insurance payments) as a large pool. Each, (the corporation and Health insurers) most likely, has subsidiary lending corporations which can practice usury and fractional reserve. Lending from these pools, they are thus able to generate untold amounts of (hollow) money on this money, (withheld from the workers by the "union") utilizing clandestine lending circles between each other and affiliates.

There is an argument that the busting of corrupt unions along with corrupt companies will lower all wages. With the knowledge of self sufficiency people will not need to work, thus will not go to work unless the pay is high, there for it is likely that the pay will be substantially higher within the Individualistic society. People with business ideas will need the people as workers, but the people will not need them, thus the power will be in the people's hands without need for a middleman to represent them.

The Populus itself is the largest union, the union of all the people of the nation, requiring no dues. With the removal of privatized insurance and usury, one cannot offer private health insurance or pensions. Even still, The Individualist does not outlaw the unions. It simply competes against existing unions to offer the best services to workers of all skills, unlike many unions whose members sit on lists, never contacted but still pay dues, sometimes forbidden to solicit for their own work, utterly controlled. The action of the Populus is to balance this present strict control of labor and place the control in the hands of the people. All individuals will be able to work on any Populus projects, union or not, to which they are qualified. In the light of freedom, the private sector always retains the right to refuse to hire anyone on any private project for any reason.

V. Returns

A. RETURNS FROM DISMANTLEMENT

Initially, the amount of employed people in the Individualistic society will be very similar to the amount of people employed in the original system. For example, the number of people dislocated from the banking industry will become the HVR employees. Overall the society is exactly the same, except that most business is now owned equally by the citizens. Those whose jobs are made obsolete have self-sufficiency knowledge to rely upon until they find a new direction. The amount of work actually needed by the people to survive will be lessened due to the substantial burdens lifted from them by these dismantlements.

a. Usury

$182.2 billion in Mortgage interest (42% of 9.7 Trillion in outstanding mortgages over an average of 22.5 years)
$165.4 billion in Credit card interest (13.8 Billion/mo (aver APR 22.5% = 1.875%/mo on 735B total US credit card debt))
$ 45.0 billion in Auto interest (9% on 500 Billion in outstanding auto loans)

Totaling: **$392.6 Billion** per year (not including 211 Billion-dollar national debt interest or various other interest)

b. Government Waste

$544.8 billion in Social Security
$359.5 billion in Unemployment and welfare
$345.7 billion in Medicare
$268.4 billion in Medicaid and other health
$ 38.4 billion in Foreign affairs
$ 88.7 billion in Education

Totaling: **$1.8566 Trillion** (approximately 71% of the US federal government spending)

c. Public Waste

$ 50 billion in Return from jail dismantlement per year
$500 billion in Processing and distributing foods
$120 billion in Profit to unnecessary industrial farms
$147 billion in Health (761 Billion removed by Populus Health. (Minus the Medicare and Medicaid already listed above))
$ 88 billion in Structures (now towards *Public* Health Structures and equipment as permanent assets of the public)

Totaling: **$905 Billion**

Subtotal: $3.1542 Trillion

B. RETURNS FROM NEW TAXES

These returns will be short lived as they are actually set up to assist the dismantlement of destructive habits. The revenue generated will be used to establish the foundations of the Individualistic society, so that it is secure when this revenue runs out in 5 to ten years.

$ 2.0 billion in Junk mail taxes
$ 88.2 billion in Fossil fuel taxes
$109.9 billion in Unnatural foods taxes
$ 49.7 billion in Controlled substance taxes

Simplifying taxes:

$300 billion (stopped evasion techniques and reduced administration costs)
$125 billion (simplified processing of complex tax law guidelines)

Totaling: **$675 Billion**

Not including: excess land tax, Foreign soil tax, Hazardous material tax, Large entity tax, Packaging tax, Primitive Vehicle tax, and Waste tax. Each of these taxes requires too much data to accurately estimate for this work. The total revenue of all of these taxes is expected to be in the hundreds of billions if not surpassing a Trillion, being that they mostly affect large businesses.

C. RETURNS FROM POPULUS FACILITIES

The Amount saved by the various "at cost" products and services of the Populus has too many variables to accurately estimate, but could be figured as a percentage of the US 13.2 Trillion dollar Gross Domestic Product. That percentage is left up to the reader to decide. Some in business ensure themselves a 10% profit, others much higher.

$261.3 billion in College education due to free education. (Annual 350 Billion in college education, minus 88.7 government student aid (already included above) from the 135 Billion in total annual student aid.)

Totaling: **$261.3 Billion**

D. GRAND TOTAL

Grand Total: **$4.1 Trillion** **burden** removed from the people.
(Not including the above mentioned taxes and product savings, both possibly being around one trillion dollars a piece)

This is approximately $1,139 per month for every man woman and child in the US. Equivalent to the entire population, even infants and the disabled, working full time at $7.12 per hour.

VI. Summary of Part Two

It has been shown that strictly the people, wholly and fully, must compose the government. A system of "representatives" can only be effectually implemented in small systems. Within large systems, a small group of people is to easy to influence in order to manipulate an entire government. (440 people, 100 US senators, 335 House representatives, 4 delegates and 1 resident, ruling over 300 Million people's lives.)

Irresponsibility leads to dependence which increases sloth and ignorance. These are preyed upon by profiteering minds increasing the growth of corporations, who directly corrupt any government that is not a complete direct democracy. In such a setting, the purpose of life becomes lost, and markets and occupations become hollow. However, this can be remedied by Unrestricted Free Knowledge.

Education and responsibility for one's own actions are key to creating a society wherein each individual, bar none, is competent and involved in the undertakings of the society at all levels. Private businesses must be limited in size to prevent control or bias in social decision making, favoring those private forces. Corporate market control can be eliminated by simply making Populus businesses which are wholly owned and equally contributed to by the citizens. Such facilities yield lower prices, and are easily monitored for facts.

It is stressed that when setting up these systems one is never deceived into ownership by "the government". These things must always be owned fully and equally by all of the citizens, not a separate entity, and utterly without a "board of directors". The people themselves, all of them, must be the responsible owners. The instant that one is lazy, and allows a "representative" to take one's place, one has taken a step towards servitude and opened the door for future deceit.

It has been shown that complexity is proportionate to corruption, and that simplicity should be maintained in all areas especially law and government. The simplicity of these two should be made so that all of the people, even the children, clearly understand them. The people should practice the governing of themselves and none other, and encourage all to do the same.

The great wastes and servitude of usury has been shown, along with the deceit of fractional reserve, repossessions, and various lending circles of banks, and other large pools of public money, allowed to be gathered by a private force, converting public power into private power. For this reason the Individualists disallow any private pool of money, keeping all of the power in the hands of the people, not a private interest and not a government separate from the people.

An attempt has been made to reveal great evils in this world suggesting that the United States, and the rest of the world, has already been conquered, whilst they slept, by The United Corporations of the World. Further effort was made to show the reader that there is more to life than slavery, presenting an alternative method to the fast paced nonsense, which is a peaceful sanity, at a calm pace. With self-sufficiency, and one tax-free acre, one is free to pursue whatever one chooses, and has no need to work for another if desired. With prices and demands of society lower and cooperation higher, one's dreams are closer in reach.

The people must band together and inform each other of all suspect practices while simultaneously sharing innovative ideas. Deception to higher solutions, to maintain old systems for the profit of the few has kept mankind burdened for too long. There will occur a massive shift in man's priorities, goals will become more meaningful, and an important purpose to life will be realized. With practice, the world can move away from doing things for money, and instead, do them for love and wisdom.

Such peace is not to be mistaken for a passivist society, easily conquered by avenging, prospecting, and aspiring corporations. Contrarily, the Individualistic society is an entire standing army, each well trained and supplied. Each homestead a strategically placed and constructed, fortified structure, independent of all others and self sustaining. There would be no single significant target for an invading enemy.

There are those readers now raising an eye, those who have benefited and been made comfortable by their dealings with the machine and its caretakers, regardless of the blood upon their hands, or their trampled brethren at their feet. Those who fear the dismantling of the machine which now sustains them. In their fear and lack of confidence in their abilities to sustain themselves, they remain adamantly loyal to

146

their heinous provider. Willing to use whatever labels to attach to opposing systems to demonize them and prevent public sway. It is for this very reason that this system is already christened with a new label – Noble Individualism.

The ultimate goal is to have every citizen being either self-sufficient and/or an employee of one of the four departments. 95% of the world's population will no longer possess only 10% of the world's wealth while performing 90% of the world's work. They have been rivaled against each other falsely for centuries only to impede their coming together under one unified banner. The Grey Flag of Individualism. It has no color, so as not to draw attention away from the colors of one's soul. It is not white symbolizing surrender or claiming perfect purity. It is not black as the corruption which it opposes. It has no symbols defining it, which would only serve to limit its infinite abilities. And it is one solid shade to symbolize the unity of All. All men, all races, all beliefs, all powers to infinity, the unity of the Creator.

"An ignorant people are easily betrayed, and a wicked people can never be ruled by the mild influence of their own laws." - Arthur J. Stansbury

--- PART THREE ---

Brief Overview of the Individualistic Homestead

This is an ideal model of the average Individualistic homestead. The method presented is purely a rough example, and is not intended to restrict any other designs, as every individual is entitled to build and live however they wish. Individualistic houses are built from all natural materials, avoiding plastics, petrochemical paints, synthetic fiber carpet, etc. Electricity should be generated by solar cells, as well as wind and water turbines at the homestead. Fuels should be hydrogen and biodiesel manufactured by the users (electrolysis and fuel crops) themselves, when possible, and used strictly as backup power. Wood or petrol based heating oil should be avoided if possible, but if used, employ efficient burning stoves with baffled chimney systems. Food and livestock should be raised onsite by the user. Water should be from wells, rain collectors and natural sources. Communication will be had by various wireless devices.

This is not to imply a nation of farmers. It is to give people control over their welfare and life. The amount of work done in this manner for just one individual is far less than the eight-hour day of common toil. (a 1,000 ft² garden worked for 30 minutes a day will feed 2 people all year) Thus, these individuals will have more time on their hands to explore higher learning and higher skills, thereby assisting to develop higher technologies. Therefore, this society will actually be a faster evolving and more technologically advanced civilization than the present world. Not a nation of antisocial, uneducated mountain men as some suggest.

Using one acre per person (36.8 billion earth acres) with the modern day population (6.55 billion people) translates into leaving 80% of the Earth's total land wild. Thus assisting the Earth to heal itself from the ravages we have afflicted it with. One acre is not only enough to sustain one person, but enough to make one feel comfortable while offering sufficient space for specialty practices, such as minor metallurgy, glass-working, etc. It is a natural right to be entitled to one tax free acre required to Independently sustain oneself. One should not be forced to depend on, or work within, a society that claims ownership over God's land, especially if its practices are in conflict with one's view of right and wrong. When the option of independence is not offered, the society is practicing forced servitude, no matter how it is justified.

This spread out nature of the Individualistic society impairs the mass effectiveness of enemy forces, from infantry to aircraft. Furthermore, 1. each individual unit is self-sustaining, thus no single strategic target could shut down the many. In times of war the Individualistic homestead is never deprived of food and fuel by producing them on site. Their machines would never be useless as long as the wind blows and the sun shines, as other nations could be crippled with a single bomb to a single refinery, and 2. many homesteads will be similar to fortified structures, as pre-cast concrete is stronger and faster to build with when taking advantage of geothermal principles by utilizing partially submerged structures. Thus a nation of Individualists, each schooled in strategic defense, would be much more challenging to conquer as opposed to common housing plans filled with untrained citizens. Therefore the Individualists design all zoning and building codes around self-sufficiency, renewable resources, and a strategic layout for defensive maneuvers.

Lastly, There will be no need to establish any new infrastructure for the conversion to this society. This argument is utilized to combat many alternative energy solutions by fossil fuel lobbyists and their vassals. In fact, it will cause many infrastructures to be dismantled and their remains recycled for use in loftier goals.
(All of the following are "generous" averages for one Individual on one acre. One acre = 43,560 sq feet)

A. Living Space

1,250 sq ft of living space per individual equates to a dwelling with the dimensions of 25 X 25, having a basement and a first floor. This only removes 625 sq ft from the total acre, and is spacious and comfortable for one individual. The home suggested below would cost about $52,000 unfinished, $90,000 finished (assuming 30/ft2) and another $30,000 for an electrical system generating about 8,000kWh per year, ($15,000 wind system and $15,000 solar), totaling $120,000, and taking less than 5 months to build. This is less than the present average purchased home. Depending on the resourcefulness of the owner, it could be a fully independent dwelling. Furthermore, there are occasionally rebates which may lower the cost of a renewable energy system.

Efficiency and Independence Solutions:

A. A solid concrete pre-cast wall home (about $35,000 just for the steel and concrete, but livable in at this stage). The basement and half of ground floor is sunken utilizing geothermal and solar thermal principles for air and water temperature assistance. Solar thermal collectors are mounted amidst photovoltaic panels, and are coupled with a geothermal loop, fed to a heat vault sunken beneath the basement, wherein also sits the hotwater tank and a heatpump (possibly a stove). Strategically placed glass block over metal grating, used on the roof, minor side windows, and first floor, utilizing sun lighting all the way to the basement.

B. Electricity

The average electricity consumption for a single individual is approximately 3,500 kWh/yr (Not used as Heat) amounting to 9.6kWh which need to be generated per day.

Efficiency and Independence Solutions:

A. A Wind Turbine producing 3,500 kWh of power over a year with average wind speeds of 10 mph will cost around $13,000, for the turbine, tower and accessories. *Maximum wind turbine tower height is 88' in the center of a square acre with a home on a corner of the property.*
B. A photovoltaic (solar cell) system generating 3,500kWh per year will cost about $14,000
C. Emergency and backup energy supplied by hydrogen and biofuel (and other fuel if unavoidable) generators, as well as biomass (and other fuels, plus excess heat vault heat) heated Stirling type generators.
E. Water turbines where applicable
F. Additional electricity will be produced by a Stirling cogenerating process wherein the heat from winter heating will heat the engine first and then proceed to the home. Furthermore, the massive heat built up in the vault in summer months, will also be used. This electricity will be converted to hydrogen, successfully saving summer heat for the winter.

C. Water

The average water consumption for a single individual is approximately 24,000 gal/yr. This includes showers and laundry. (There are 7.48 gallons of water per cubic foot.)

Efficiency and Independence Solutions:

One inch of rain over one acre produces 27,154 gallons of water. Most regions in the world have at least 20 inches of rain per year. In addition to the entire acre being contoured to collect rain, a 2,178 sq feet section is dedicated to rain collection, if one has no well. Besides common filters within the system, all drinking water is passed through an electric distiller which requires 0.6kwh per distilled gal. The average individual drinks less than 400 gal per year, amounting to a 240 kWh per year consumption.

A. Rain collectors (2,178 ft2 per individual)

Any non-saturable area, funneling water to a drain leading to a Detention tank ($3,000 for the storm system). A corrugated metal cylindrical tank 10 feet in diameter and 22 ft long ($5,000) will hold 12,918 gal of water. This is assuming consumption will be similar to rainfall. This system could include various methods of water transfer to the house through multiple filters, most likely by an electric pump, coupling it with a geothermal and solar thermal system ($10,000).

B. Common Wells

D. Heating

The largest challenge to energy independence is winter heating. A great deal of needed heating is removed with a fully or partially submerged house, taking advantage of solarthermal and geothermal principles. The average Heat consumption in BTU (effected by environment, this estimate uses the Midwest US climate) is 92,790,000 BTU/yr, which translates to 27,211 kWh per year. The average present day individual and homes are not very energy conscious, nor efficient, thus this figure can be reduced with little effort. The Individualist and home are both a minimum of 30% more energy efficient than this average. Thus the winter backup energy (for heat) required will be 10,000 to 16,000 kWh. (Or possibly less depending on the efficiency of the home and individual, as well as the climate). Splitting the maximum up would amount to 448 lbs of hydrogen (2,237m^3) and 214 gallons of biodiesel needed. Both impractical values as shown below. Therefore the Individualist employs a number of these systems in tandem to achieve a high degree of energy efficiency if not total independence.

(1 BTU raises 50 ft3 of air 1 degree F)

Efficiency and Independence Solutions:

A. A large wind turbine will produce 31,500 kWh per year with winds of 18 mph, and a 100 ft tower. This is highly impractical for most, and costs around $60,000. It is more feasible to utilize a smaller turbine (if your average annual wind is only around 10mph) in tandem with many other systems.

B. A Photovoltaic array (solar cells) will collect 10% of the solar energy in an environment. The average solar radiation is 0.42 kWh/ft2/day, or 153.3kWh/ft2/year, making the average amount collected with photovoltaic panels approximately 15kWh/ft2/year. Or 1,814 ft2 of solar panels (over $100,000) to meet the above demand, which is also impractical. Thus, this system should be used in tandem with the below devices.

C. Solar thermal heat is water heated by sunlight in various ways, used to transfer heat. It can be coupled with a heat vault system which stores the heat in an array of water tanks. The necessary materials are inexpensive. The temperatures within these vaults can reach over 170 degrees in summer months.

D. Geothermal heat provides a consistent temperature base to water or air by using the average ground temperature of approximately 50 degrees F. By looping conduits repeated through the earth, it thus warms water or air cooler than this, and cools water or air warmer than this. Saving the energy of another system from doing the same. This system can also be relatively inexpensive (not including the drilling variety).

E. Heat from wood. The average piece of wood contains about 7,500 BTU/lb (about 2.2kWh). Burning at approximately 80% efficiency one would need around 7.75 tons of seasoned wood per year (to meet the Midwest average above). This is about 24 average trees. Thus, this method is to be minimized.

F. Biodiesel burned as or with heating oil, possibly in a combination wood/oil stove within the heat vault. It would require over 4 acres of land, and a good deal of effort to single-handedly produce 214 gallons of biodiesel from oil crops, and it amounts to only half of the expected efficient heat requirement, and only a quarter of the larger average. Thus, it is an impractical heating solution to rely upon (there is research into oil producing algae that are claimed to produce 100 times the amount of conventional oil crops, this would undoubtedly change things).

G. Hydrogen. To produce and store 4,475 m3 of hydrogen (the entire amount needed for winter backup) one would need 110 1000 gal storage tanks at 200psi. This would take up an enormous amount of space, and is thus also impractical. There is also roughly a 40% energy loss in converting water to hydrogen (thus, for every 10 kWh one converts, one will only get 6 kWh back when burnt at 100% efficiency). This amounts to a feasible method to store surplus electricity, but is impractical to rely upon fully, requiring an electrical generating system 3-4 times the sizes above, as well as storage ($120,000 system plus a $6,000 electrolyser, and $2,000 per 1,000 gallon tank = $346,000).

E. Motive Fuels

The average octane consumption for a single individual is approximately 1,000 gal/yr

Efficiency and Independence Solutions:

A. An average electric vehicle can be run for 3,800 kWh per year to travel 15,000 miles, with no other
    fuel needed. With current gas rates at $3/gal, and the average US gas mileage around 18 mpg, this would
    save $2,500 per year in fuel (driving 15,000 miles), and only cost $342 in electricity (0.09 cents per kWh).
    Therefore, Octane may be abandoned.
B. Biodiesel from plants and waste is marginally acceptable when there is no other alternative. It should be
    used as emergency and backup fuel only and produced by the user when possible.
C. Surplus hydrogen is marginally acceptable when there is no other alternative. It should be used as
    emergency and backup fuel only, generated with the homestead's surplus electricity by electrolysis.

F. Waste

The average waste production for a single individual is approximately 1,850 lbs/yr of which:

#	Waste Type	0	Avoided	Recycled at paying scrap yard	recycled	Burned as heat for electricity producing Stirling engine, or composted
1.	Aluminum	12		yes		
2.	Dense plastic	69	yes			
3.	Garden waste	332				yes
4.	Glass	149			yes	
5.	Iron	35		yes		
6.	kitchen waste	298				yes
7.	Misc. combustible waste	46				yes
8.	Misc. non-combustible waste	23	yes			
9.	Miscellaneous metal	23		yes		
10.	Miscellaneous plastic	35	yes			
11.	Packaging paper	103				yes
12.	paper	240				yes
13.	Sanitary wastes	446				yes
14.	Textiles	35	Yes*			
	TOTALS	1846	162	70 (less than $12/yr)	149	1465 (673lbs water)
						792 lbs converted

* Synthetic textiles are avoided, organic materials such as cotton or wool utilized instead, preferably not dyed. Burned in small quantities when needing disposed.

Efficiency and Independence Solutions:

When each individual has to personally deal with the waste they create, a greater awareness evolves now that the waste doesn't conveniently disappear. The individual is more prone to be conscious of what, and how much, is used, and conserves more wisely. Many of these common wastes will not exist in the Individualistic society, as listed in the avoided column. A small amount will be recycled, and the rest is either burned as fuel for a Stirling engine in a cogeneration process, or composted, creating a practically waste free homestead, and society.

Many of the organic materials, apart from the paper products, are most likely 60% - 70% water with an energy yield of about 2,500 BTU/lb. The paper will yield around 6,500 BTU/lb. (When combusting damp items as these, they can be placed in a metal heat box and then placed into the burner. The heat box allows the water to vaporize yet not extinguish the fire. When completely dry, the materials will combust on their own within the box releasing their heat energy.) Burning clean and natural organic material produces few dioxins contrary to popular belief. Dioxins can be formed only when matter is burned in the presence of chlorine. In clean natural organic material, the way this would happen would be from chloride ions, which will not occur without the presence of water. When heated in a heat box, the water vaporizes and the chlorides revert back to salts, rendering them inert for chemical interaction in combustion. The temperature inside the box will not exceed that of water's boiling point until the water is gone. The cause of dioxin release from modern incineration plants is the combination of filth and unnatural man made chemicals that bond in abnormal ways creating anomalous compounds in the unusually high heat of the incineration process. However, if one still fears the release of dioxins whatsoever, composting is suggested, and by the slow generation of these wastes (about 4lbs/day, half of which is water) it may be more convenient to compost in the long run. (Human wastes should be dehydrated fully and used separately)

G. Food

The average food consumption for a single individual is approximately 728 lbs/yr of fruit and vegetables, 200 lbs/yr in meat, 400 lbs/yr in dairy, and 52lbs/yr in breads.

Efficiency and Independence Solutions:

For the ease of self-sustainability upon one acre, it is not recommended to raise large animals on site as they require much of the acre. For example, one acre is needed for the care of one cow, yet a quarter of that area supports two goats. Because of the numerous methods to divide up one acre, different climates, and individual food preferences, the following figures are listed only for basic purposes. Obviously, these values cannot produce these acreage yields all at the same time. They are listed by acreage output merely for ease in dividing them proportionately across an acre. Lastly, chemical fertilizers need not be used. The native Americans were farming with inter-cropping techniques, and producing some 200 bushels per acre, long before the advent of such chemicals.

1. PLANTS

These values may assist in dividing up one's acre depending upon climate, green house use etc. One acre of land can produce: 20 tons of strawberries, 18 tons of peaches, 18 tons of potatoes, 14 tons of navel oranges, 12 tons of tomatoes, 10 tons of carrots, 10 tons of celery, 8 tons of apples, 8 tons of beets, 7 tons of sweet corn, 6 tons of cabbage, 5 tons of peppers, 5 tons of cucumbers, 3 tons of straw, 2.5 tons of grapes, 2 tons of rice, 2,300 lbs of soybeans, 1 ton of almonds, 1 ton of peanuts, 1 ton sugar, 1 ton of tea, 1 ton of tobacco, 1400lbs coffee, 1,300lbs of cotton lint, 1500lbs sunflower seed, 1000lbs wheat, 700lbs cashews, 500lbs pecans,11,000 heads of lettuce. One acre of hemp (4 tons) yields the same quantity of fiber, able to be used as pulp, as one acre of 20 year old trees, for use as paper etc. (the fiber can also be used as rope and the seed for oil).

A possible milk substitute for those unable, or unwilling, to raise a dairy animal is nut milk. Which is cleaned seeds and/or nuts in water, blended until smooth, then filtered. The result has more calcium than milk, no cholesterol, and does not need pasteurized. It can be sweetened and flavored with various things, such as honey, maple syrup, fruits etc. The remaining solids can be used as spreads, seasoning, flour additives etc. It can be used as milk for drinking and recipes. (A possible egg substitute would be flaxseed)

2. ANIMALS

One acre of land can support: One 1,000 pound horse, or cow, 5 to 10 sheep or goats, or 2 to 5 pigs.

A dairy cow consumes 30 gallons of water, and 75 lbs of ensilage per day. Each year it generates 15 tons of manure, and produces 1,500 gallons of milk, taking an hour a day to milk the cow, milking three times per day.

Chickens could number 80 chickens per acre. They eat about 100 lbs of feed per year, drink a pint of water per day, and require a pen, enclosed from predators at night. Meat chickens are harvested at 3 months old, and hens can lay 300 eggs per year, which when fertilized will hatch in 21 days.

Goats can number around 8 per acre and can be used for meat, milk or fleece. They weigh 100-200 lbs and produce about 1/2 gallon of milk per day. Meat goats are slaughtered at one year of age, for around 60 lbs of meat, and useable skin. Goats can also produce 7 lbs of fleece per year. They require 12 pounds of fresh forage and a 1-2 gallons of water per day. They should be isolated from crop producing areas of the acre, for they may eat the crop. Thus an acre cropping 87% of its area leaves just enough space for an isolated goat.

Fish (aquacultue) could number 4000 per acre of 8 foot deep pond. It takes approximately 2 years to grow a 1.5lb edible fish. For control purposes, mesh cages could be employed along with feeding regimes. Feeding twice per day about a half gram of food per fish, resulting in a food to fish ratio of 1:1.

H. Self Health

For thousands of years man went without manufactured supplements and pharmaceuticals, yet they have become "essential" in the last hundred years. Compare how fit the natural wild animals are, such as a lion, with its rippling muscles, to the obesity and weakness of the disease ridden present day humans, with their supplemented foods and magic drugs, which only grant them even stranger diseases. All "drugs" needed by man have already been created, and are in the form of wild plants (herbs).

Health is simple to maintain, many ailments can be cured with just fresh food, (grown by the user is the best, especially when eaten moments after harvest), and clean water (due to today's pollution one may choose distilled as the purest) taken at about one fluid ounce per pound of body weight per day. When drinking this proper amount of water one needs about one gram of salt per 150 pounds of body weight per day.

Good hygiene (body and mouth) is hopefully an obvious item, however an area often neglected is the nasal cavity. For thousands for years yogis have practiced "neti", the rinsing of the nasal cavity with lightly salted water. This not only helps breathing but it prevents any microbial colonies from gaining a foot hold, and then migrating to other parts of the body.

40 minutes per day of exercise is required, the minimum being a walk. However vigorous exercise, too often, will have negative effects. A good balance, depending upon the individual, is a medium exercise every other day, with lighter ones in between, coupled with 2-8 vigorous workouts a month. The most important part is to stretch upon completion. Attempt to stretch every muscle group. The reason for exercise and stretching, besides the many obvious benefits, is that the lymph system is not a circulating system. Therefore by moving every part of the body, one causes the lymph to move in that area, assisting the removal of toxins and the purifying of the lymph to continue such removal.

The importance of proper breathing is, more often than not, unknown to many. Just as in a damp, dark, basement with little circulation, mold will grow upon the walls, similar occurrences will happen within lungs which do not fully inhale and fully exhale, allowing microbial life to gain a foothold. This stale air, deoxygenated, is slightly toxic by its action with the surrounding moisture and, furthermore, it hinders oxygen's ability to penetrate into theses areas causing the parts of the body relying on that part of the lung to weaken. To sit comfortably in a chair with the back straight, hands rested in the lap, feet rested on floor, and consciously breath for 5 minutes, morning and night, will add tremendous health benefits. One simply fills the lungs, without force, slowly and evenly, and pauses for as long as one comfortably can. Then exhales fully, slow and evenly, pausing again for as long as is comfortable, then the cycle is repeated.

As is breathing, the importance of consciously relaxing is also grossly neglected by humanity. Lying down on one's back with the arms out to the side, slightly tense the legs, lift them, and then spread them evenly apart about 2-3 feet, and then place them back down. Lift the buttocks, slightly tense it, and place it back down. Slightly lift the spine, then place it down. Lift the arms, slightly tense them, and then place them down. Lift the shoulders up from the floor and pull them gently towards the neck, then place them down. Raise the head slightly, pulling the chin toward the neck, and then place down. What this achieves is a symmetrical body and spine. One can practice one's breathing in this position and also add the following practice.

Start at the feet and work upwards. When the inhale is being held focus upon the foot and mentally state, "my foot is relaxed" then exhale. Repeat for each section, from the foot to the ankle, shin, knee, thigh, other leg, hips, back, abs, chest, innards, shoulders, triceps, biceps, forearm, wrist, hands, other arm, neck, head, parts of face etc. Each part can be subdivided as much as one desires and has time for (down to the cells and even the DNA etc.). When the whole body is thus covered, mentally state, "my entire body is relaxed" then exhale. This should be done once per day.

Tension causes the build up of localized Lactic acid (a waste product of muscles), which over long periods, can be a foundation for numerous ailments. Furthermore, the body is a building, a tension in one area throws the entire structure out of balance, causing strain upon other areas to maintain the balance, these, in turn, throw other parts off of balance, and so on, until ailments arise far removed from the location of the initiating tension.

Apart from physical care one must also practice mental care. In the present hectic world this is much more important. Just as one should cause the body to be active at least 40 minutes per day, one should exercise and relax the mind for 40 minutes per day. One should find a quite, solitary spot to carry out this work without interruption. After one has completed either the breathing or relaxation exercise above, one might add the following practice.

First, to gain an appreciation of the size of infinity, visualize a glass sphere filled with sand. Then visualize each grain of sand being a tiny glass sphere of sand just as the first. Similarly, the grains of sand within these are also glass spheres of sand. Continue this as long as desired. Then visualize the glass sphere of sand as being Earth, and it is composed of countless Earths no bigger than a grain of sand. Focusing upon one grain and visualize that it too is made up of countless Earths, and so on. Continue this as long as desired. Then visualize each grain of sand, instead of them being Earths, are each unique worlds, and each one is composed of unique worlds, and each of those components likewise is composed of endless unique worlds, and so on. This is one simple recursive exercise, which exercises the imagination's capabilities and grants one an appreciation of infinity. One can easily create one's own such exercises, limited only by the imagination.

The Individualist is encouraged to often, if not constantly, deeply ponder Infinity and God, and practice being aware of that awesome presence. A final basic exercise to assist this is: After any of the above exercises, close the eyes and ponder, "If God is Infinite, and infinity is every thing, including even void itself, then all is God". After a few moments pondering this, and all it relates to, open the eyes. Behold, one is looking at God. Open the ears, one is hearing God. Feel, one is feeling God. You, and every part of you, is made of God, because there is only God, the ever present Now. From the local surroundings to the cosmos, all things are made up of the fabric of God's body. God is not separate from the Creation, God is the Creation. Furthermore, this Creation is much bigger than what humans can perceive with their senses. This entire physical world is an infinitely small speck in Its ocean of light. Practice this presence of God vigilantly and constantly, and one will experience the majesty of the Creator of All.

The effects of these practices are numerous, increasing health, strength, and clarity, in the mind, body and spirit, granting peace and understanding to the practitioner. With this society increasingly demanding more time from the citizens for nonsense, time for these important exercises is often challenging to secure. Those who begin to practice these simple techniques will understand the Individualists' emphasis upon them and a society which gives the people more time. The more time spent with these practices the more probable it is that one will attain notable results, and the more profound those results will be.

"All of Mans troubles stem from his inability to sit quietly in a room alone" – Blaise Pascal

I. Final Summary

Be Alarmed!

"Only after the last tree has been cut down and the last river poisoned, only then will you find that money cannot be eaten." – Prophecy of the Cree Indians

This document has been designed to increase the people's awareness of the lack of advancement in present day society, the lack of motivation to be more efficient and responsible, the lack of the use of technologies that have existed for decades, which could have already solved much of today's energy wastes, the general lack of evolution of mankind and its misplaced priorities, (all impeded for the private profit of the few) and to alert the people and move them into freedom. But they all must move, save not one. Regardless of political affiliation, religion, race or other separating beliefs, mankind must drop all labels and prejudices and ban together in love as one people, bar none. Knowledge must be freely distributed and shared as rapidly as possible exposing those that only survive by withholding knowledge from their fellow man. Else, the meek shall inherit the Earth only after it has been destroyed, and they robbed of everything.

The Individualistic society brings out the brilliance of each individual, developing them to the high ideals of Individualism so as to then be able to assist their fellow humanity, making a society of adepts living in harmony with each other and the Earth. Individualism removes all crutches to get one on one's feet to be responsible for one's own destiny and realize the massive power inherent within, which will never be realized by relying on others as the need suppliers insist.

The Individualists regularly ask themselves if they are being a worthy soul upon the earth. Upon death, what will be declared to the Creator as one's deeds are compared to the deeds of all other souls, from Masters to inept failures? Where will one stand? Was the gift of life wasted, or every single second utilized to the fullest? Was the self sculpted to the highest ideal in mind, body and spirit, or did one waste away and contribute nothing to humanity?

Some may be too attached to the old world to take up the responsible life of the Individualist, blinded by their captor, and defending it to their death. They may scoff at Individualistic points and notions declaring them ridiculous or impossible because of their ignorance, fears and doubts of sustaining themselves and assuming a global responsibility. The Individualists encourage them to voluntarily step out of the old machine before it dies, inevitably leaving them to fend for themselves, thus is its fate. The public continues to do less and less, and grow fatter and weaker. Even more become unskilled and incapable outside of serving their niche within the machine. The continual nursing of weaknesses causes weakness to grow to a fatal magnitude. As the machine collapses, the abandoned people have no abilities or strength to survive on their own.

In a mere 200 years the entire world has been enslaved and is now on a runaway train. Some complain but do nothing, others don't want to hear about it, and thus the problems grow. Too many perform their occupation just because of the dollar figure as opposed to doing what they love, pawns blown about by the forces of other people's wills. Working only for the money needed to procure food, shelter, fuel, land taxes, material goods and occasionally knowledge, ensuring their welfare. With the knowledge of self-sufficiency, one's welfare is secured better than it ever was, removing the need to depend upon any other for any reason.

One has no right to complain about the world if one is not doing something to change it with all of one's might. Individualism starts with you, The Individual. Blazing a trail and being an example for others to gain courage from. Rise, therefore, and work against these forces. Be an active creator of the utopian world to come. Rise and create such a world, undeterred, remembering one's infinite power because of being made in the image of The Infinite Creator. Work not in violence, anger, or haste, as these are powers of darkness, baring only fruits of darkness. Expose all corruption to the light, with truth, so that none allow themselves to be subjected to its parasitical practices in any of its shadowy forms. Rise and be a dispenser of light and free your brothers from the blackness! There is no excuse to not assist in the dismantlement of the corrupt old world.

During the time of transition from the ways of the old world to that of the Individualists, an obligation of every Individualist is to thwart any and all attempts of monopoly, oppression, control or things of a similar nature, by devising unbeatable solutions systematically dismantling the need suppliers. For instance – the technologies of electrical generation and storage significantly developed to make all fossil fuels obsolete, the stopping of all organizations and individuals that take advantage of their less informed brethren by spreading knowledge for free, etc. Such are the tasks that the mind of Individualist will be apply to.

The only resistance to Individualistic simplicity is from those who benefit from the complexity of inequality. These few are the most powerful materialistically, yet spiritually and rationally impoverished. Regardless of their intellect and wisdom, they possess much of the world's money, amounting to great material power. They therefore control 99% of the hearts and minds of men, who, not understanding Individualistic philosophy, will do anything for money, even small amounts. These global need suppliers have no concern for human life. Using whatever the people hold dear to rally them to their obedience. Whether it is their god, their Loves, or their children. They will utilize compromised government institutions in the guise of the greater good, to usurp the Individualist way of life. For example, the environmental protection agency could be employed by fantastic systems of reasoning that it is unhealthy, or environmentally unsound for each individual to be independent by producing one's own food and power, and dealing with natural waste, etc.

Be especially aware of those who by utilizing popular "Green" solutions of the new world, veil their intent to prey upon their brethren. Promoting the "only" way and the "best" way to utilize green solutions, and those ways will always be their own. An example is ethanol. Another unneeded system of waste and consumption instead of simply moving to the end solution of fully electric. Motive fuels are only needed as a secondary energy source. Fuels are pushed by corporations to keep control of an economy wherein they profit off of perpetual waste and consumption.

Not wasting time on non-constructive projects, the Individualists are active in government, keeping track of the actions of politicians and the members of large corporations, as well as who they affiliate with from past to present. They regularly contact all of their representatives, local to national, mayors to presidents. Not asking, but demanding direct control by the people, reminding them that they are employed by the people. They use laws such as the Sherman Antitrust Act to disperse resistant collusion.

The Sherman Antitrust Act:

This Act declares that "Every contract, combination in the form of trust or otherwise, or conspiracy, in restraint of trade or commerce among the several States, or with foreign nations, is declared to be illegal". As well as "Every person who shall monopolize, or attempt to monopolize, or combine or conspire with any other person or persons, to monopolize any part of the trade or commerce among the several States, or with foreign nations, shall be deemed guilty of a felony . . . " The Clayton Act extended the right to sue under the antitrust laws to "any person who shall be injured in his business or property by reason of anything forbidden in the antitrust laws."

All citizens, especially the learned such as, doctors, scientists, engineers, lawyers, etc. who do not apply their knowledge to the new world are only assisting corruption, the destruction of the earth and their fellow brethren, as well as themselves. Their minds should focus on a future of efficiency, and harmony, assisting the evolution of one's fellow man to return to a Golden Age of boundless inventiveness, instead of focusing on solely self-profit, prolonging the system of waste and consumption.

"Be bold and mighty forces will come to your aid"
- Basil King

All patriots, such as the Individualists, are demonized when they present plans for peace and harmony, wisdom and love. As Christ they are nailed up in display of dissidence, and their friends deny knowing them. For all power one returns to the people, one will be lied about and demonized by the need suppliers and their massive array of minions. Be prepared to be assailed by every sort of evil, for they will seek to destroy such works along with its designer. Thus, steps should be prepared wisely, protecting oneself from all angles from their well-funded movement to thwart Individualism and maintain global suppression.

"You are a den of vipers and thieves. I intend to rout you out, and by the Eternal God, I will rout you out."
- Andrew Jackson (in reference to bankers at the state of his administration)

Be ever vigilant to prevent the following acts which lead to servitude:

1. Any law that assumes an individual is not responsible enough to handle a product or service or action, thus makes illegal the product, service, or action. True **L**iberty
2. Any product or service which the majority has become dependent upon. True **I**ndependence
3. Any individual or group who withholds knowledge from others in order to maintain control or superiority. True **F**reedom
4. Any individual or group that has laws made for them that differ from the laws applied to all of the individuals of the union. True **E**quality
5. Any individual or group attempting to collect pools of money from many individuals apart from a true direct democracy <u>wholly</u>
    <u>of the people</u>.

The government of **LIFE** wholly of the people: Individualism.

   Know that we are the caretakers of Earth, not the owners or exploiters.   Unite with the growing force of the Individualists of all nations and all creeds, for the time for Change is long past due.
– May this be the final trumpet.

Hear All Yea Children - God is One - We are One

You are commanded to awaken!

$$\infty = 1$$

So Let It Be Written
So Let It Be Done

This entire document has been the opinion of one individual exercising the freedom of speech

This has been a

MASS MEDIA PUBLICATION

To Contact the Publisher or to have mail forwarded to the author, please write to:

PR@MassMedia.Space

Thank You For Your Purchase!

&

Please Visit MassMedia.Space for more products and services!

www.ingramcontent.com/pod-product-compliance
Lightning Source LLC
Chambersburg PA
CBHW080519030426
42337CB00023B/4569